Foundations Spanish 1

Cathy Holden
Tutor at the Institute for Applied Language Studies,
University of Edinburgh and formerly Lecturer in Spanish
at Manchester Metropolitan University
and Staffordshire University

Series Editor
Tom Carty
Formerly IWLP Programme Leader at Staffordshire University
and the University of Wolverhampton

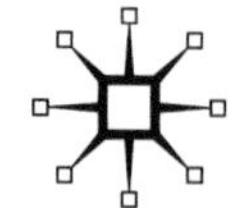

First published 2001 by
PALGRAVE MACMILLAN
Houndmills, Basingstoke, Hampshire RG21 6XS and
175 Fifth Avenue, New York, N.Y. 10010
Companies and representatives throughout the world

PALGRAVE MACMILLAN is the new global academic imprint of St. Martin's Press LLC Scholarly and Reference Division and Palgrave Publishers Ltd (formerly Macmillan Press Ltd).

ISBN 0–333–80267–5 book
ISBN 0–333–80299–3 cassettes

This book is printed on paper suitable for recycling and made from fully managed and sustained forest sources.

A catalogue record for this book is available from the British Library.

Audio Production: University of Brighton Media Centre.
Produced by Brian Hill.

Voices: Javier García Sánchez, Xavier Ribas, Inés Sal, César Martínez, Adriana Montes

Original design by Wendi Watson

Formatted by
The Ascenders Partnership, Basingstoke

10 9 8 7 6 5
10 09 08 07 06 04

Printed and bound in China

CONTENTS

Acknowledgements

The following illustration sources are acknowledged: Lisa Bates p.48; Helen Bugler pp. 1, 13, 15; Jo Marshall p. 29; Helen Phillips p. 4; Quo, Hachette Filipacchi, S.A. pp. 33, 93, 142; Spanish Tourist Office pp. 2, 6, 20, 28, 44, 55, 64, 72, 85, 86, 103, 112; Esther Thackeray pp. 111, 115.

Every effort has been made to trace all copyright holders, but if any have inadvertently been overlooked the publishers will be pleased to make the necessary arrangements at the first opportunity.

The author would like to dedicate this book to Elisabeth Dimock and Jeff Holden.

INTRODUCTION

Mainly for the tutor

Foundations Spanish 1 is a Spanish language course for beginners aimed at students taking a language option or similar module on an Institution-Wide Language Programme (IWLP) or equivalent programme. It is part of the *Foundations Languages Series* which is specifically designed for such programmes. Its structure and content are informed by market research and consultation within the sector. All the authors are experienced tutors on IWLP-style university courses.

Many of the textbooks used on beginners' and intermediate language courses in higher education were not designed for that purpose and it shows. Tutors and students particularly complain of inappropriate topics and excessive length (with units and sections having to be skipped or the book not completed). Tutors often also find they have to supplement the textbook to make up for deficiencies in the coverage of skills, tasks or grammatical topics required by university or college module descriptors.

This textbook is designed to fit the typical 24-week teaching year and assumes two or three hours of class contact per week. There are ten units (five per semester if your academic year is organised that way), the first nine structured in the same way. Unit 10 is a revision unit and has a slightly different structure. In each unit the core material is supported by partner work, extension work, grammatical exposition and exercises, as well as a vocabulary page. For further work and private study there are supplementary exercises relating to each unit. Answers are provided to all exercises, whether core or supplementary. There is a global grammar summary, a vocabulary section and an index. Items marked with a headphone icon are on the accompanying cassettes, the price of which includes the right to duplicate the cassettes for the use of students within your institution.

For more details on the structure of the book and how it is designed to be used, see the "Mainly for the student" section of this Introduction. Encourage your students to read that section in connection with the practical tips on learning a language which follow it. Both the Introduction and the tips stress to the student that this is a taught course and they must be guided by you, the tutor.

Mainly for the student

What follows is a guide to the textbook. Take time to read it so you get maximum benefit from your course. You should also read the section "Learning a language" which begins on page ix.

1. Structure

There are ten **units**. Units 1–9 have the same clear, consistent structure, which you will soon get used to. (Unit 10 is slightly different because it is a revision unit and doesn't introduce new material.) At the start of a unit, there is a brief **summary** of what you will learn to do in it. Then comes the core, several pages in which new material is introduced, then practised and used in various ways. Each unit is divided into numbered items or sections. Audio cassettes accompany the textbook.

The core is followed by a page headed **Extra!** As the heading implies, this material, while on the same topics as in the six-page core, makes extra demands and is that bit more challenging.

Two pages are then devoted to the **grammatical structures** you have encountered in the unit, with exercises to practise them.

The next page is the **new vocabulary** from the unit.

Then come two pages of **partner work**, communication exercises where you are given prompts for half a conversation (Partner A page) and your partner has the prompts for the other half (Partner B page).

Beginning on page 123 there are **supplementary exercises** for each unit. These are for work outside the classroom. Your tutor may sometimes set work from these pages or you can use them as and when suits you to consolidate what you have done from the unit core.

For reference there is a **guide to grammatical terms**, an overall **grammar summary** and a **vocabulary** section. Also at the end of the book, you will find **answers** to all the exercises.

2. Using the book

Each **unit** is focused on one or more themes or situations in which the language is used. The short **summary** at the start of the unit tells you what the themes are and describes what you will be able to do with the language once you have completed the unit. That's a key word ("do"): while language-learning requires and develops knowledge and understanding, it above all means developing the capability of using the language in given circumstances.

The **core** contains the "input" (new language) for the unit as well as a range of tasks designed to help you master it and make it your own. The key inputs come in various forms such as: *presentation*, when you are given, for example, the numbers or the system for telling the time; *listening exercises*, especially involving gap-filling; *matching exercises*, where you are introduced to new words or structures by matching up a Spanish word or phrase with a picture, a person with an activity or by questions and answers in a dialogue; *reading exercises*, where you may, for example, be asked to re-arrange the order of a dialogue or narrative; *using a model*, the best example of which is working on your pronunciation and intonation using the audio material.

Whatever the form of input, it is absolutely vital to spend time and effort mastering this material. Be guided by your tutor. He or she will introduce it in class or ask you to prepare it in advance. If there's a word or phrase you're unsure of, turn to the vocabulary page for the unit and check. If a grammatical point puzzles you, refer to the unit grammar pages or the grammar summary towards the end of the book. If you wonder what a grammatical term means, look it up in the guide to grammatical terminology just before that grammar summary.

The material introduced in an input exercise flows into exercises in the section(s) immediately following, enabling you to practise, use and master this language. After you have done these exercises in class (or gone over them there, having prepared them in advance), make sure you revise the input material and key structures in your private study time.

The exercises practising and applying the input material are carefully devised to enable you to progress and consolidate in manageable steps. They are very varied, as the following examples show. They include above all many *speaking exercises*, typically involving you working with a partner. Here, you are communicating in a controlled situation, using the language introduced in the input sections. There are also *listening and reading exercises* involving gap-filling, answering questions and re-ordering information or correcting errors. *Grammar exercises* develop your ability to deduce rules from examples as well as to recognize and use the structures of Spanish correctly. Grammatical points are highlighted in boxes throughout the core pages of each unit. As to *writing* in Spanish, work in the unit core is mostly carefully controlled.

The **Extra!** page in each unit gives you the opportunity of further developing your Spanish, taking in particular listening and reading skills beyond the confines of the core input material while staying on related topics. The listening material is lively and natural and you have to extract specific information from it. In such exercises, it is important to avoid the temptation to fret over every word: check out the information you are being asked for and listen with that in mind.

The **grammar** pages follow. In each unit, the first gives you a clear overview of the grammar content of the unit, the second provides a set of short exercises so you can test yourself (answers at the back of the book). Don't skip these pages: they simply clarify and check off grammatical structures you have met with and used in the course of the unit. This is how you become aware of the Spanish language as a system.

The **vocabulary** page gives the new words occurring in the unit. Learn them as you go along and revise them regularly. Note that you can use a noun in Spanish properly only if you know whether it is masculine or feminine.

The **partner work** material can be used in or out of the classroom to develop communication skills. The scenarios are always based on the material in the unit core, so you are securely in a known context. The challenge is to use the language you have learnt to communicate information your partner needs and to respond to what he or she says.

The **supplementary exercises** give further practice on a unit-by-unit basis and are designed to be used in private study. Answers are given at the back of the book. As the section "Learning a Language" stresses, work outside the classroom, both that set by the tutor and that done on your own initiative to meet your own priorities, is an essential part of a taught language course.

Now you have a clear idea of how this book is designed to be used, read the section on "Learning a language" which follows. It gives detailed practical advice which will help you to get maximum benefit from your Spanish course.

The Introduction on the previous pages outlines the structure of this book and indicates how it is designed to be used: make sure you read it. The aim here is to give more general guidance on language learning. You should read it before you begin your course and refer to it regularly.

The advice which follows takes into account that you are beginning a taught course rather than a course of self-tuition. You're probably taking a Spanish language option or elective alongside your main subject, or maybe your higher education course has a compulsory, if minor, language element.

1. A practical point first. Check the course or module guide and/or **syllabus** to see exactly what's required of you by your university or college. In particular, find out how the course or module is assessed.
   The course guide and assessment information will probably be expressed in terms of the four language skills of listening, speaking, reading and writing. The relative importance of these skills can vary between institutions.

2. Remember this is a taught course – you're not on your own. **Your tutor** is there to guide you through the course. Using the material in the book, he or she will introduce new structures, ensure you practise them in class and then enable you to produce similar language until you develop the capacity to work autonomously. The first rule of a taught language course, then, is to follow your guide.

3. Of course a guide can't go there for you. While your tutor will show you the way, **only you can do the learning**. This means hard work both in the classroom and outside the timetabled hours.

4. **Regular attendance** at the language class is vital. This isn't like a lecture-based course, where you can miss one session and then catch up from a friend's notes or even live with the fact that there's going to be a gap in your knowledge. A language class is a workshop. You do things. Or to put it more formally, you take part in structured activities designed to develop your linguistic competence.

5. But mere attendance isn't enough. Being there isn't the same thing as learning. You have to **participate**. This means being an active member of the class, listening carefully, working through the exercises, answering questions, taking part in simple dialogues, contributing to group work, taking the risk of speaking without the certainty of being right. It also means preparing before classes and following up afterwards ...

6. … because what you do **outside the classroom** is vital, too. While new topics will normally be introduced in class, your tutor will also set tasks which feed in to what you will be doing in the next session. If you don't do the preparation, you can't benefit from the classroom activity or the tutor will have to spend valuable time going over the preparation in class for the benefit of those who haven't done it in advance. Classroom contact time is precious, normally no more than two or three hours a week, and it's essential to use that time to the best effect. Similarly, the tutor will sometimes ask you to follow up work done in class with tasks designed to consolidate or develop what you have done.

7. You should also take time to **review** and reflect on what you have been doing, regularly going over what you have done in class, checking your learning. This will also enable you to decide your priorities for private study, working on areas you find difficult or which are particular priorities for you (see point **9** below).

8. This assumes that you are **organised**: keep a file or notebook, in which you jot down what you have done and what you plan to do. It's a good idea to work for several shortish bursts a week than for a long time once a week.

9. While a lot of out-of-class work will be done at home, your university or college will probably have a Learning Centre, **Language Centre** or similar facilities in the library. Check this out and use whatever you can to reinforce and supplement what you are doing in class and from this textbook. Make sure any material you use is suitable for your level: it will probably be classified or labelled using categories such as Beginners, Intermediate and Advanced.

   Possible resources: audio cassettes, videos, satellite TV, computer-based material, the internet, books (language courses, grammar guides, dictionaries, simple readers), magazines and newspapers, worksheets. Possible activities: listening comprehension, pronunciation practice, reading comprehension, grammar exercises, vocabulary exercises. Computer-based materials and worksheets will usually have keys with answers.

   It's possible your tutor will set work to be done in the Language Centre or that you will be expected to spend a certain amount of time there, otherwise you should find times during your week when you can drop in.

10. Don't be afraid of **grammar**. This is simply the term for how we describe the way a language works. Learn it and revise it as you go along. There are boxes with grammar points throughout each of the units in this book, a grammar summary for each unit and a grammar summary for the whole book. You probably feel hesitant about grammatical terms such as "direct object" or "definite article" but they are useful labels and easily learned. There is a guide to such terms towards the end of the book.

11. In addition to listening-based work in class, you should regularly work in your own time on the accompanying audio cassette material. Try to reproduce the **pronunciation and intonation** (the "music" of the language) of the native speakers on the recording. It's easier if you work at this from the start and establish good habits than if you approximate to the sounds of the language and have to correct them later. It is important that you repeat and speak out loud rather than in your head.
12. Always bear in mind that, in learning a foreign language, you can normally **understand** (listening and reading) more than you can **express** (speaking and writing). Test yourself by seeing whether you can do some of the exercises where you have to **produce** some Spanish. It's a good idea to practise with a fellow-student.
13. When listening or reading, remember **you don't have to be sure of every word** to get the message. Above all, you don't need to translate into your native language.
14. Universities and colleges are increasingly international and you will almost certainly be able to make contact with **native speakers** of Spanish. Try out your language, get them to correct your pronunciation, find out about their country and culture.
15. Above all, **enjoy** your language learning!

To summarize:

1. Check the syllabus.
2. Remember your tutor is your guide
3. ... but you do the learning!
4. Attend the class regularly
5. ... and participate actively.
6. Work outside the classroom,
7. constantly reviewing your learning.
8. Be organized.
9. Use the Language Centre or other private study facilities.
10. Learn the grammar and don't be afraid of grammatical terms.
11. Work from the start on getting pronunciation and intonation right.
12. Remember understanding isn't the same as producing the language
13. ... but you don't have to be sure of every word to get the message.
14. Meet fellow-students who are native speakers of Spanish.
15. Enjoy yourself!

Tom Carty, *Series Editor*

In this unit you will learn how to give and understand basic information about yourself and others and to ask questions.

1 Saludos. / Greetings. **Escucha y lee.** / Listen and read.

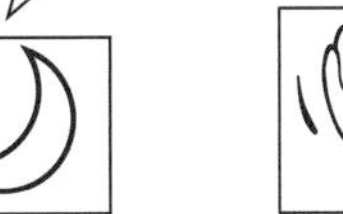

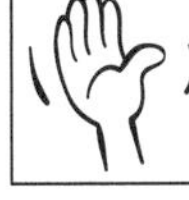

2 Greet your partner. Then greet two or three other people and say goodbye.

3 Escucha y lee.

Hola, buenos días.
Me llamo Carmen Salguero Ramírez.
Vivo en Birmingham. Soy de Madrid.
Soy española. Soy profesora.

– ¿Cómo te llamas? – Me llamo Carmen Salguero Ramírez.
– ¿Dónde vives? – Vivo en Birmingham.
– ¿De dónde eres? – Soy de Madrid; soy española.
– ¿Cuál es tu profesión? – Soy profesora.

Buenas tardes. Me llamo Eduardo Gutiérrez Ramos. Vivo en Nueva York. Soy de Buenos Aires. Soy argentino. Soy profesor.

– ¿Te llamas Pablo? – No. Me llamo Eduardo.
– ¿Vives en Manhattan? – No. Vivo en Nueva York.
– ¿Eres de Chile? – No. Soy de Argentina.
– ¿Eres argentino? – Sí. Soy argentino.
– ¿Eres estudiante? – No, no soy estudiante. Soy profesor.

gramática

¿Cómo te llamas? What are you called?	**Me llamo ...** I am called ...
¿Dónde vives? Where do you live?	**Vivo en ...** I live in ...
¿De dónde eres? Where are you from?	**Soy de ...** I am from ...
¿Eres español/a? Are you Spanish?	**No, no soy ... / Sí, soy ...** No, I'm not ... / Yes, I'm ...
¿Cuál es tu profesión? What is your job?	**Soy ...** I am (a) ...

The personal pronouns ('I', 'you', 'he', 'she' etc) are often omitted in Spanish.

4 Take on the roles of Carmen and Eduardo, and introduce yourself to a partner.

A **Hola, buenos días. ... Carmen Salguero Ramírez. ... en Birmingham. ... de Madrid. ... española. ... profesora.**

B **Buenas tardes. ... Eduardo Gutiérrez Ramos. ... en Nueva York. ... de Buenos Aires. ... argentino. ... profesor.**

5 ¿Quién eres? / Who are you?

Practise with a partner. Introduce yourself as one of the people below. Your partner has to work out which one you are. For example:

A **Soy inglesa. Soy de Inglaterra pero** (but) **vivo en Florida. Soy administradora.**

B **Eres** (You are) **Yasmin Patel.**

Eva Herrmann	alemana	Alemania	Glasgow	pintora
Josef Blum	alemán	Alemania	Glasgow	pintor
Yasmin Patel	inglesa	Inglaterra	Florida	administradora
Frank Hanley	inglés	Inglaterra	Florida	administrador
Anne Fornells	francesa	Francia	Cardiff	estudiante
Paul Maurizot	francés	Francia	Cardiff	estudiante
Sarah Duffy	irlandesa	Irlanda	Torquay	mecánica
Martin McNally	irlandés	Irlanda	Torquay	mecánico

Gran Vía desde la calle de Alcalá

6 **Escucha las preguntas y respuestas.** / Listen to the questions and answers.

– ¿Cómo te llamas?	– Soy Mario.
– ¿Dónde vives?	– Vivo en Cartagena.
– ¿De dónde eres?	– Soy de Alicante.
– ¿Eres español?	– Sí, soy español.
– ¿Cuál es tu profesión?	– Soy médico.

7 **Soy estudiante.** / I am a student.

Ask two classmates the questions below and fill in the table.

PREGUNTA	COMPAÑERO/A 1	COMPAÑERO/A 2
¿Cómo te llamas?		
¿De dónde eres?		
¿Eres español/a?		
¿Dónde vives?		
¿Cuál es tu profesión?		

8 Write out the questions in Spanish.

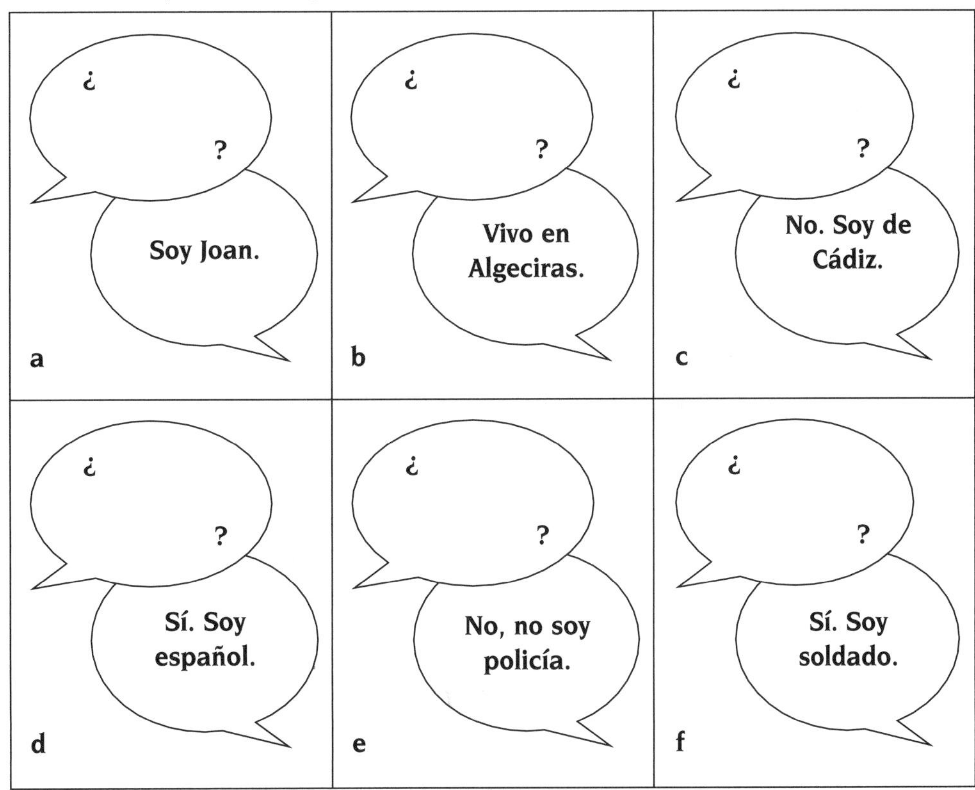

9 **¿Quién es?** / Who is s/he?

Escucha y lee.

Se llama Carmen Salguero Ramírez. Vive en Birmingham. Es de Madrid. Es española. Es profesora.

Se llama Emilio Gómez y es colombiano de Bogotá. Vive en Edimburgo y es investigador.

Es Ianis. Es griego, de Atenas, pero vive en Cardiff. Es ingeniero.

Es Krystyna de Polonia. Es polaca pero vive en Dublín y es abogada.

10

Choose one of the people described above. Your partner has to find out who it is by asking questions. For example:

B **¿Es ingeniero?**	A **No, no es ingeniero.**
B **¿Es española o polaca?**	A **Es polaca.**
B **¿Vive en Dublín?**	A **Sí. Vive en Dublín.**
B **¿Es Krystyna?**	A **Sí. Es Krystyna. /No, no es Krystyna.**

gramática

¿Cómo se llama? What is s/he called?	**Se llama ...** S/he is called ...
¿Dónde vive? Where does s/he live?	**Vive en ...** S/he lives in ...
¿De dónde es? Where is s/he from?	**Es de ...** S/he is from ...
¿Es español/a? Is s/he Spanish?	**No, no es ... /Sí, es ...** No, s/he isn't ... /Yes, s/he is ...
¿Cuál es su profesión? What is his/her job?	**Es ...** S/he is (a) ...

11 Escucha y lee.

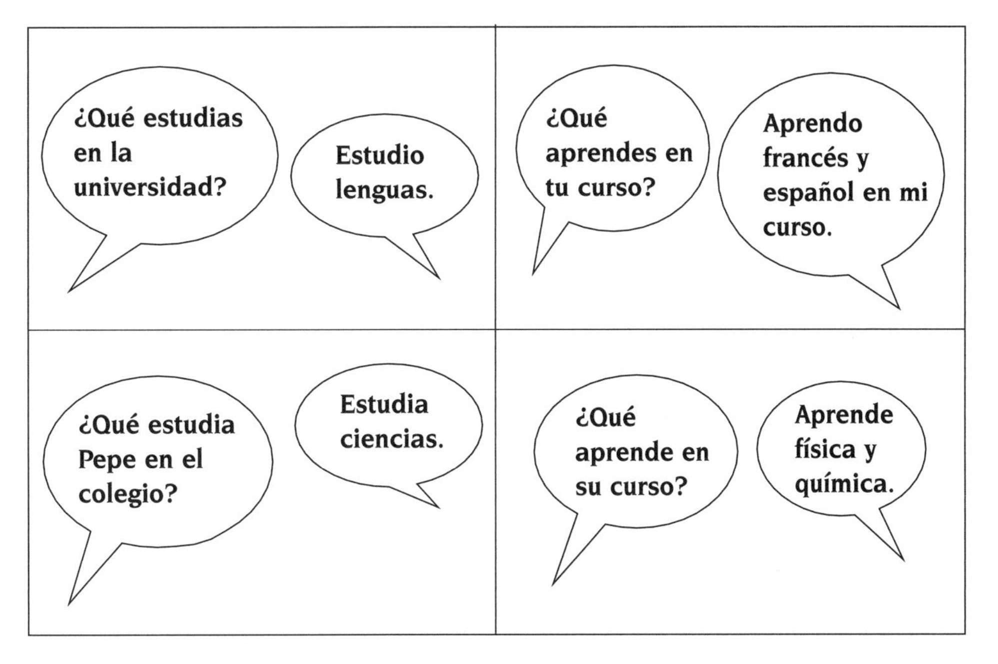

12

In groups of three ask about someone else as follows. A asks B what s/he is studying or learning. B answers. C asks A what B is studying. A answers. For example:

1 A to B: **¿Qué estudias?** 2 B to A: **Estudio geografía.**
3 C to A: **¿Qué estudia B?** 4 A to C: **B estudia geografía.**

In the same way A can ask B other questions and tell C about B.
You can find other subjects in the vocabulary section on page 10.

13

Read the letter from Marta Serrat, and answer your partner's questions.

For example: B **¿De dónde es Marta?** A **Es de Venezuela.**

Soy Marta Serrat. Soy venezolana pero vivo en El Salvador. Soy funcionaria y estudio Relaciones Internacionales. En mi curso aprendo sociología, economía y psicología.

gramática

Yo (I)	**Tú** (You)	**Él/Ella** (He/She)
estudio ...	**estudias ...**	**estudia ...**
aprendo ...	**aprendes ...**	**aprende ...**

14 Escucha y repite los números. / Listen and repeat the numbers.

LOS NÚMEROS

1 uno	6 seis	11 once	16 dieciséis	21 veintiuno
2 dos	7 siete	12 doce	17 diecisiete	22 veintidós
3 tres	8 ocho	13 trece	18 dieciocho	23 veintitrés
4 cuatro	9 nueve	14 catorce	19 diecinueve	24 veinticuatro
5 cinco	10 diez	15 quince	20 veinte	25 veinticinco

15 Escucha y lee.

– ¿Cuántos años tienes? – Tengo veinticinco años.
– ¿Cuántos años tiene Carmen? – Tiene veintiún* años.
– ¿Eduardo tiene veintitrés años? – No. Tiene veinticuatro.

*__Veintiuno__ loses the **o** before **años**.

gramática

		tener	to have	
tengo	I have	BUT	**Tengo X años.**	I *am* X years old.
tienes	you have		**Tienes X años.**	You *are* X years old.
tiene	s/he has		**Tiene X años.**	S/he *is* X years old.

16 Escucha y escribe su edad. / Listen and write their age.

a Federico, … años **b** Manuel, … años **c** Alberto, … años **d** Jacinta, … años

17

Practise counting with a partner, one of you taking the even numbers and the other taking the odds.

18 Me presento. / I introduce myself.

a Write a few sentences about yourself (name, age, nationality, course, etc).
b Write a few sentences about someone else.

Avenida Gaudí, Barcelona

19 ¡Bienvenidos! / Welcome!

Escucha y rellena el formulario. Listen and fill in the form. Four people want to enrol on a course in a language school in Barcelona.

NOMBRE	Segoshi Tanizaki	Carla Bertolini		Xavier Marchand
NACIONALIDAD				senegalés
PROFESIÓN		diseñadora	periodista	ingeniero
ESTUDIOS		arte y diseño		
DOMICILIO ACTUAL		Llobregat		
DOMICILIO NORMAL	Tokio			Senegal

20

Read the postcards and answer the questions in English.

Querida Eulalia

Acabo de matricularme en un curso de inglés. Vivo en el centro de la ciudad en una casa grande con 5 estudiantes de la universidad. Trabajo en un hotel para pagar el curso. No está mal.

Un abrazo,

Fernando

Querido Fernando

Yo también aprendo inglés, aquí en Durham. Vivo con un danés que estudia filosofía y una china que trabaja en la oficina de la universidad.

Hasta luego; un abrazo,

Eulalia

acabo de matricularme	I have just enrolled	**trabajo**	I work
la ciudad	town	**pagar**	to pay for
la casa	house	**también**	also

a Give three facts about where Fernando lives.
b What does he do to finance his studies?
c What is Eulalia studying, and where?
d How many people does Eulalia share her house with?
e What nationality are they and what are their jobs?

Gramática

- **Verbs**
  - All Spanish verb infinitives ('to go', 'to have', etc) end in **-ar**, **-er** or **-ir.**

estudiar	to study	**aprender**	to learn	**vivir**	to live
estudio	I study	**aprendo**	I learn	**vivo**	I live
estudias	you study	**aprendes**	you learn	**vives**	you live
estudia	s/he studies	**aprende**	s/he learns	**vive**	s/he lives

As there are often no personal pronouns ('I', 'you', 'he', 'she', etc) to help you, you have to look at the endings of the verbs in order to know who the subject is. For example **estudio** ends in **-o** so it means 'I study'. See page 34 for a list of personal pronouns.

Ser 'to be' is very irregular. It does not follow the same pattern as other **-er** verbs. See page 34.

- **How to ask a question**
  - You can use a verb. Verbs can be both questions and statements:

Vive S/He lives **¿Vive?** Does s/he live?

You can also use question words. For example:

¿Quién?	Who?	**¿Dónde?**	Where?	**¿Dónde vives?**	Where do you live?
¿Qué?	What?	**¿Adónde?**	(To) where?	**¿Quién es?**	Who is s/he?
¿Cómo?	How?	**¿Cuál?**	Which?	**¿Qué estudias?**	What do you study?

- **Nouns**
  - All nouns are masculine or feminine in Spanish. Masculine nouns frequently end in **-o** and feminine ones in **-a**. Some, however, look the same for both genders: **estudiante**, **periodista**, etc.

	singular		plural	
masculine	**el secretario**	*the* secretary	**los secretarios**	*the* secretaries
feminine	**la secretaria**		**las secretarias**	
masculine	**un colegio**	*a* college	**unos colegios**	*some* colleges
feminine	**una academia**	*an* academy	**unas academias**	*some* academies

Ejercicios de gramática

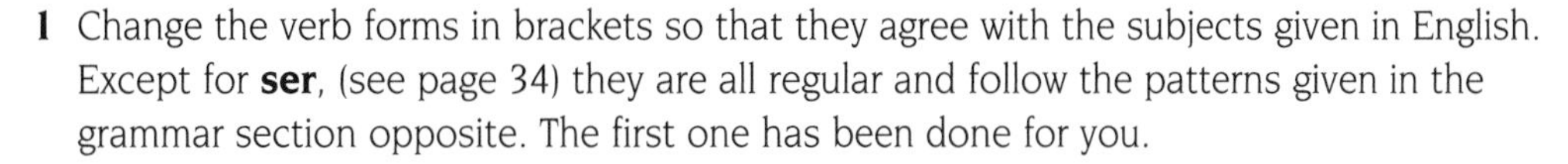

1 Change the verb forms in brackets so that they agree with the subjects given in English. Except for **ser**, (see page 34) they are all regular and follow the patterns given in the grammar section opposite. The first one has been done for you.

a (I) (Ser) *Soy* irlandesa y (vivir) en Dublín. (Ser) novelista y (escribir) novelas. También (trabajar) en una universidad y (aprender) turco.

b (You) ¿(Trabajar) en el hotel Bienestar? (Ser) recepcionista y (comer) en el restaurante, ¿no?

c (She) Lola (estudiar) lenguas y (trabajar) mucho. (Vivir) en Toledo y (ser) mexicana.

escribir to write **trabajar** to work **comer** to eat

2 What questions could you ask someone in order to fill in this form …

a about himself or herself?
For example: **¿Cómo te llamas?**

b about someone else?
For example: **¿Cómo se llama?**

NOMBRE ______
EDAD ______
NACIONALIDAD ______
PROFESIÓN ______
ESTUDIOS ______
DOMICILIO ______

3 Find the appropriate nouns from the list below to fill the gaps and make sense.

Maribel es (**a**) en la universidad y aprende francés. Es (**b**) pero vive en España. Su (**c**) se llama Pierre y es (**d**). Maribel también estudia economía, y su (**e**) se llama Ana, y es (**f**), de Buenos Aires.

profesor/a	**estudiante**	**francés**
francesa	**mexicano/a**	**argentino/a**

Vocabulario

Saludos	Greetings
Buenas tardes	Good afternoon
Buenos días	Good morning
Buenas noches	Good night/evening
Hola	Hello
Adiós	Goodbye
Hasta luego	See you soon
Bienvenido/a	Welcome

Verbos ('yo')	Verbs ('I')
Aprendo	I learn
Estudio	I study
Soy	I am
Tengo X años.	I am X years old.
Trabajo	I work
Vivo en ...	I live in ...

Preguntas ('tú')	Questions ('you')
¿Cuál es tu profesión?	What is your job?
¿Cuántos años tienes?	How old are you?
¿De dónde eres?	Where are you from?
¿Dónde vives?	Where do you live?
¿Eres ...?	Are you ...?
¿Qué aprendes?	What are you learning?
¿Qué estudias?	What are you studying?
¿Quién eres?	Who are you?

Verbos ('él/ella')	Verbs ('s/he')
Aprende	S/He learns
Estudia	S/He studies
Es	S/He is
Tiene X años.	S/He is X years old.
Trabaja	S/He works
Vive en ...	S/He lives in ...

Nacionalidades (*f pl*)	Nationalities
alemán/alemana	German
argentino/a	Argentinian
chino/a	Chinese
colombiano/a	Colombian
escocés/escocesa	Scottish
español/a	Spanish
francés/francesa	French
galés/galesa	Welsh
griego/a	Greek
inglés/inglesa	English
irlandés/irlandesa	Irish
italiano/a	Italian
japonés/japonesa	Japanese
norteamericano/a	American
polaco/a	Polish
senegalés/senegalesa	Senegalese
sudamericano/a	South American
turco/a	Turkish
venezolano/a	Venezuelan

Profesiones (*f pl*)	Professions/Job(s)
abogado/a	lawyer
actriz/actor	actress/actor
administrador/a	administrator
artista	artist
diseñador/a	designer
estudiante	student
funcionario/a	civil servant
ingeniero/a	engineer
investigador/a	researcher
mecánico/a	mechanic
médico	doctor
músico/a	musician
periodista	journalist
pintor/a	painter
policía	police officer
profesor/a	teacher
recepcionista	receptionist
secretario/a	secretary
soldado	soldier

Asignaturas	Subjects
arte (m)	Art
ciencias (f pl)	Science
diseño (m)	Design
economía (f)	Economics
estudios (m pl)	Studies
filosofía (f)	Philosophy
física (f)	Physics
geografía (f)	Geography
lengua (f)	Language
matemáticas (f pl)	Mathematics
política (f)	Politics
psicología (f)	Psychology
química (f)	Chemistry
relaciones internacionales (f pl)	International relations
sociología (f)	Sociology

For more vocabulary turn to the Appendix on p. 181.

Práctica en parejas/PARTNER WORK

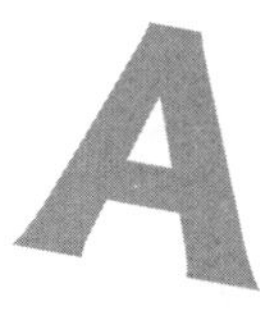

1 **a** Greet your partner and ask her/him questions in Spanish to find out the following information. Without writing anything down, try to remember the details s/he has given you.

Name
Age
Nationality
Where s/he is from.
Where s/he lives.
What job (if any) s/he does.
What s/he is studying.

b Now tell your partner what you remember: ('Eres francés, eres profesor,' etc). S/He will correct you if you are wrong.

c Your partner will now ask you some similar questions about yourself. Answer in Spanish. S/He has to remember what you say without writing anything down.

d Check that your partner has remembered correctly the information you gave her/him, and correct her/him if s/he is wrong: ('No soy argentino, soy de Colombia', etc).

2 **a** Answer your partner's questions about Oreste and June in Spanish so that s/he can fill in a table like the one below.

- Oreste Bertona, 21, Italian, lives in Milan, studies sciences and works in a hotel.
- June Thompson, 19, Scottish, lives in Glasgow, studies psychology and works in a hospital (**un hospital**).

b Ask your partner questions about Iñaki and Elena in Spanish and fill in the table below.

NOMBRE	Iñaki Romero	Elena Fernández
EDAD		
NACIONALIDAD		
DOMICILIO		
ESTUDIOS		
TRABAJO		

Práctica en parejas/PARTNER WORK

1 **a** Answer your partner's questions about yourself in Spanish. S/He has to remember what you say without writing anything down.

b Your partner will now check that s/he has your details correct. Give her/him the right information if s/he is wrong ('No, no soy francés, soy italiano', etc).

c Now ask your partner questions in Spanish to find out the following information. Without writing anything down, try to remember the details s/he has given you.
Name
Age
Nationality
Where s/he is from.
Where s/he lives.
What job (if any) s/he does.
What s/he is studying.

d Tell your partner what you remember ('Eres griego, eres estudiante', etc). S/He will correct you if you are wrong.

2 **a** Ask your partner questions about Oreste and June in Spanish and fill in the table below.

NOMBRE	Oreste Bertona	June Thompson
EDAD		
NACIONALIDAD		
DOMICILIO		
ESTUDIOS		
TRABAJO		

b Answer your partner's questions about Iñaki and Elena in Spanish so that s/he can fill in a table like the one above.

- Iñaki Romero, 22, Spanish, lives in Jerez, studies economics and works in a bar.
- Elena Fernández, 15, Argentinian, lives in Buenos Aires, studies languages.

In this unit you will add to the personal details you can discuss with others. You will learn how to describe your family and where you live.

1 La familia de Carmen / Carmen's family

Escucha y repite.

La familia

masculine	feminine	plural	
el padre	**la madre**	**los padres**	the parents
el hijo	**la hija**	**los hijos**	the children
el hermano	**la hermana**	**los hermanos**	the brothers and sisters
el marido	**la mujer**	**el matrimonio**	the married couple
el novio	**la novia**	**los novios**	boyfriend and girlfriend

2 Escucha y lee.

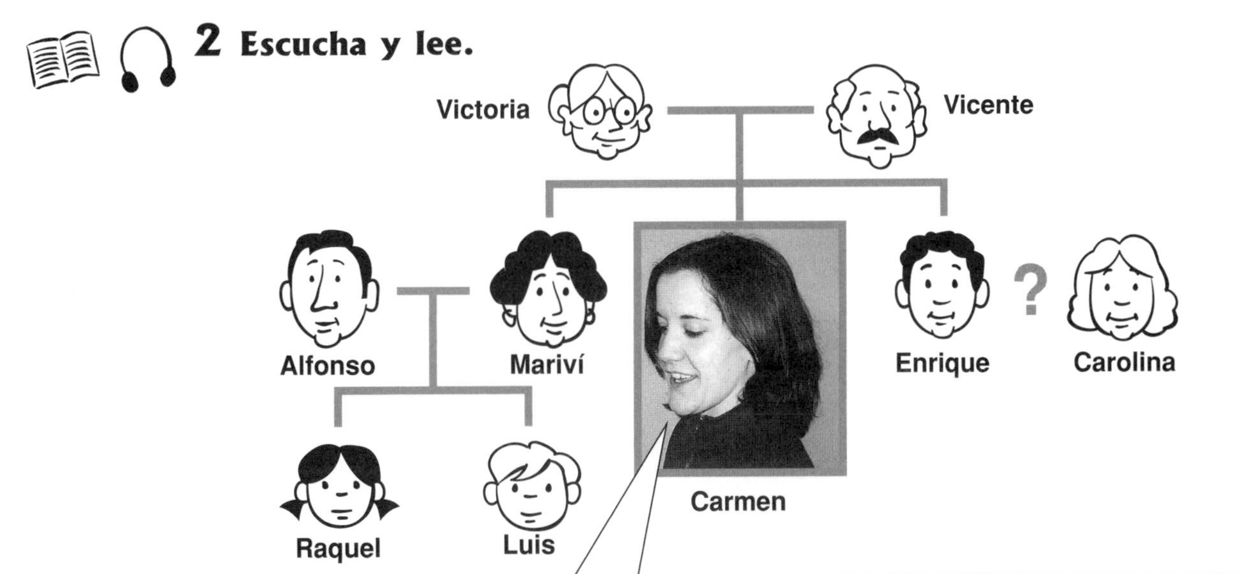

Victoria y Vicente son mis padres. Mariví es mi hermana mayor. Tiene 30 años y está casada. Su marido se llama Alfonso, y tienen dos hijos, Raquel y Luis. Enrique es mi hermano menor. Está soltero, pero tiene novia. Su novia se llama Carolina.

son	(they) are	**está casado/a (con)**	s/he is married (to)
tienen	(they) have	**está soltero/a**	s/he is single
mayor	older	**menor**	younger

gramática

How to say someone or something belongs to you.

Talking about one person			Talking about more than one person		
mi	**padre**	my father	**mis**	**padres**	my parents
tu	**hijo**	your child	**tus**	**hijos**	your children
su	**hermano**	his/her/their brother	**sus**	**hermanos**	his/her/their brothers and sisters

3 Escucha y contesta a las preguntas. / Listen and answer the questions.

Carmen is being asked about her family. For example:

¿Cómo se llama tu madre? Mi madre se llama ...

a ¿Cómo se llama tu madre? ________

b ¿Cómo se llama tu padre? ________

c ¿Cómo se llaman tus hermanos? ________

d ¿Tu hermana está casada o soltera? ________

e ¿Tu hermano está casado o soltero? ________

f ¿Enrique tiene hijos? ________

g ¿Cuántos hijos tienen Mariví y Alfonso? ________

4 With a partner, practise asking and answering questions like the ones above, taking it in turns to be Carmen.

gramática

Talking about one person		Talking about more than one person	
Es	**la madre.**	**Son**	**los padres.**
She is	the mother.	They are	the parents.
Está	**casada.**	**Están**	**casados.**
She is	married.	They are	married.
Tiene	**dos hijos.**	**Tienen**	**dos hijos.**
S/He has	two children.	They have	two children.
Se llama	**Mariví.**	**Se llaman**	**Raquel y Luis.**
She is called	Mariví.	They are called	Raquel and Luis.
Negative			
No tiene	**hijos.**	**No tienen**	**hijos.**
S/He doesn't have	children.	They don't have	children.

5 **Más números.** / More numbers.

Escucha y repite los números.

26	veintiséis	32	treinta y dos	50	cincuenta
27	veintisiete	33	treinta y tres	51	cincuenta y uno etc.
28	veintiocho	34	treinta y cuatro	60	sesenta
29	veintinueve	35	treinta y cinco, etc.	70	setenta
30	treinta	40	cuarenta	80	ochenta
31	treinta y uno	41	cuarenta y uno etc.	90	noventa

6 **¿Cuántos años tienen?** / How old are they?

Escucha y escribe su edad. / Listen and write their age.

a Anita, ... años
b Jesús, ... años
c Fernando, ... años; José, ... años
d Doña Isabel, ... años
e Hermanos, ..., ..., y ... años; hermana, ... años; María ... años

7 Draw Eduardo's family tree like Carmen's in Section 1.

Soy Eduardo. Inés e Ignacio son mis padres. Tienen 64 y 59 años. Tomás es mi hermano mayor. Es médico. Tiene 35 años y está casado. Su mujer se llama Trini, y tienen dos hijos. Sus hijos se llaman David y Dolores. Marta es mi hermana menor. Tiene 20 años. Está soltera, pero tiene novio y viven juntos. Su novio se llama Manolo y tiene 29 años.

gramática

In the following types of sentences with 'apostrophe s' you need to use **de**:

Inés e Ignacio son <u>los padres de Eduardo.</u>
Inés and Ignacio are Eduardo's parents.
<u>La hermana de Eduardo</u> se llama Marta.
Eduardo's sister is called Marta.

8 Answer the questions using the possessive **su(s)**. For example:

¿Cómo se llama *el hermano de* Eduardo? Su hermano se llama Tomás.

a ¿Cómo se llama *la hermana de* Eduardo? ____
b ¿Quién es *el hijo de Tomás y Trini*? ____
c ¿Cuántos años tiene *el marido de Trini*? ____
d ¿Cuántos años *tienen los padres de* Eduardo? ____

9 Ask your partner about his or her family using questions like the ones in Section 3. Remember to ask people's ages.

10 ¿Quién vive dónde? / Who lives where?

Escucha y escribe el número debajo de la imagen. Listen and write the number under the picture.

el campo	the country	**grande**	big
una urbanización	housing estate	**pequeño/a**	small

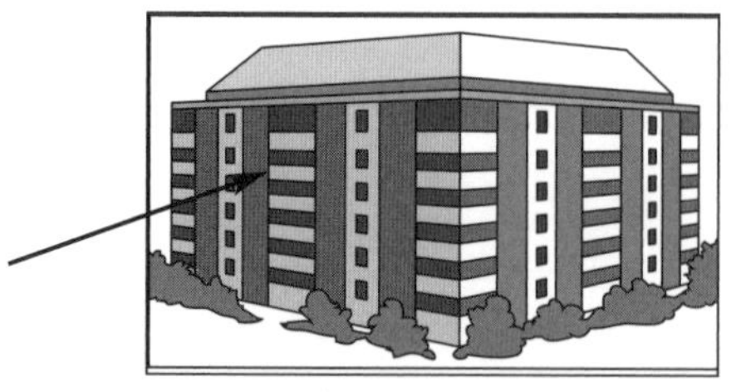

a ...un piso

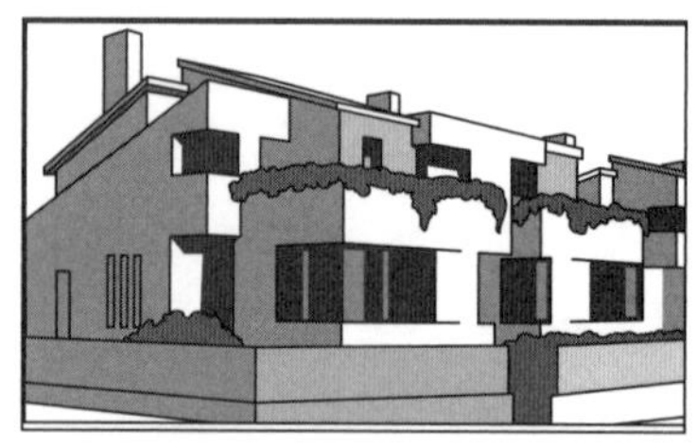

c ... un chalet

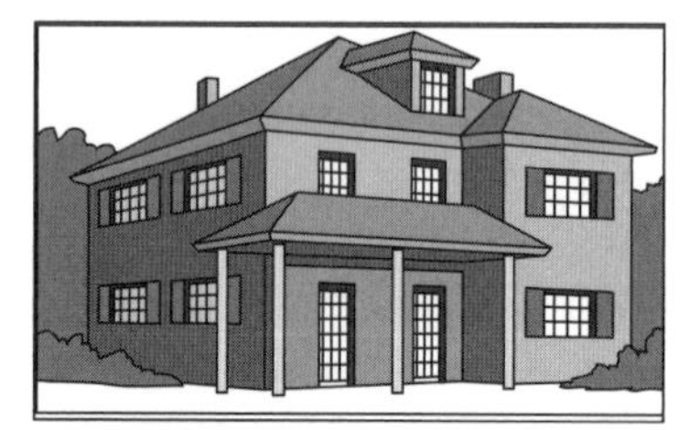

b ... una casa

d ... una habitación amueblada

11 Escucha y rellena los espacios. / Listen and fill in the gaps.

Mariví y Alfonso viven en un chalet (a) __________ y (b) __________ en una urbanización (c) __________ . Victoria y Vicente, los padres de Mariví, viven en el campo. Tienen una casa (d) __________ con dos dormitorios (e) __________ .

grande	**pequeño/a**	**moderno/a**	**viejo/a**
grandes	**pequeños/as**	**modernos/as**	**viejos/as**

gramática

How to describe something or someone.
Adjectives have to agree in number and gender with the noun.

	masculine	feminine
singular	**un piso pequeño**	**una casa pequeña**
	a small flat	a small house
plural	**unos pisos pequeños**	**unas casas pequeñas**
	some small flats	some small houses

Adjectives usually go after the noun they describe, but **pequeño** can go before.
Grande does not change in the singular: **un piso grande; una casa grande.**

12 ¿Cómo es tu casa? / What is your house like?

Label the rooms in the house with the words in the box.

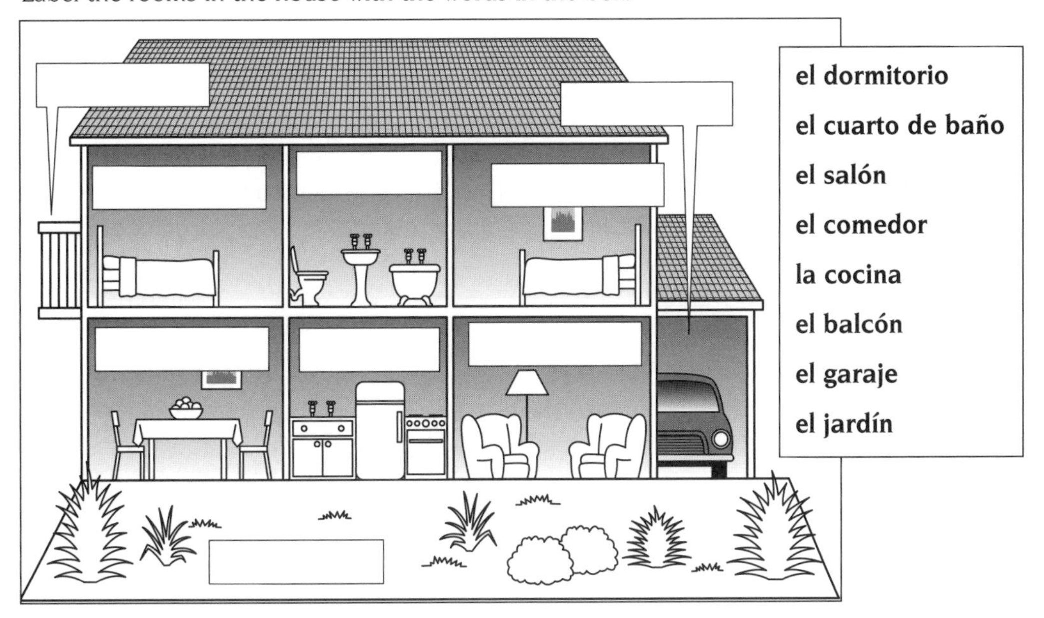

13

The transcripts of these two conversations contain a total of five mistakes.

a Escucha y subraya los errores. Listen and underline the mistakes.

Conversación 1

– ¿Vives en una casa o un piso?
– Vivo en un piso.
– ¿Es moderno o viejo?
– Es bastante viejo, muy grande.
– ¿Cuántos dormitorios tiene?
– Tiene tres dormitorios.
– ¿Tiene garaje?
– Hay aparcamiento abajo.
– ¿Tiene jardín?
– No, pero tiene balcones.

Conversación 2

– ¿Cómo es tu casa?
– Es muy vieja, y muy bonita.
– ¿Cuántos dormitorios tiene?
– Tiene tres dormitorios, uno muy pequeño.
– ¿Qué más tiene?
– Tiene cocina, dos cuartos de baño, uno arriba y el otro en la planta baja, y salón-comedor. También tiene jardín y garaje.

b Da la versión correcta. Give the correct version. For example:

El piso no es bastante viejo. Es bastante moderno.

bastante	quite/rather	**bonito/a**	pretty
muy	very	**el aparcamiento**	car park
arriba	upstairs	**la planta baja**	the ground floor
abajo	downstairs	**más**	more/else

14 En una agencia inmobiliaria / At an estate agent's

Escucha y contesta en inglés. Elisa quiere alquilar un piso amueblado.
Elisa wants to rent a furnished flat.

a Describe the one she is offered.
b How much is it per month?

Quisiera alquilar ...	I would like to rent/hire ...	**mil**	thousand
¿Cuánto es al mes?	How much is it per month?	**caro/a**	expensive
¿Quiere?*	(Do) you want?	**euro**	euro

*This is a formal way of addressing someone.

15

Take on the roles of estate agent and client. The client wants to rent a furnished flat with three bedrooms. The estate agent offers her/him one in the centre of town with three bedrooms, two bathrooms, a kitchen and sitting room, for €5,000 a month.

16 Escucha y señala los muebles que Elisa tiene en su salón. / Listen and tick the items of furniture that Elisa has in her sitting room.

Los muebles Furniture

la ventana	window	☐	**la puerta**	door	☐
la silla	chair	☐	**el sillón**	armchair	☐
el balcón	balcony	☐	**el sofá**	sofa	☐
la alfombra	carpet	☐	**el televisor**	TV set	☐
la mesa	table	☐	**el estéreo**	stereo	☐
la estantería	shelves	☐	**el vídeo**	video	☐

17

Now imagine you are offering your own house or flat for rent, and your partner is a prospective tenant. S/He has to find out what it is like, how many bedrooms it has, and how much it is a month. S/He might also like to know what you have in your sitting room. For example:

A **¿Hay televisor en el salón?** B **No, no hay televisor.**
A **¿Cuánto es el alquiler?** B **Son €500 al mes.**

gramática

tiene	s/he has, it has	**¿tiene?**	does s/he have? does it have?
hay	there is / there are	**¿hay?**	is there? / are there?

¡Extra!

18 Escucha y completa.

Listen to Juana describing her family. Fill in her family tree below with the appropriate names and ages of her relatives.

Nombres	
Isabel	Carlos
Juana	Jorge
Roberto	Juan

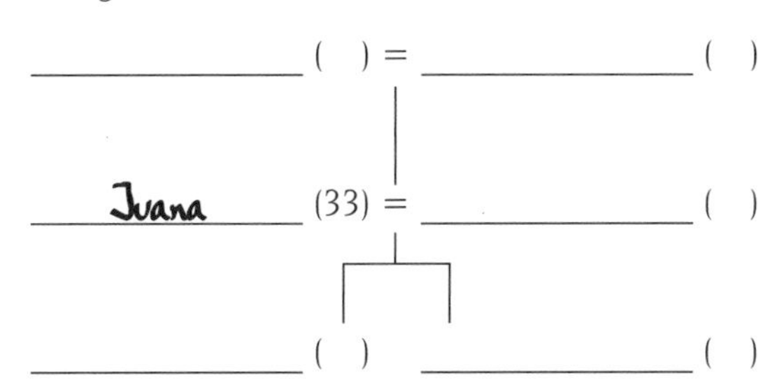

19

Read the descriptions below and match them to the rooms in the box.

a Hay una mesa en el centro con cuatro sillas. También hay dos sillones y un sofá. En el suelo hay una alfombra y en las paredes hay tres cuadros.
b Hay una cama grande de matrimonio, un armario viejo y un tocador, viejo también, con un espejo grande. En el tocador hay una lámpara.
c Tiene ducha y bañera. También hay un wáter y un lavabo con un espejo.
d Hay una mesa con cuatro sillas, una cocina, una lavadora y un frigorífico.

la cocina	el cuarto de baño	el salón	el dormitorio

20

Match the Spanish to the English. The descriptions above should help you. Try to use guesswork and a process of elimination rather than a dictionary.

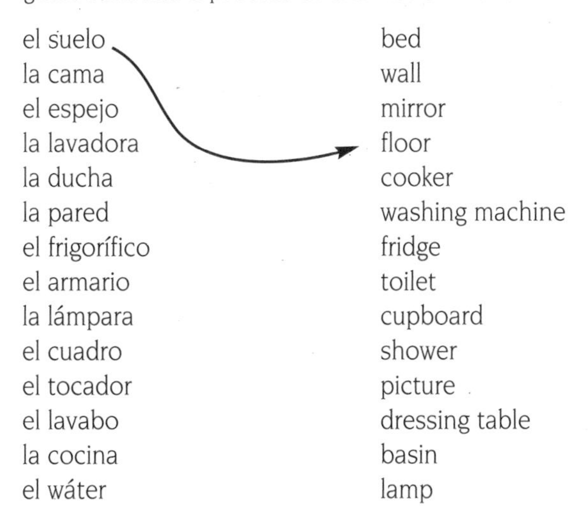

el suelo	bed
la cama	wall
el espejo	mirror
la lavadora	floor
la ducha	cooker
la pared	washing machine
el frigorífico	fridge
el armario	toilet
la lámpara	cupboard
el cuadro	shower
el tocador	picture
el lavabo	dressing table
la cocina	basin
el wáter	lamp

Gramática

- **How to say something or someone belongs to someone**

One thing owned	More than one thing		Also	
mi	**mis**	my	**La madre de Ana**	Ana's mother
tu	**tus**	your	**Los padres de Ana**	Ana's parents
su	**sus**	his/her/their		

- **Verbs**

Ser and **estar** are not interchangeable, although they are both translated by 'to be' in English. Note how they are used.
Ser is used when someone or something is in a permanent state:
Soy una mujer española. (I am and always will be a Spanish woman)
Ser is always the verb 'to be' that you use with a noun: **Es una casa.**
Estar is used when someone or something is in a temporary state:
Estoy casado/a. (I was not born married, and I could get divorced.)

- **How to talk about more than one person: 'they'**

-ar	**estar**	to be	**están**	they are	
	llamarse*	to be called	**se llaman**	they are called	(Reflexive)
-er	**aprender**	to learn	**aprenden**	they learn	
	ser*	to be	**son**	they are	(Irregular)
	tener*	to have	**tienen**	they have	(Root-changing)
-ir	**vivir**	to live	**viven**	they live	

*See page 34 for reflexive and irregular verbs. See page 46 for root-changing verbs.

- **How to describe people, places and things**

Adjectives describe nouns and have to agree with them in number and gender. Thus if a noun is masculine and singular, the adjective has to be the same. Most adjectives go after the noun.

	singular	plural
masculine	**un piso moderno**	**unos pisos modernos**
feminine	**una casa moderna**	**unas casas modernas**

Calle Guipúzcoa, Barcelona

Ejercicios de gramática

1 Answer the questions as if you were Diana. For example:

¿Rita es la madre de Lena? No, Rita es mi madre

Rita = Pablo

Carmen | Román | Juan | Diana = Andrés

Lena | Laura

a ¿Andrés es el marido de Carmen? ______________

b ¿Lena y Laura son las hijas de Román? ______________

c ¿Román y Juan son los hermanos de Rita? ______________

2 A new friend has written telling you about her family and asking about yours. Fill in the gaps with **mi**, **mis**, **tu**, **tus**, **su** or **sus**.

(a) __________ padres viven en Puerto Rico con (b) __________ hermana menor, pero (c) __________ hermano y (d) __________ mujer viven en Carolina. Tienen una hija y un hijo. (e) __________ hijos son estudiantes en la universidad.

¿Dónde viven (f) __________ padres? ¿(g) __________ familia es grande o pequeña? (h) __________ hermano mayor es abogado, ¿verdad? Y (i) __________ hijos, ¿cuántos años tienen?

3 Use the correct forms of the verbs **ser** or **estar** in the following paragraph.
Elena (a) __________ profesora. (b) __________ muy atractiva y (c) __________ casada con Manolo. Elena y su marido (d) __________ argentinos, de Buenos Aires. Los padres de Elena (e) __________ divorciados y su hermana Rosa (f) __________ separada.

4 Read about Eulalia, and then write a similar short paragraph about Eulalia and her sister Eugenia, making the necessary changes.
Se llama Eulalia y es estudiante. Estudia ciencias y aprende mucho en la universidad. Está soltera pero tiene muchos amigos.
For example: **Se llaman Eulalia y Eugenia y** __________ .

5 Change some of the adjectives in brackets in order to make them agree with the nouns they are describing.

Tengo una casa (grande) y (bonito) con tres dormitorios (cómodo). En el salón hay tres (pequeño) ventanas, un sofá (viejo) y unos sillones (moderno). La cocina también es (moderno) pero no muy (grande).

Vocabulario

Familia (f)	Family
hermano/a	brother/sister
hijo/a	son/daughter
hijos (m pl)	children
madre (f)	mother
marido (m)	husband
matrimonio (m)	married couple
mujer (f)	wife (woman)
novio/a	boy/girlfriend
padre (m)	father
padres (m pl)	parents
casado/a/s	married
divorciado/a/s	divorced
separado/a/s	separated
soltero/a/s	single
viven juntos	they live together

Possessive adjectives

mi/s	my
tu/s	your
su/s	his/her/their/your

Talking about more than one person (they)

están	they are
se llaman	they are called
son	they are
tienen	they have
viven	they live

Alojamiento (m)	Housing
casa (f)	house
chalet (m)	house
habitación (f)	room
h. amueblada	bedsit
piso (m)	flat
afueras (f pl)	outskirts
campo (m)	country
ciudad (f)	city/town
urbanización (f)	housing estate

En casa	At home
cocina (f)	kitchen
comedor (m)	dining room
cuarto (m)	room
c. de baño	bathroom
dormitorio (m)	bedroom
salón (m)	sitting room
abajo	downstairs
arriba	upstairs
planta (f) baja	ground floor

En el exterior	Outside
aparcamiento (m)	car park
balcón (m)	balcony
garaje (m)	garage
jardín (m)	garden

Adjetivos	Adjectives
amueblado/a/s	furnished
atractivo/a/s	attractive
bastante	quite
bonito/a/s	pretty
grande/s	big
moderno/a/s	modern
muy	very
pequeño/a/s	small
tradicional/es	traditional
viejo/a/s	old

En una agencia inmobiliaria	In an estate agency
Quisiera alquilar	I'd like to rent
¿Cuántos quiere?	How many do you want?
¿Cuánto es?	How much is it?

Muebles (m pl)	Furniture
alfombra (f)	carpet
armario (m)	cupboard/wardrobe
azulejo (m)	tile
bañera (f)	bath
cama (f)	bed
cocina (f)	cooker
cuadro (m)	picture
ducha (f)	shower
espejo (m)	mirror
estéreo (m)	stereo
frigorífico (m)	fridge
lámpara (f)	lamp
lavabo (m)	basin
lavadora (f)	washing machine
mesa (f)	table
mesita (f)	little table
mesita de noche (f)	bedside table
pared (f)	wall
puerta (f)	door
silla (f)	chair
sillón (m)	armchair
sofá (m)	settee
suelo (m)	floor
televisor (m)	TV set
tocador (m)	dressing table
ventana (f)	window
wáter (m)	toilet

Práctica en parejas/PARTNER WORK

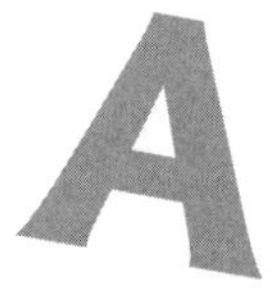

1 **a** Imagine you are Penélope or Felipe and describe your family tree below. Your partner has to fill in a family tree with details you give. Check that your partner has recorded the information correctly.

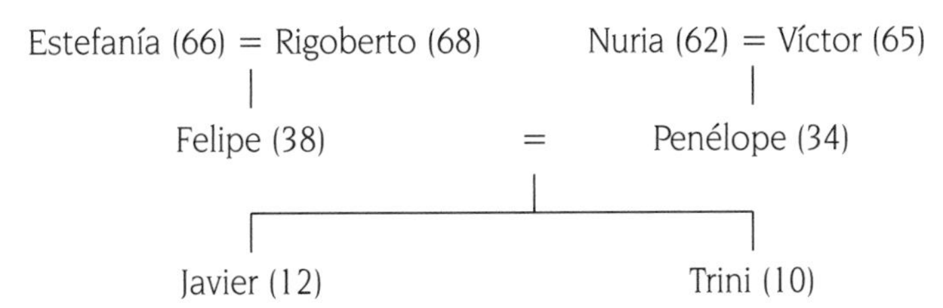

b Now your partner will describe his/her family tree to you. Fill in the family tree below with the names and ages of his or her relatives. Check the information with your partner.

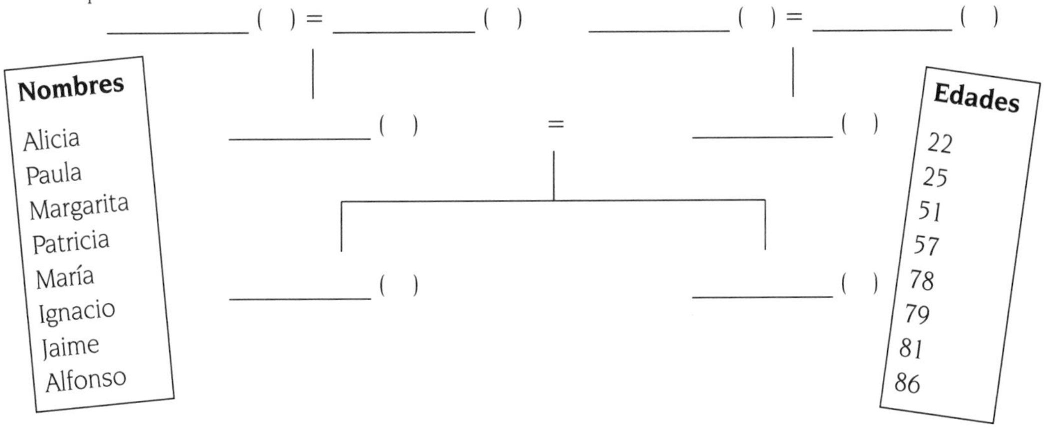

2 **a** You are an estate agent and your partner is the client. S/He wants to rent a flat. Describe this one in answer to his/her questions.

> Piso grande, 3 dormitorios, 2 baños, cocina, salón, comedor pequeño, balcón. Centro de la ciudad. Aparcamiento. €700 al mes.

b You want to rent a flat. Your partner is the estate agent. Find out if s/he has a small flat in town. Ask how many bedrooms it has and if it has a garage and a balcony. Ask how much it is.

3 **a** Describe a room containing all the furniture below. Your partner has to draw the items you mention and then tell you what room it is.

- double bed, small chair, lamp
- wardrobe, dressing table, mirror

b Draw the items listed by your partner and work out what room they are in.

Práctica en parejas/PARTNER WORK

1 **a** Your partner will describe his/her family tree to you. Fill in the family tree below with the names and ages of his/her relatives. Check the information with your partner.

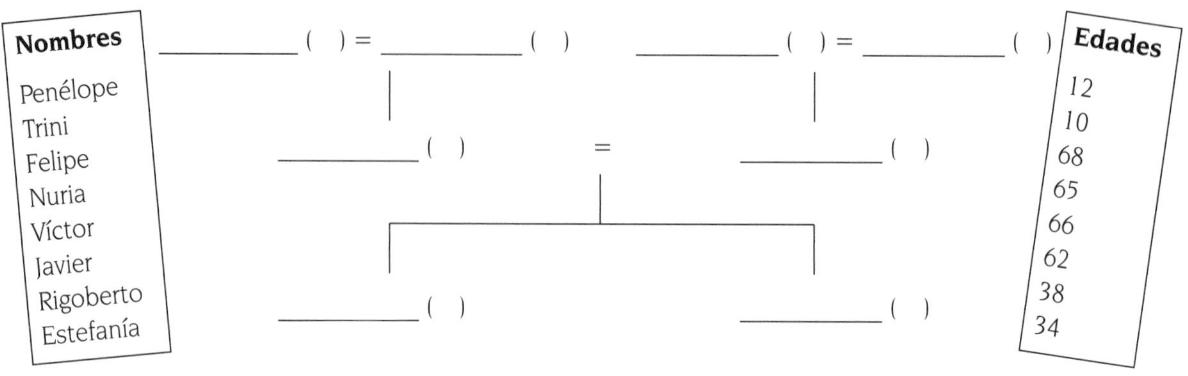

b Imagine you are Margarita or Jaime and describe your family tree below. Your partner has to fill in a blank family tree with the details you give. Check that your partner has recorded the information correctly.

Alicia (78) = Ignacio (81)   Paula (79) = Alfonso (86)

Margarita (51) = Jaime (57)

Patricia (25)   María (22)

2 **a** You want to rent a flat. Your partner is the estate agent. Find out if s/he has a large flat in the centre of town. Ask how many bedrooms it has and if it has a garage and a balcony. Ask how much it is.

b You are an estate agent and your partner is the client. S/He wants to rent a flat. Describe the one below in answer to his/her questions.

> Piso pequeño, 1 dormitorio, baño, cocina, salón-comedor. En el centro de la ciudad. €500 al mes.

3 **a** Draw the items of furniture listed by your partner and work out what room they are in.

b Describe a room containing all the furniture below. Your partner has to draw the items you mention and then tell you what room it is.

- large table with four chairs, cooker, fridge, washing machine, large window

3 La rutina

In this unit you will learn how to tell the time and describe your own and other people's daily routine. You will also find out how to say what someone is doing now.

1 **¿Qué hora es?** / What time is it?

Es la una.

Son las dos.

Son las siete menos cuarto.

Son las cinco y media.

Write these times in numbers. For example:
Son las dos menos veinte de la tarde. 13:40

a Son las siete y diez de la mañana.

b Son las cuatro y cuarto de la tarde.

c Son las once y veinte de la noche.

d Son las ocho menos cinco de la mañana.

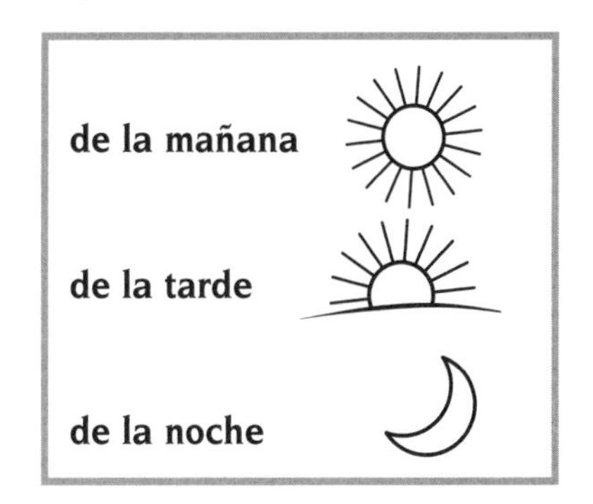

2 **Escucha y subraya la hora correcta.** / Listen and underline the correct time.

a 10:00 10:10

b 02:10 12:10

c 16:15 15:45

d 15:05 14:55

e 24:00 00:20

f 02:20 09:40

3 **Escucha y completa las frases.** / Listen and complete the sentences.

Carmen is saying what she does each day. For example:

a **Me levanto a las siete y media.**
b **Desayuno a las ...**
c **Salgo de casa ...**
d **Llego a la universidad ...**

e **Voy a clase ...**
f **Como en la cantina ...**
g **Vuelvo a casa ...**
h **Ceno ...**

4 **Escucha y completa las frases.**

Carmen wants to know about Eduardo's daily routine.

Carmen	**Eduardo**
a ¿A qué hora te levantas?	Me levanto …
b ¿A qué hora desayunas?	Desayuno …
c ¿A qué hora sales de casa?	Salgo de casa …
d ¿A qué hora vas a clase?	Voy a clase …
e ¿A qué hora comes?	Como …
f ¿A qué hora vuelves a casa?	Vuelvo a casa …
g ¿A qué hora cenas?	Ceno …

5

Ask your partner the same questions.

6 Escucha y rellena el horario. / Listen and fill in the timetable.

It is the start of term and Carmen is being given her timetable.

	9:00	10:00	11:00	12:00	13:00	17:00	18:00	19:00	20:00
lunes		*Español*							
martes		*Ciencias (laboratorio)*							
miércoles	*Informática*					*Deportes*			
jueves									
viernes									

la ciencia	science	**el seminario**	seminar	**los deportes**	sports
la conferencia	lecture	**la informática**	IT	**la biblioteca**	library

lunes	Monday	**jueves**	Thursday	**domingo**	Sunday
martes	Tuesday	**viernes**	Friday		
miércoles	Wednesday	**sábado**	Saturday		

Days of the week are not written with capital letters in Spanish. All are masculine.

7 Eduardo is asking Carmen about her course. Put the answers in the right order.

Eduardo	**Carmen**
a ¿A qué hora empiezas los lunes?	Voy a la biblioteca.
b ¿Terminas temprano los viernes?	Empiezo a las diez.
c ¿Qué haces los jueves por la mañana?	Tengo 16 horas en total.
d ¿Adónde vas los miércoles por la tarde?	No. Termino a las siete.
e ¿Cuántas horas de clase tienes en total?	Voy al centro deportivo.

8 Ask your partner similar questions about his or her own timetable.

9 Escucha y señala las respuestas correctas. / Listen and tick the correct answers.

Pepe and Ana are taking part in a game show for couples. How well does Pepe know his wife? Which of his answers are correct?

- Se levanta a las ocho y media. ☐
- Por la mañana trabaja. ☐
- Por la tarde va de compras. ☐
- Come en casa. ☐
- Vuelve a las siete. ☐
- Ve la televisión. ☐
- Se acuesta temprano por la noche. ☐

por la mañana	in the morning
por la noche	at night
ir de compras	to go shopping
temprano	early

10

Test your memory. Give the correct answers to these questions about Ana.

a ¿A qué hora se levanta Ana? Se levanta a las ...

b ¿A qué hora empieza a trabajar? Empieza ...

c ¿Dónde come a mediodía? Come ...

d ¿A qué hora termina por la tarde? ______

e ¿Adónde va después del trabajo? ______

f ¿A qué hora vuelve a casa? ______

Terrazas en la plaza de la Paz, Castellón de la Plana

11 ¿Qué trabajo hace? / What job does s/he do?

Match what the people do every day to their job.

a Limpia la casa y va de compras por la mañana.
Por la tarde prepara la comida y trabaja en el jardín.

b Trabaja por la noche y duerme durante el día.
Sabe quién entra y quién sale del edificio.

c Llega a la oficina a las nueve. Escribe cartas por la mañana.
Por la tarde asiste a las reuniones. Habla mucho por teléfono.

d Trabaja mucho. Se levanta temprano, a las seis, y llega al hospital a las siete y media. Normalmente termina muy tarde, a las once o a medianoche.

secretaria	portero/a	ama de casa	médico

12

Describe what one of these people does.
Your partner has to guess who you are talking about. For example:

A **Trabaja en un hospital. Empieza a las seis.**
B **¿Es enfermera?**
A **Sí. Es enfermera. / No, no es enfermera.**

estudiante	jardinero	enfermera	periodista	camarero/a	profesor/a

La universidad de Barcelona

13 ¿Qué está haciendo Carmen? / What is Carmen doing?

Carmen is having a day off. Choose a suitable caption for each pair of pictures.

a Normalmente Carmen vuelve a casa a las 8.00, pero hoy está saliendo de casa.

b Normalmente Carmen come en la cantina, pero hoy está comiendo en casa.

c Normalmente a las 7.30 Carmen se levanta, pero hoy está durmiendo en la cama.

d Normalmente a las 9.00 Carmen va a clase, pero hoy está desayunando.

1  

2  

3  

4  

14

Pick a time at random from the pictures above. Your partner says what Carmen is doing at that time today.
For example:
A **Son las nueve.**
B **Carmen está desayunando.**

gramática

To describe what someone is doing now, use the present continuous:
estar (to be) + present participle

estoy hablando	I am speaking
estás comiendo	you are eating
está saliendo	s/he is leaving

15 ¿Qué dice Carmen que está haciendo? / What does Carmen say she is doing?

Carmen doesn't want to see Ignacio. Listen and complete her excuses.

a lunes Estoy trabajando.
b martes ________ comiendo.
c miércoles ________ .
d jueves ________ la cena.
e viernes ________ un informe.
f sábado ________ la tele.
g domingo ________ .

ver **trabajar**
comer **escribir**
preparar **desayunar**
estudiar

16 ¡A comer! / Let's eat!

With a partner, see how quickly you can match the words to the pictures.

la sopa	**la fruta**
el café	**el agua**
el vino	**las galletas**
las verduras	**el pan**
los cereales	**la mantequilla**
la carne	**el bocadillo**
la cerveza	**la mermelada**
el zumo	**el pescado**
la ensalada	**la leche**

17

Ask your partner what s/he has for each meal.
For example:

A **¿Qué tomas para el desayuno?**
B **Como cereales y bebo café con leche.**

el desayuno	breakfast
el almuerzo	lunch
la cena	dinner
tomar	to have/to take
beber	to drink

18 Escucha y señala (✓✗) las respuestas correctas.

Pepe and Ana are comparing eating habits.

		Pepe	Ana
a	¿Come carne?	✓	✗
b	¿Es vegetariano/a?	☐	☐
c	¿Come muchas verduras?	☐	☐
d	¿Toma azúcar en el café?	☐	☐
e	¿Bebe vino?	☐	☐

yo sí	I do
yo no	I don't
yo también	so do I
yo tampoco	nor do I

19

Compare your own eating habits with those of your partner.
For example:

A **¿Comes carne?**
B **No, no como carne.**
A **Yo sí.**

20 Escucha y escribe lo que piden Juana y Lucía en un bar. / Listen and write what Juana and Lucía order in a bar.

a Juana pide …

b Lucía pide …

BAR LA PLAYA
Las bebidas
la limonada el whisky
la Coca-Cola la tónica
el jerez el coñac
Las tapas
los champiñones la tortilla
las patatas fritas las olivas
los calamares el jamón

21 Escucha y rellena los espacios. / Listen and fill in the gaps.

Águeda is in a restaurant. What does she order?

Camarero	¿Qué quiere tomar señora?
Águeda	Quisiera (a) … y (b) … .
Camarero	¿Quiere algo de beber?
Águeda	Quiero (c) …, por favor.
	¿Qué hay de postre?
Camarero	Hay (d) …, (e) …
Águeda	No, no quiero (f) … .
	La cuenta, por favor.

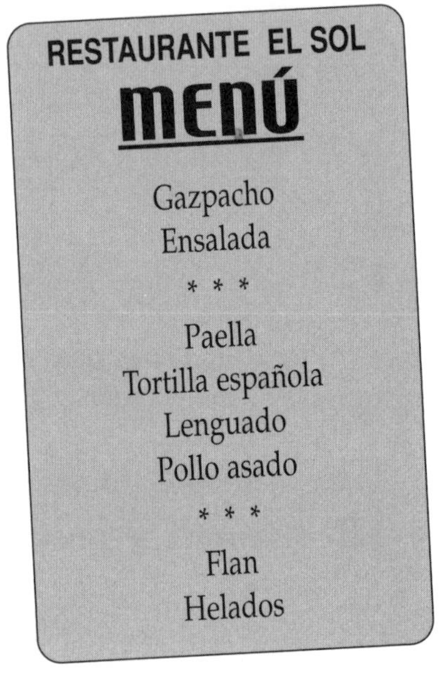

22

Take on the roles of waiter/ress and customers. Practise ordering items from the menu above in pairs or groups.

gramática

To talk formally to a person, use the same verb forms as for *he/she* or *they*, if you are talking to more than one person. You can omit the word for *you* (**usted/es**) if it is clear you are talking *to* someone:

¿Qué quiere?	What does *s/he* want? What do *you* want?
Usted quiere vino.	You want wine.
¿Qué quieren?	What do they want?/What do you (more than one person) want?
Ustedes quieren vino.	You (more than one person) want wine.

23 La buena vida / The good life

Read this extract from a radio interview with Manuel Ibarra.

a **Busca la traducción correcta.** Find the correct translation.

"No hacer absolutamente nada puede ser más sano que trabajar. Los momentos de relax fortalecen el sistema inmunológico, y dormir la siesta todos los días ayuda a reducir el estrés."

no hacer nada	more healthy
puede ser	doing nothing
más sano	relaxation
relax	can be
fortalecen	to sleep
dormir	stress
todos los días	helps
ayuda	strengthen
el estrés	every day

b **Escucha la entrevista y escribe los porcentajes.** Listen to the interview and write in the percentages

el tiempo	time
una vez por semana	once a week

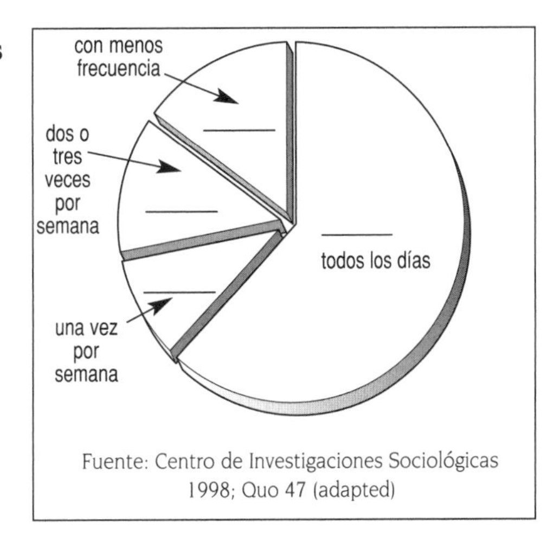

Fuente: Centro de Investigaciones Sociológicas 1998; Quo 47 (adapted)

24 Lee y contesta en inglés.

What makes Juan ill once a week?

Cómo evitar trabajar

Juan no quiere trabajar. Pasa horas en el wáter pensando en cómo puede evitar el trabajo. Hoy le está diciendo al director que tiene demasiado trabajo, y no puede hacer más. En efecto, con el estrés de tanto evitar trabajar se pone enfermo un día por semana.

evitar	to avoid
pensando	thinking
puede	he can
diciendo	telling
demasiado	too much
tanto	so much
se pone enfermo/a	s/he gets ill

Gramática

- **Regular Verbs**

-ar		**-er**		**-ir**	
Singular					
estudiar	to study	**comer**	to eat	**vivir**	to live
estudio	I study	**como**	I eat	**vivo**	I live
estudias	you study	**comes**	you eat	**vives**	you live
estudia	s/he studies	**come**	s/he eats	**vive**	s/he lives
	you (formal) study		you (formal) eat		you (formal) live

For the plural forms of the verbs ('we', 'you' when speaking to more than one person, and 'they') see Unit 4.

- Reflexive verbs have the normal **-ar**, **-er** or **-ir** endings, but also have a reflexive pronoun to indicate that the person is doing something to, by or for him/herself.

llamarse	to be called (to call oneself)		
me llamo	I am called (I call myself)	**nos llamamos**	we are called
te llamas	you are called	**os llamáis**	you are called
se llama	s/he is called; you are called	**se llaman**	they/you are called

- Personal pronouns indicate *who* is doing something.

yo	I	**nosotros/as**	we
tú	you	**vosotros/as**	you
él/ella	he/she	**ellos/ellas**	they
usted*	you (formal)	**ustedes***	you (formal)

*Also written **Vd. / Vds.**

- **Two irregular verbs**

ser	to be	**ir**	to go
soy	I am	**voy**	I go
eres	you are	**vas**	you go
es	s/he is	**va**	s/he goes
somos	we are	**vamos**	we go
sois	you are	**vais**	you go
son	they are	**van**	they go

- **How to describe what someone is doing at the moment**

Present continuous

Estar + present participle		Present participle
Estoy llegando (I am arriving)	**llegar:**	**llegando**
Estás bebiendo (you are drinking)	**beber:**	**bebiendo**
Está saliendo (s/he is leaving)	**salir:**	**saliendo**

Ejercicios de gramática

1 Fill in the gaps with the verbs in the box.
Yo (a) __________ en Navarra y (b) __________ ciencias generales en la Universidad de Pamplona. También (c) __________ francés. (d) __________ por la mañana y (e) __________ en la cantina. Por la tarde (f) __________ novelas. Después de cenar (g) __________ la tele o (h) __________ con amigos.

aprendo	**estudio**	**trabajo**	**veo**	**vivo**	**escribo**	**salgo**	**como**

2 Change the verbs in brackets into the appropriate form. For example:
¿Dónde (vivir/tú)? ¿Dónde vives?

a ¿Dónde (vivir, tú)?	(Vivir, yo) en Almería.
b ¿A qué hora (levantarse, tú)?	(Levantarse, yo) a las ocho.
c ¿Cuándo (llegar, tú) al trabajo?	(Llegar, yo) al trabajo a las tres.
d ¿Dónde (comer, tú) a mediodía?	(Comer, yo) en un restaurante.
e ¿A qué hora (terminar, tú)?	(Terminar, yo) a las ocho.

3 What informal and formal questions would you ask to get the following answers?

(trabajar)	**¿Dónde trabajas?**	**¿Dónde trabaja usted?**	**En el banco.**
a (levantarse)			A las siete.
b (comer)			En un bar.
c (terminar)			A las dos.
d (salir mucho)			No.

4 Make at least five sentences by combining items from each column.
For example: **Los niños están escuchando a la profesora.**

Los niños	estoy	comiendo	a la profesora.
Vosotros	estás	mirando	un bocadillo.
Julio	está	saliendo	por la ventana.
Yo	estamos	hablando	con Javier.
Tú	estáis	escuchando	de la clase.
Nosotros	están	escribiendo	en el libro.

5 Write five sentences describing what the people in your class are doing at the moment.

Vocabulario

Verbos	Verbs
(Some of these are given in full on page 46.)	
acostarse*	to go to bed
almorzar*	to have lunch
aprender	to learn
asistir	to be present at
beber	to drink
cenar	to have dinner
comer	to eat
decir*†	to say/tell
desayunar	to have breakfast
dormir*	to sleep
empezar*	to start
entrar	to enter
escribir	to write
estar†	to be
estudiar	to study
hablar	to speak
hacer†	to do
ir†	to go
levantarse	to get up
limpiar	to clean
llegar	to arrive
pasar	to spend
pensar*	to think
preparar	to prepare
quedarse	to stay
querer*	to want
salir†	to go out
ser†	to be
tener*†	to have
terminar	to finish
tomar	to take/have
trabajar	to work
ver	to see/watch
vivir	to live
volver*	to return
hay	there is/are

* root-changing
† irregular

Lugares (*m pl*)	Places
cantina (f)	canteen
centro (m) deportivo	sports centre
cine (m)	cinema
edificio (m)	building
gimnasio (m)	gymnasium
hospital (m)	hospital
oficina (f)	office

El día	The day
mañana (f)	morning
noche (f)	night
tarde (f)	afternoon/evening
tarde	late
temprano	early

Profesiones (*f pl*)	Professions/Jobs
ama (f) de casa	housewife
camarero/a	waiter/ress
enfermero/a	nurse
jardinero/a	gardener
portero/a	porter

Comidas (*f pl*)	Meals
almuerzo (m)	lunch
cena (f)	dinner
desayuno (m)	breakfast
postre (m)	dessert
vegetariano/a	vegetarian

Comida (*f*)	Food
aceituna (f)	olive
azúcar (m)	sugar
bocadillo (m)	sandwich
calamares (m pl)	squid
carne (f)	meat
cereal (m)	cereal
champiñón (m)	mushroom
ensalada (f)	salad
flan (m)	crème caramel
fruta (f)	fruit
galleta (f)	biscuit
gazpacho (m)	cold soup
helado (m)	ice cream
jamón (m)	ham
lenguado (m)	sole
mantequilla (f)	butter
mermelada (f)	jam
oliva (f)	olive
paella (f)	paella
pan (m)	bread
pan (m) tostado	toast
patata (f) frita	chip/crisp
pescado (m)	fish
pollo (m) asado	roast chicken
sopa (f)	soup
tortilla (f)	omelette
verduras (f pl)	greens

For more vocabulary turn to the Appendix on p. 181.

Práctica en parejas/PARTNER WORK

1 Say the times. Your partner writes them down. You check they are correct. For example:
A 10.00 **Son las diez de la mañana.**

a 10.10 **b** 12.45 **c** 02.20 **d** 14.25 **e** 12.30

2 You want to go out for a drink with your partner. By referring to your diary below, try to find a time when you are both free (**libre**).
For example:
A **¿Estás libre el martes por la tarde?**
B **No. El martes por la tarde no estoy libre. Tengo clase.**

	Por la mañana	Por la tarde	Por la noche
lunes	Trabajo	Trabajo	Teatro con Chus
martes	Trabajo		Cine
miércoles		Trabajo	Trabajo
jueves	Trabajo	Gimnasio	
viernes	Trabajo	Trabajo	Bar con Charo
sábado	De compras		Cine con Pedro
domingo	En casa de mis padres		

3 Mime an activity from the box. Your partner has to say what you are doing.
For example:
A (doing an action) **¿Qué estoy haciendo?**
B **¿Estás escribiendo?**
A **Sí, estoy escribiendo. / No, no estoy escribiendo.**

escribir	**pintar**
salir	**entrar**
comer	**beber**
leer	**escuchar**
estudiar	**hablar**

4 Have a conversation in a bar in which you are the customer and your partner is the barman or barmaid. Your partner speaks first.

B ______________________ A Say, 'I want a beer, please'.

B ______________________ A Ask what there is. **(¿Qué hay?)**

B ______________________ A Say, 'I want some olives, please'.

Práctica en parejas/PARTNER WORK

1 Say the times. Your partner writes them down. You check they are correct. For example:
17.00 **Son las cinco de la tarde.**

a 15.10 **b** 16.45 **c** 05.15 **d** 20.25 **e** 02.30

2 You want to go out for a drink with your partner. By referring to your diary below, try to find a time when you are both free (**libre**).
For example:
A **¿Estás libre el martes por la tarde?**
B **No. El martes por la tarde no estoy libre. Tengo clase.**

	Por la mañana	Por la tarde	Por la noche
lunes	Clase	Clase	
martes		Clase	Trabajo
miércoles	Clase	Clase	Gimnasio
jueves	Clase	Clase	
viernes		Clase	Cine con Miguel
sábado	De compras		Bar con Carlos
domingo	En casa de mis abuelos		

3 Mime an activity from the box. Your partner has to say what you are doing.
For example:
A (doing an action) **¿Qué estoy haciendo?**
B **¿Estás escribiendo?**
A **Sí, estoy escribiendo. / No, no estoy escribiendo.**

escribir	**pintar**
salir	**entrar**
comer	**beber**
leer	**escuchar**
estudiar	**hablar**

4 Have a conversation in a bar in which you are the barman or barmaid and your partner is the customer. You speak first.

B Say 'Hello' and ask 'What do you want?' A ________

B Ask 'Do you want anything to eat?' A ________

B Say 'There are mushrooms, ham, squid, olives, sandwiches …' A ________

4 El tiempo libre

In this unit you will learn how to discuss the things you like doing in the evenings and at weekends. You will also learn how to make, accept and reject invitations and to buy tickets for shows.

1 ¿Qué te gusta hacer? / What do you like doing?

Escucha y junta a la persona con lo que le gusta. Listen and match the person to what s/he likes.

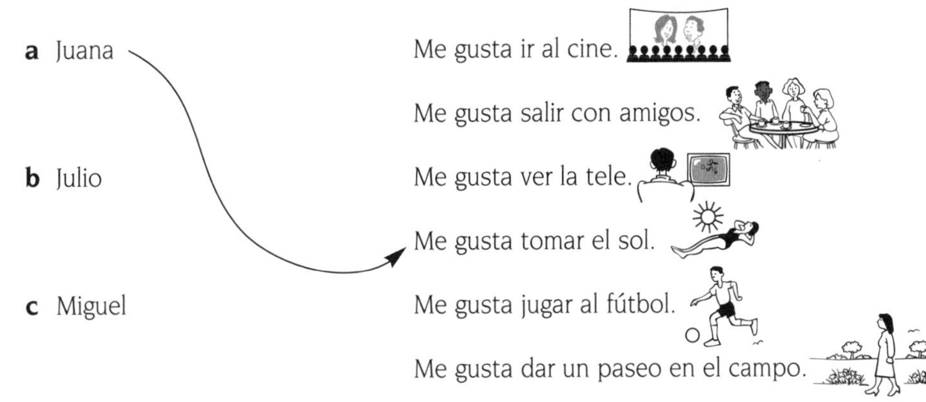

2 ¿Cómo responde Julio? / How does Julio reply?

Julio is being asked if he likes certain activities. Write his answers. For example:

¿Te gusta escuchar música? **Sí, me gusta.**
¿Te gusta jugar al tenis? **No, no me gusta.**

a ¿Te gusta fumar cigarros?
...
b ¿Te gusta ir de compras?
...
c ¿Te gusta hacer ejercicio?
...
d ¿Te gusta trabajar?
...
e ¿Te gusta bailar?
...
f ¿Te gusta leer?
...

3

Ask your partner if s/he likes the activities in Sections 1 and 2 above. For example:

A **¿Te gusta ver la tele?**
B **Sí. Me gusta./No, no me gusta.**

gramática

Me gusta.
I like it (it pleases me).
Te gusta.
You like it (it pleases you).

4 ¿Te gusta el deporte? / Do you like sport?

Match the pictures to the sports. Look up any you can't guess in the vocabulary section on page 48.

a el canotaje **b** el banyi **c** el squash **d** la equitación **e** el patinaje

5 Escucha y junta las preguntas con las respuestas.

Juana wants to know what Miguel thinks of these sports.

Juana	Miguel	
a ¿Te gusta el ciclismo?	Sí, me encanta.	✓✓✓
b ¿Te gusta el aerobic?	Sí, me gusta mucho.	✓✓
c ¿Te gusta el montañismo?	Sí, me gusta bastante.	✓
d ¿Te gusta el críquet?	No, no me gusta mucho.	✗
e ¿Te gusta el kárate?	No, no me gusta nada.	✗✗

6

Ask your partner the questions in Section 5 above.

7

Test your memory. What did Miguel say about the sports?

	Verdad (True)	**Falso** (False)
a A Miguel le encanta el críquet.	☐	☐
b No le gusta nada el kárate.	☐	☐
c Le gusta bastante el montañismo.	☐	☐
d Le encanta el aerobic.	☐	☐
e No le gusta mucho el ciclismo.	☐	☐

gramática

Le gusta.
S/He likes (it) (it pleases him/her).
A Miguel le gusta.
Miguel likes (it).

8

Find out which sports in Sections 4 and 5 your partner likes and be prepared to tell your tutor. For example:

A Fred le encanta ... Le gusta ... No le gusta nada ...

9 **Me gustan.** / I like them. **No me gustan.** / I don't like them.

Me gusta el vino.

No me gustan las mañanas.

No me gusta el trabajo.

Me gustan las vacaciones.

10

Ask your partner:

¿Te gusta **el vino?**
el curso?
el trabajo?
¿Te gustan **las vacaciones?**
las clases?
las mañanas?

gramática

To say someone likes more than one thing:

Me gustan.	I like *them*.
Te gustan.	You like *them*.
Le gustan.	S/He likes *them*. You like *them*. (formal)

11 **Escucha y rellena los espacios.**

Three people are telling you about themselves.

	Andrés	Bea	Carlos
le gusta		ir de compras	
le gustan			las clases
no le gusta			
no le gustan	los coches		

12

Who would say the following? For example:

«A Bea le gusta ir de compras y a mí también.» Carlos

a «A Andrés no le gusta hacer deporte y a mí tampoco.» __________

b «A Carlos le gustan las clases pero a mí no.» __________

c «A Andrés no le gustan los coches pero a mí sí.» __________

gramática

To emphasize or specify who likes something: **a mí, a ti, a él, a ella**, etc

A mí me gustan las comedias pero a ti no (te gustan).

I like comedies but *you* don't (like them).

A ella no le gusta la música pop pero a él sí (le gusta).

She doesn't like pop music but *he* does (like it).

13 **¿Quieres ir al cine?** / Do you want to go to the cinema?

Escucha y lee.

Juana	**Carlos**
¿Quieres ir al cine?	Sí, quiero. ¿Qué ponen?
Perdita Durango de Álex de la Iglesia.	¿Cuándo es?
El viernes.	¿A qué hora empieza?
A las diez.	¿Dónde nos encontramos?
En la entrada del cine.	Vale.

14

Invite your partner out. S/He must say whether s/he wants to go or not.
For example:

A **¿Quieres ir al cine? (a + el = al)**
B **Sí, quiero. / No, no quiero.**

el cine	**el teatro**
el club	**el concierto**

15

a Invite your partner to the cinema.

Carne trémula
Dir. Pedro Almodóvar
sábado a las 22.30h

A	B
Ask 'Do you want to come to the cinema'?	Say 'Yes, I do', and ask what's on.
Say '*Carne trémula* by Pedro Almodóvar'.	Ask 'When is it?'
Say 'Saturday.'	Ask 'What time does it start?'
Say 'At 10.30.'	Ask 'Where shall we meet?'
Say 'In the cinema foyer.'	Say 'OK.'

b Your partner can now invite you to see *Los amantes del círculo polar*.

Los amantes del círculo polar
Dir. Julio Medem
viernes a las 23.00h

16 **¿A qué club deciden ir?** / Which club do they decide to go to?

Juana and Carlos are wondering how to spend the evening.

Club	**Hora**	**Música**	**Entradas**
La Boite	23.00 h	Los Stompers	€12
Luz de Gas	24.30 h	Tandoori Lenoir	€15
El Mojito	24.00 h	Orquesta sabor cubano	€16
El Moog	24.00 h	Los Taxi Boys. Noche Latin-Lover	€10

17 ¿Qué prefieres hacer? / What do you prefer to do?

Escucha y junta a la persona con lo que prefiere. Four people are trying to find something to do together that they all enjoy.

a Juana	**1** No quiero salir. Prefiero quedarme en casa y ver la tele.
b Carlos	**2** No me gustan los clubs. Prefiero ir al centro deportivo.
c Lucía	**3** No quiero bailar. Prefiero charlar en un bar.
d Marco	**4** No me gustan los bares. Prefiero ir al cine.

18

Ask your partner if s/he wants to do something. S/He will say s/he prefers to do something else. For example:

A **¿Quieres ver la tele?** B **No. Prefiero escuchar la radio.**

a ¿Jugar al fútbol? (Jugar al tenis) **b** ¿Hacer gimnasia? (Hacer footing)

c ¿Dar un paseo? (Ir de compras) **d** ¿Salir? (Quedarme en casa)

19 Tengo que trabajar. / I have to work.

¿Qué tienen que hacer? What do they have to do?
Sometimes you can't accept an invitation because you have to do something else.

a Esther: «Tengo que ...»

b Bea:

c Carlos:

> **gramática**
>
> These are all root-changing verbs See page 46.
>
> **quiero** I want
> **prefiero** I prefer
> **puedo** I can
>
> Irregular in the **yo** form:
> **tengo que** I have to

20 Quiero pero no puedo. / I want to but I can't.

Invite your partner to do the things below. S/He has to refuse, giving a different excuse each time. For example:

A **¿Quieres venir al cine esta noche?**
B **Quiero pero no puedo. Tengo que trabajar.**

A	B
¿Quieres ...	**Quiero pero no puedo. Tengo que ...**
venir al club esta noche?	**quedarme en casa.**
ver una película?	**preparar la cena.**
dar un paseo en el campo?	**estudiar.**
ir al gimnasio?	**ir de compras.**

21 ¿Queréis venir? / Do you want to come?

Escucha y rellena los espacios en las preguntas.
Julio and Lucía are inviting Juana and Carlos to the concert below.

CONCIERTO
Manuel García, ex-componente de El Último de la Fila toca el 24 de septiembre en la Plaza de Toros de Las Ventas (Madrid). 22.30h. Entradas € 20.

Julio	Lucía y yo vamos a un concierto. ¿Tú y Carlos queréis venir?
Juana	¿ (a) __________ vais?
Julio	Vamos esta noche.
Juana	¿ (b) __________ ?
Julio	Manuel García de El Último de la Fila.
Juana	Sí, queremos ir con vosotros. ¿ (c) __________ ?
Julio	Empieza a las diez y media.
Juana	¿Cuánto cuestan (d) __________ ?
Julio	Las entradas cuestan €20.

¿Qué hay? What's on?

gramática

nosotros	we	**vamos**	we go	**queremos**	we want
vosotros	you (pl)	**vais**	you (pl) go	**queréis**	you (pl) want

22

This conversation does not make sense. Match the questions to the right answers.

- **a** Tú y Bea, ¿qué hacéis vosotros mañana por la tarde?
- **b** Ana y yo vamos al cine el jueves. ¿Queréis venir?
- **c** ¿Podéis venir el viernes?
- **d** ¿El sábado estáis libres?
- **e** ¿El domingo?

1. El viernes no podemos. Vamos a un concierto.
2. El sábado preferimos ir a un restaurante.
3. No. El domingo no. Hay un programa muy interesante en la tele.
4. ¿Nosotros? Mañana por la tarde estudiamos.
5. Queremos pero no podemos. El jueves tenemos que trabajar.

Plaza De Castilla, Madrid

¡Extra!

23 Entrevistas con estrellas / Interviews with stars

Read this magazine interview with María Magnolia, a (fictional) film star. Put the programmes she mentions into the correct groups, according to whether she loves, likes, dislikes or hates them.

Periodista ¿Te gusta la tele?

María Magnolia La tele, la adoro. La veo todas las noches, sobre todo los culebrones que grabo durante el día en vídeo. Me encantan también los dramas psicológicos y las series policíacas – pero no me gustan nada las películas violentas y si creo que me van a dar miedo, la apago o cambio de canal.

Periodista ¿Te interesan las noticias?

María Magnolia Bastante. Pero no me gusta mucho ver las noticias en la tele – prefiero escuchar la radio o leer un periódico para saber lo que pasa en el mundo. Tampoco veo los documentales.

Periodista ¿Y las comedias?

María Magnolia Me gustan mucho. También las entrevistas con estrellas y los programas concurso.

a Le encantan

b Le gustan mucho

c No le gustan

d Aborrece

el culebrón	soap opera
el concurso	competition (game show)
las noticias	the news

24

Judging by their tastes in sports, music and films, how compatible are these couples? Put ✓ if they will get on well together and ✗ if not.

a Miguel and Bea ☐ **b** Juana and Jaime ☐ **c** Julio and Ángela ☐

25

Interamor is an organization which gets people together on the Internet. Which of these two people do you have most in common with? Say why.
For example: **A Iñaki le gusta el jazz y a mí también.**

¡Hola! Me llamo Iñaki, y me encanta la música - sobre todo el rock duro. El jazz me gusta bastante también, pero no me gusta nada el heavy, ni el punki tampoco. El tecno me gusta para bailar.

¡Hola! Soy Itziar. ¿Qué tal? ¿Te gusta la música? Pues a mí también, sobre todo el soul y la música latinoamericana. No me gusta mucho la música pop. Me encanta el flamenco.

Gramática

- **How to say you like something**

Gustar 'to please'

To say you like one thing:

(a mí) me gusta	**(a ti) te gusta**	**(a él/ella/usted) le gusta**
I like it	you like it	he/she likes it; you (formal) like it

To say you like more than one thing:

me gustan	**te gustan**	**le gustan**
I like them	you like them	he/she likes them; you (formal) like them

Because **gustar** means 'to please' and not 'to like', in Spanish you have to say 'X pleases me', rather than 'I like X'. Thus to say you like more than one thing, you need to say 'they please me'. For emphasis you can add **a mí**, **a ti**, **a él**, **a ella** or **a usted**.

- **How to express obligation, desire and ability**

You need to use two verbs, the second of which is an infinitive.

Tener que	**Querer**	**Poder**
to have to	to want	to be able
tengo que trabajar	**quiero salir**	**puedo jugar**
I have to work	I want to go out	I can play

Personal pronouns (plurals)

vosotros	you (informal)	**ustedes**	you (formal)
nosotros	we	**ellos/ellas**	they (male/female)

- **Plural forms of verbs**

-ar	**estamos**	we are
	estáis	you (informal) are
	están	they/you (formal) are
-er	**comemos**	we eat
	coméis	you eat
	comen	they/you eat
-ir	**salimos**	we leave
	salís	you leave
	salen	they/you leave

- **Root-changing verbs**

These have a vowel in the 'root' of the verb which changes in all parts of the present tense except for the **nosotros** and **vosotros** forms.

Querer

quiero	**queremos**
quieres	**queréis**
quiere	**quieren**

Poder

puedo	**podemos**
puedes	**podéis**
puede	**pueden**

Tener and **venir** are root-changing verbs which are also irregular in the **yo** form: **tengo** (I have); **vengo** (I come).

Ejercicios de gramática

1 Fill in the gaps in the sentences with the words from the box.

me	**te**	**le**
gusta		
gustan		

– A mí (a) _____ _____ las novelas policíacas.
¿Qué tipo de novelas (b) _____ _____ a ti?
– A mí no (c) _____ _____ leer. Prefiero ver la tele.
¿Cuáles son los programas que (d) _____ _____ a ti?
– Los programas que a mí (e) _____ _____ más son las noticias.
A Julieta (f) _____ _____ los programas de entrevistas, ¿verdad?
– Sí, pero a ella también (g) _____ _____ los programas concurso.

2 Refuse the following invitations for the reasons indicated in brackets.
For example:
¿Quieres ir al campo? No, no quiero. Prefiero ir a la ciudad.

a ¿Quieres ir al cine? (preferir) … (al teatro)

b ¿Quieres jugar al fútbol? (querer) … (al tenis)

c ¿Quieres salir? (tener que) … (estudiar)

d ¿Quieres ver la película en la tele? (preferir) … (las noticias)

3 Complete the table.

estamos	we are	**estáis**	you are
_________	we want	**queréis**	_________
_________	_________	_________	you prefer
_________	we have	_________	_________

4 Change the verbs in brackets to the correct forms. For example:
Lo siento. (Querer) pero no (poder). **Lo siento. Quiero pero no puedo.**

a ¿(Querer, tú) venir al cine mañana? (Preferir, yo) ir al teatro.

b Juan no (poder) venir al cine. (Tener) que lavarse el pelo.

c ¿Cuándo (ir) vosotros al concierto?

d Bea y yo (querer) venir, pero no (poder).

Vocabulario

Lugares (*m pl*)	Places
bar (m)	bar
club (m)	club
concierto (m)	concert
discoteca (f)	disco
entrada (f)	entrance
teatro (m)	theatre

Actividades (*f pl*)	Activities
apagar	to turn off
bailar	to dance
cambiar de canal	to change channels
charlar	to chat
dar miedo	to frighten
dar un paseo	to go for a walk
escuchar música	to listen to music
fumar cigarros	to smoke cigars
hacer ejercicio/gimnasia	to work out
ir de compras	to go shopping
ir de vacaciones	to go on holiday
jugar al fútbol	to play football
leer un libro/una revista	to read a book/ magazine
poner una película	to put on a film
preparar la cena	to make supper
quedarse en casa	to stay at home
tomar el sol	to sunbathe

Deportes (*m pl*)	Sports
aerobic (m)	aerobics
banyi (m)	bungee-jumping
canotaje (m)	canoeing
ciclismo (m)	cycling
críquet (m)	cricket
equitación (f)	horse-riding
kárate (m)	karate
montañismo (m)	mountaineering
patinaje (m)	skating/roller-blading
squash (m)	squash
tenis (m)	tennis

Música (*f*)	Music
flamenco (m)	flamenco
heavy (m)	heavy metal
jazz (m)	jazz
punki (m)	punk
rock (m) duro	hard rock
soul (m)	soul
tecno (m)	tecno

Programas (*m pl*) de televisión	TV Programmes
culebrón (m)	soap opera
drama (m) psicológico	psychological drama
serie (f) policíaca	detective series
noticias (f pl)	news
documental (m)	documentary
comedia (f)	comedy
concurso (m)	competition

Adverbios	Adverbs
bastante	quite
mucho	a lot
nada	not at all/nothing

Práctica en parejas/PARTNER WORK

1 **a** Find out if your partner likes the following activities:
canoeing   cycling   dancing   bungee-jumping   football

b Your partner will ask you for your opinion on types of music.

2 Your partner wants to know what your friend, Ana, likes to eat and drink. Answer his/her questions.
For example:
B **¿Le gusta a Ana el café?**   A **Sí, le gusta el café.**

- Ana likes coffee and green vegetables and she doesn't like wine or ice cream.

3 **a** Invite your partner to the events below.

Ask 'Do you want to go to the sculpture exhibition?'

Say when it is.

Say 'It is free.' **(Es gratis)**.

Ask 'Do you prefer to go to a concert?'

Say 'It is a charity concert organized by the United Nations.'

Say what the tickets cost.

'La gran vía de las esculturas'
(31 obras de artistas del siglo XX)
Gran vía Marqués de Turia (Valencia)
Miércoles
Entrada gratis

Viena en Madrid
Concierto benéfico organizado por Las Naciones Unidas
Auditorio Regional (Valencia)
Entradas €12 – €21

b Your partner wants to invite you out. S/He speaks first.

Ask 'When is it?'

Ask 'How much are the tickets?'

Say 'No, I don't want to go.'

Say 'Yes', and ask what's on.

Ask how much the tickets cost.

4 Someone you don't like is going to ask you out. With your partner think of as many excuses as possible in three minutes.

Práctica en parejas/PARTNER WORK

1 **a** First answer your partner's questions about your sports interests.

b Then find out if your partner likes the following types of music:
punk opera salsa rock heavy metal

2 Ask your partner what his/her friend, Ana, likes to eat and drink.
For example:
B **¿Le gusta a Ana el café?** A **Sí, le gusta el café.**

- You want to know if she likes coffee, wine, green vegetables and ice cream.

3 **a** Your partner wants to invite you out. S/He speaks first.

Ask 'When is it?'

Ask 'How much are the tickets?'

Say 'No, I don't want to go.'

Say 'Yes.' Ask what's on.

Ask 'How much do the tickets cost?'

b Invite your partner to the events below.

Ask 'Do you want to go to the Planetarium?'

Say when it is.

Say 'It is free.' **(Es gratis)**.

Ask 'Do you prefer to go to the Visual Theatre Festival?'

Say 'It is an exhibition: *The Monster's Smile*.'

Say what the tickets cost.

Planetario Observación con telescopios
(para ver la luna, Júpiter y Saturno)
Parque Tierno Galván, Madrid
Viernes, Entrada gratis.

Festival de Teatro Visual
Exposición: ***'La sonrisa del monstruo'***
Centro de Cultura Contemporánea
Jueves, Entrada €5

4 Someone you don't like is going to ask you out. With your partner think of as many excuses as possible in three minutes.

5 El dinero

In this unit you will learn how to spend money on clothes and presents. You will also learn how to talk about holidays and what you are going to do.

1 ¡Voy a viajar por el mundo! / I am going to travel round the world!

¿Qué va a hacer Ramón con el dinero? What is Ramón going to do with the money? Ramón is being interviewed after winning the lottery. In English, give five ways in which he plans to spend his fortune.

Periodista	¿Qué vas a hacer con el dinero?
Ramón	Voy a viajar por el mundo y voy a comprar una casa grande en el campo.
Periodista	¿Vas a comprar un coche nuevo?
Ramón	Voy a comprar un avión, un yate de lujo, ¡y muchos coches!
Periodista	¿No vas a ahorrar un poco?
Ramón	No, no voy a ahorrar. Voy a gastar todo el dinero, y voy a empezar inmediatamente – ¡champaña, por favor!

ahorrar	to save
empezar	to start
gastar	to spend

gramática

To say what you are going to do:
Ir (to go) + **a** + infinitive. (All the forms of the verb **ir** are in the grammar section on page 53.)

Voy a gastar mucho dinero.	I am going to spend a lot of money.
Vas a viajar por el mundo.	You are going to travel round the world.

2

You are the lucky lottery winner and your partner is interviewing you. Have a conversation like the one in Section 1. Your partner speaks first.

B Ask 'What are you going to do with all the money?'
A Say 'I am going to travel round the world.'
B Ask 'Are you going to buy a big car?'
A Say 'I am going to buy a plane, a yacht and a lot of cars.'
B Ask 'Aren't you going to save a little?'
A Say 'No, I'm not going to save. I'm going to spend all the money immediately!'

3 Escucha y repite los números.

Más números

cien	100	setecientos	700
doscientos	200	ochocientos	800
trescientos	300	novecientos	900
cuatrocientos	400	mil	1000
quinientos	500	un millón	1000.000
seiscientos	600		

4 Write these numbers in figures.

a Ciento uno 101
b Doscientos cincuenta 205
c Quinientos cuarenta y cinco 545
d Mil novecientos noventa y cinco 1995
e Tres mil ochocientos ochenta y seis 3886
f Siete millones, setecientos treinta y tres mil, quinientos setenta y uno 6733,571

5 Take the roles of Ramón and a friend. Look at Ramón's accounts and talk about how much he is going to spend on each item.

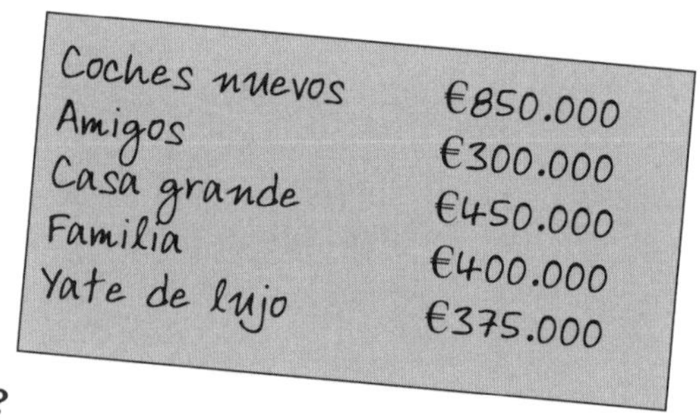

For example:

A (friend) **¿Cuánto vas a gastar en los coches nuevos?**
B (Ramón) **Voy a gastar €850.000 en los coches nuevos.**
A **¿Cuánto vas a dar a tus amigos?**
B **Voy a dar ...** etc

6 Ramón viaja por el mundo. / Ramón is travelling round the world.

¿Cuándo va a estar en cada lugar? When is he going to be in each place?

a Argentina **en agosto**
b Los Estados Unidos ______
c Rusia ______
d China ______
e Australia ______
f India ______
g África ______
h España ______

Los meses del año The months of the year

enero	**abril**	**julio**	**octubre**
febrero	**mayo**	**agosto**	**noviembre**
marzo	**junio**	**se(p)tiembre**	**diciembre**

la fecha the date: **lunes 24 de diciembre de 2032**

7 Escucha y rellena los espacios con las fechas de salida y vuelta.

These three people are also off on holiday. Fill in the gaps with their departure and return dates.

NOMBRE	DESTINO	SALIDA	VUELTA
Señor Cid	Marruecos	10 de octubre de 2001	
Juana Laloca	Lisboa		
Pepe Botella	París		

8

You and your partner are both going on holiday. Ask and answer questions about each holiday.
For example:

México	Nairobi	Tokio
Salida 11/4	Salida 28/1	Salida 19/2
Vuelta 10/5	Vuelta 14/3	Vuelta 20/6

A	B
¿Adónde vas a ir?	**Voy a ir a México.**
¿Cuándo vas a salir?	**Voy a salir el 11 de abril.**
¿Cuándo vas a volver?	**Voy a volver el 10 de mayo.**

9

Read Juana's letter, then ask and answer the questions below taking the roles of Juana and Lucía. For example:

A (Lucía): **¿Adónde vais a ir tú y Miguel durante las vacaciones?**
B (Juana): **Vamos a viajar por América.**

a ¿Adónde vais a ir tú y Miguel durante las vacaciones?
b ¿Cuánto tiempo vais a pasar viajando, en total?
c ¿Quién va a reservar los billetes?

Querida Lucía

El curso termina en junio y Miguel y yo vamos a viajar por América. Primero vamos a ver a mis amigos en Colombia. Luego ellos van a acompañarnos a Ecuador y Perú. Vamos a pasar tres meses en total viajando por todas partes.

Miguel va a reservar los billetes mañana. ¿Y vosotros? ¿Qué vais a hacer tú y Julio este verano?

Un abrazo

Juana

10

Have a similar conversation about Lucía's plans. (She and Julio are going to spend three months travelling round Africa. Julio is going to book the tickets on Wednesday).

gramática

To remind you: **Ir** (to go)

voy	I go
vas	you go (sing)
va	s/he goes; you go (sing)
vamos	we go
vais	you go (pl)
van	they go; you go (pl)

11 Comprando ropa / Buying clothes

With a partner see how quickly you can put the correct labels on the garments below. Make a guess before you use the **Vocabulario** Section.

El hombre	**La mujer**
el traje	el vestido
los pantalones	la chaqueta
los zapatos	el monedero
el abrigo	el bolso
la camisa	las botas
la corbata	la falda
la cartera	las medias

12 ¿Cuál es su talla? / What size are you?

Escucha y rellena el cuadro. Fill in the table. What size are these customers?

Cliente	1	2	3
Prenda	una falda		
Talla		44	

13 Los colores / The colours

Match the English to the Spanish. Check in the **Vocabulario** Section.

rojo negro amarillo azul naranja verde blanco violeta gris

blue white red yellow black grey orange green purple

14 ¿Qué color quiere? / What colour do you want?

Escucha y rellena los espacios. Listen and fill in the gaps.

1 – ¿Qué color quiere?
– Me gusta esta falda ______ .

2 – ¿Le gusta este traje ______ ?
– Prefiero el traje ______ .

3 – ¿De qué color?
– Me gustan estos pantalones ______ .

4 – Estas botas ______ están muy de moda.
– Prefiero las ______ .

15

Practise asking and giving the prices of the garments below.
For example:

A **Me gusta esta camisa violeta.**
¿Cuánto cuesta?
B **Esta camisa cuesta €25.**

purple shirt (€25)
orange suit (€285)
brown coat (€195)
yellow shoes (€68)
white tights (€5)
grey jacket (€90)

gramática

est_e_ vestid_o_ roj_o_
this red dress
est_a_ camis_a_ roj_a_
this red shirt
est_os_ zapat_os_ roj_os_
these red shoes
est_as_ bot_as_ roj_as_
these red boots

Centro comercial 'La Vaguada', Madrid

16 Esta camisa es demasiado grande. / This shirt is too big.

Escucha y corrige la falta en cada frase. Correct the mistake in each sentence.
What is wrong with these garments?

a «Esta falda es demasiado pequeña.»

b «Estos pantalones son demasiado caros.»

c «Este abrigo es demasiado barato.»

d «Estas botas son demasiado grandes.»

caro/a/s	expensive
barato/a/s	cheap
grande/s	big
pequeño/a/s	small

17

Your partner is very difficult to please. S/He finds something wrong with each of the items below. For example:

A **¿Te gusta esta camisa roja?**
B **No, no me gusta. Es demasiado cara.**
A **¿Te gustan estos pantalones negros?**
B **No, no me gustan. Son demasiado grandes.**

red shirt
black trousers
white boots
yellow suit
green shoes

18 Vamos a comprar regalos. / We're going to buy presents.

Escucha y coloca la persona con el regalo sugerido que le corresponda y escribe el precio. Match the person to the suggested present and write in the price. Ramón and his new girlfriend Carolina are discussing what presents to buy.

Mariví Alfonso Raquel Luis

una pulsera	una cartera	una pintura	un florero
€ _____	€ _____	€ _____	€ _____

19 Escucha otra vez la conversación de Ramón con Carolina y contesta las preguntas. / Listen again to Ramón's conversation with Carolina and answer the questions.

a What does Carolina say is wrong with each of Ramón's suggestions?

b What does he end up buying?

20 ¿Cuánto es, y cuál es el problema? / How much is it, and what is the problem?

Ramón has been stocking up for a party, and he wants to pay at the till.

How to pay	Cash only
¿Puedo pagar con un cheque?	**Pagos únicamente en efectivo.**
¿No aceptan ustedes tarjetas de crédito?	**Hay que pagar en metálico.**
	Sólo dinero en efectivo.

21 ¡Fiesta! / Party!

In pairs, ask and answer questions about Ramón's party. For example:

A **¿Cuántas personas van a venir?** B **600 personas van a venir.**

¿Cuántas personas van a venir?	(600)
¿Cuánto dinero va a costar la fiesta?	(€10.000)
¿A qué hora va a empezar?	(11.00h)
¿Cuántas cajas de champaña va a comprar Ramón?	(75)
¿Vais a venir, tú y tus amigos?	(Sí, o No)

22 La lotería y los juegos de azar. / The lottery and games of chance.

Este año cada español va a gastar €186 en juegos de azar; €117 de ellos en la lotería. ¿Por qué nosotros los españoles gastamos tanto en sueños e ilusiones? Porque es una forma de evadirse de la realidad. La sociedad actual tiende mucho hacia valores materialistas y el consumismo, pero la ilusión, los sueños no van a desaparecer nunca.

a How much will each Spanish person spend this year on
  1 games of chance and
  2 the lottery?

b Why do people spend so much on hopes and dreams?

el sueño	dream
la ilusión	hope
evadirse	to escape
nunca	never

23 ¿Qué va a hacer cada uno para ahorrar dinero?

Juana and Miguel are broke. What are they each going to do to save money? Who says what?

a Yo voy a tirar mis tarjetas de crédito. Juana /Miguel
b Yo voy a pagar siempre en efectivo. Juana /Miguel
c Antes de ir de compras voy a hacer una lista de lo que necesito y no voy a comprar nada más. Juana /Miguel
d Vamos a comer en casa. Juana /Miguel
e Tú vas a dejar de fumar, ¿no? Juana /Miguel
f Tú no vas a salir todas las noches, ¿verdad? Juana /Miguel
g ¿Cuándo vamos a empezar? Juana /Miguel

tirar	to throw out	**a menos que**	unless
elevado	high	**dejar de**	to stop
menos	except	**no hay prisa**	there's no hurry
salvo	except	**la semana que viene**	next week

24 Rank these money saving ideas in order of the amount of money they would save you:

Comprar de segunda mano
Dejar de beber alcohol
Ahorrar gasolina
Utilizar el transporte público
Dejar de ir al cine
Arreglar tu vehículo tú mismo
Vivir más cerca de la universidad
Llamar por teléfono los fines de semana

Gramática

- **How to talk about the future**

  1 Use the present tense to express the future:

  Abre a las once. It opens at 11.
  Empieza a las cinco. It starts at 5.

  2 Use **IR** + **A** + infinitive to say what you are *going* to do:

  voy a ir **vamos a llegar**
  vas a salir **vais a viajar**
  va a volver **van a venir**

  With a reflexive verb:
  voy a quedarme

- **How to specify a particular object or person**

	masculine	feminine
this	**este**	**esta**
these	**estos**	**estas**

- The personal **'a'**

  When the direct object of the verb is human:
  Voy a ver a Juan.

- **How to describe people and things**

  In Unit 2 you saw that adjectives have to change according to the number and gender of the noun they are describing:

  una camisa roja **un abrigo rojo**
  unas camisas rojas **unos abrigos rojos**

  Some exceptions:
  Adjectives ending in **-e** change only in the plural, when you must add **-s**:

  una corbata verde **un vestido verde**
  unas corbatas verdes **unos vestidos verdes**

  Adjectives ending in a consonant only change in the plural, when you must add **-es**:

  una falda azul **un traje azul**
  unas faldas azules **unos trajes azules**

- **How to ask 'How much?' or 'How many?'**

  ¿Cuánto? means 'How much?' and it doesn't change when asking the price.

  ¿Cuánto es la falda? **¿Cuánto son los pantalones?**

  ¿Cuántos? means 'How many?' and it does change:

  ¿Cuántos coches tienes? **¿Cuántas personas van a venir?**

Ejercicios de gramática

1 Fill in the gaps in the conversation with the appropriate part of the verb **ir**, as indicated in the brackets. For example:

¿Qué (a) (**tú**) a hacer durante las vacaciones? (b) (**yo**) a viajar por Europa.
¿Qué (a) ***vas*** a hacer durante las vacaciones? (b) ***Voy*** a viajar por Europa.

¿Con quién (c) (**tú**) a ir? (d) (**yo**) con Charo.

¿Cómo (e) (**vosotros**) a viajar? (f) (**nosotros**) a viajar en tren.

¿Cuánto tiempo (g) (**vosotros**) a pasar en Europa? Un mes, pero Charo (h) (**ella**) a volver más temprano porque sus padres (i) (**ellos**) a venir a su casa.

¿Dónde (j) (**vosotros**) a quedaros? (k) (**nosotros**) a quedarnos en hostales.

2 Write down the following dates in Spanish. For example:
el lunes 14 de julio de 2002.

a Mon 14 July 2002
b Thurs 16 September 2001
c Fri 22 May 1999
d Sat 30 March 2020
e Sun 1 January 2003

14
JULIO

3 Write out the following numbers in full. For example:
263 **doscientos sesenta y tres.**

263 554 6.689 17.777 43.167 122.943

4 Put the correct form of the adjective into the spaces. For example:

Esta camisa es demasiado ***cara.***

a (Este/a/os/as) _____ camisa es demasiado _____ (caro/a/s).

b (Este/a/os/as) _____ zapatos son demasiado _____ (pequeño/a/s).

c (Este/a/os/as) _____ botas son demasiado _____ (grande/s).

d (Este/a/os/as) _____ traje no es muy _____ (barato/a/s).

Vocabulario

1

todo	all
nuevo	new
avión (m)	aeroplane
yate (m)	yacht
de lujo	luxury
coche (m)	car
poco (m)	bit
champaña (f)	champagne

8

durante	during
reservar	to book
billete (m)	ticket
primero	first
luego	then
acompañar	to go with
verano (m)	summer

10

traje (m)	suit
pantalones (m pl)	trousers
zapato (m)	shoe
abrigo (m)	coat
camisa (f)	shirt
corbata (f)	tie
cartera (f)	wallet
vestido (m)	dress
chaqueta (f)	jacket
monedero (m)	purse
bolso (m)	handbag
bota (f)	boot
falda (f)	skirt
medias (f pl)	tights

11

prenda (f)	garment

12

rojo	red
negro	black
amarillo	yellow
azul	blue
naranja	orange
verde	green
blanco	white
violeta	purple
gris	grey

13

de moda	fashionable

17

pulsera (f)	bracelet
pintura (f)	painting
florero (m)	flower vase

19

pagar	to pay
cheque (m)	cheque
aceptar	to accept
tarjeta (f)	card
crédito (m)	credit
pagos (m pl)	payment
únicamente	only
en metálico	in cash
en efectivo	in cash

20

caja (f)	box, crate

21

cada	each
¿Por qué?	Why?
porque	because
tanto	so much
forma (f)	way
realidad (f)	reality
sociedad (f)	society
tender (tiende)	to tend (tends)
hacia	towards
valor (m)	value
materialista	materialistic
consumismo (m)	consumerism
desaparecer	to disappear

22

siempre	always
antes de	before
lista (f)	list
lo que	that which
necesitar	to need
nada	nothing

23

de segunda mano	second hand
gasolina (f)	petrol
utilizar	to use
arreglar	to fix
tú mismo	yourself

Práctica en parejas

1 **a** Congratulations! You have won €1,000,000 on the lottery. Your partner wants to know what you are going to do with the money. Answer her/his questions.

b Now your partner is the lucky winner. Find out how much money s/he has won and ask her/him at least three questions like the ones below:

How much money do you have?
What are you going to do with the money?
Are you going to save a little (**un poco**)?
Are you going to spend all the money?
Are you going to buy a house in the country / a big car / a luxury flat?
Are you going to give a little to charity?
Are you going to give me (**vas a darme**) a little?

2 **a** Ask your partner what s/he is going to do in the holidays. Find out where s/he is going, when s/he is leaving and when s/he is getting back.

b Your partner wants to know about your holiday plans. Tell her/him that you are going to travel round South America. You are setting off on 16 September and you are coming back on 17 October.

3 Play a variation of B*ingo*! with your partner. Write down six numbers between 540 and 560. Your partner will try to guess them. Cross them off when s/he says them. Then your partner will write down six numbers between 770 and 790 and you will guess them.

4 Tell your partner the following dates in Spanish. S/He must write them out in figures. For example: 5/8/1977. You will say **'cinco de agosto de mil novecientos setenta y siete'**, and your partner will write **5/8/1977**.

5/8/1977 10/10/2000 1/2/2016

5 Practise buying clothes with a partner, each taking one of the roles below.

Cliente Say I like this yellow shirt. Ask how much it is.
Dependiente/a Say it is €22. Ask what is your size?
Cliente Say it is 44.
Dependiente/a Say this shirt is too big. It's size 48.

Práctica en parejas

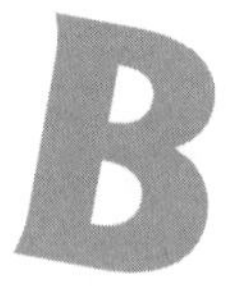

1 **a** Your partner has won the lottery. You want to know what s/he is going to do with the money. Ask at least three questions like the ones below:

How much money do you have?
What are you going to do with the money?
Are you going to save a little (**un poco**)?
Are you going to spend all the money?
Are you going to buy a house in the country / a big car / a luxury flat?
Are you going to give a little to charity?
Are you going to give me (**vas a darme**) a little?

b Now you are the lucky winner of €3,500,000. Answer your partner's questions.

2 **a** Your partner wants to know about your holiday plans. Tell her/him that you are going to travel round Africa. You are setting off on 30 June and you are coming back on 28 August.

b Ask your partner what s/he is going to do in the holidays. Find out where s/he is going, when s/he is leaving and when s/he is getting back.

3 Play a variation of B*ingo*! with your partner. S/He writes down six numbers between 540 and 560. You have to guess them. S/He crosses them off when you say them. Then you write down six numbers between 770 and 790 and your partner will guess them.

4 Tell your partner the following dates in Spanish. S/He must write them out in figures. For example: 19/6/1959. You will say '**diecinueve de junio de mil novecientos cincuenta y nueve**', and your partner will write **19/6/1959**.

19/6/1959 3/7/2012 17/8/2016

5 Practise buying clothes with a partner, each taking one of the roles below.

Cliente	Say I like this yellow shirt. Ask how much it is.
Dependiente/a	Say it is €22. Ask what is your size?
Cliente	Say it is 44.
Dependiente/a	Say this shirt is too big. It's size 48.

6 En la ciudad

In this unit you will learn how to say where things are, give directions and instructions and find your way round a town and within office buildings.

1 ¿Dónde está el banco? / Where is the bank?

Escucha y busca los edificios en el plano. Find the buildings on the map.

el banco	Correos	la estación de trenes (la RENFE)
la farmacia	el museo	la universidad

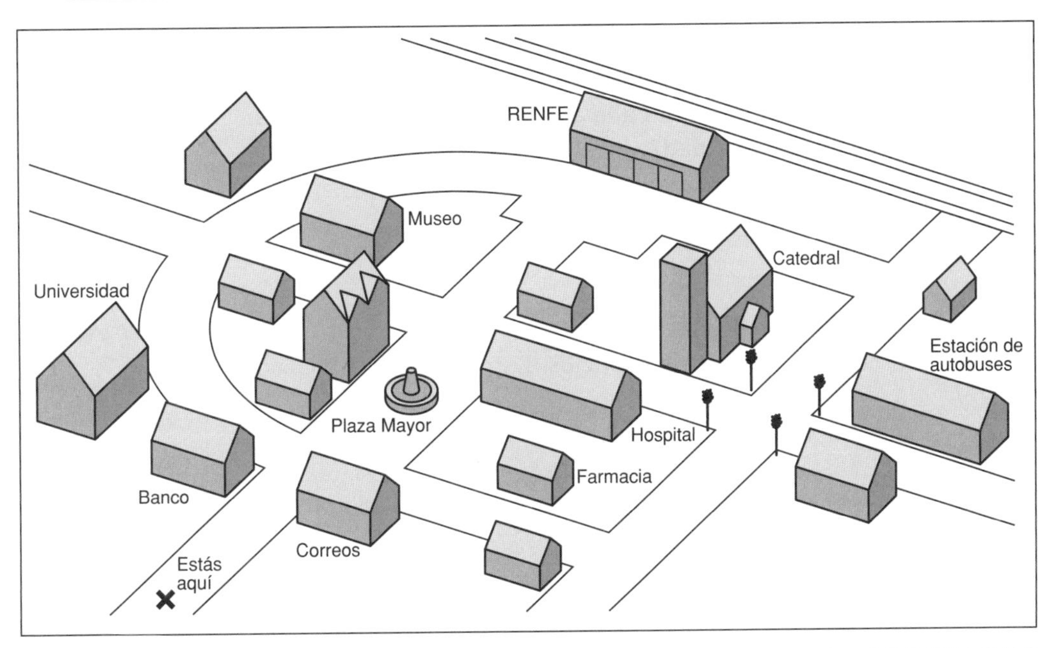

gramática

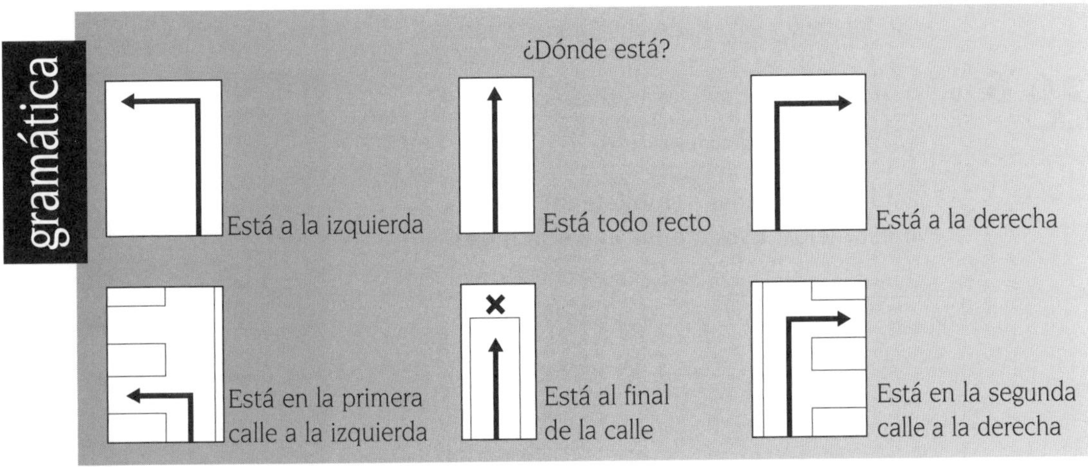

2 Using the map in Section 1, practise asking each other where places are and giving their location. For example:

A **Perdone, ¿dónde está la catedral?**
B **Está enfrente de la estación de autobuses.**

3 Escucha y escribe la letra de cada edificio en el plano. / Listen and write in the letter for each building on the map (in Section 1).

a Galería de Arte Moderno
b Oficina de turismo
c Telefónica (telephone exchange)
d Ayuntamiento (town hall)

4 Test your partner. Give the exact location of a particular building. Your partner must work out which one it is. For example:

A **Está en la primera calle a la derecha, a la izquierda.**
B **¿Es la universidad?**
A **No. Está en la primera calle a la derecha ...**
B **¿Es la farmacia?**
A **Sí.**

5 ¿Está lejos? / Is it far?

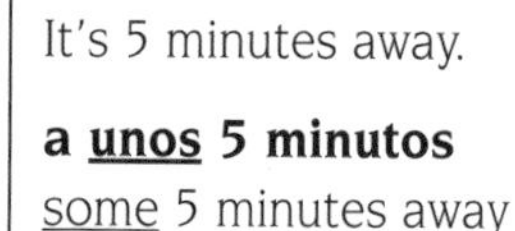

Está a 5 minutos.
It's 5 minutes away.

a unos 5 minutos
some 5 minutes away

Está cerca de aquí.
It's near here.

Escucha y rellena los espacios. Listen and fill in the spaces.

a – ¿La universidad está lejos?
– No, está muy cerca, a 5 minutos andando.

b – ¿Está cerca de aquí el centro comercial?
– No, está muy ______ . Está a unos ______ minutos en coche.

c – ¿Hay una farmacia cerca de aquí?
– Hay una bastante ______ , a unos ______ minutos a pie.

d – ¿Está lejos de aquí el centro deportivo?
– No, no muy ______ . En autobús está a unos ______ minutos.

6 With a partner ask how far away these places are from where you are now.
For example:

A **¿Está lejos de aquí la biblioteca?**
B **No está lejos. Está a unos cinco minutos.**

library
sports centre
canteen
laboratory

Galería de Arte, Barcelona

7 Without looking anything up, work out the meanings of the words underlined.

a La piscina está al lado del centro deportivo. next to

b El centro deportivo está enfrente del parque. ________

c La piscina está entre la escuela y el centro deportivo. ________

d La escuela está en la esquina. ________

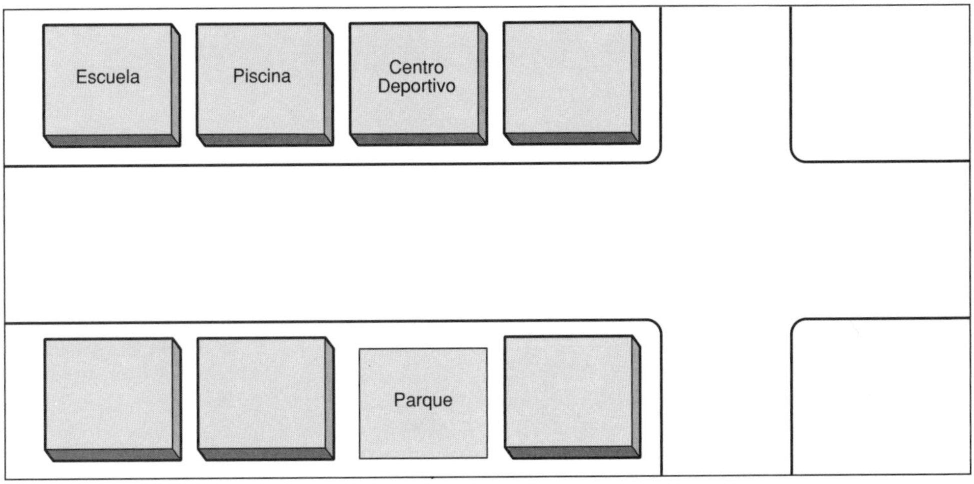

Escuela
Piscina
Centro Deportivo
Parque

8 Take it in turns to practise asking for and giving the locations of the places above. For example:

A **¿Dónde está el centro deportivo?**
B **Está al lado de la piscina.**

gramática

de + el = del

9 These places have been left off the diagram.
Decide where they are and describe their locations to your partner, who has to fill them in.
For example:

A **¿Dónde está el cine?**
B **El cine está en la esquina, enfrente de la escuela.**
(A writes **cine** where s/he thinks it is on the diagram.)

el cine
el restaurante
el bar Mundial
el supermercado

10 Escucha y completa las frases. / Listen and complete the sentences.

Listen to the people saying where particular buildings are.

a La mezquita está en la ________ calle a la ________ .
Está ________ la esquina.

b El centro comercial está en la ________ calle a la ________ .
Está ________ la catedral.

c El campo de fútbol está ________ la piscina,
en la ________ calle a la ________ .

d La iglesia de Santa María está ________ la biblioteca y la librería,
en la ________ calle a la ________ .

1° primero/a
2° segundo/a
3° tercero/a
4° cuarto/a
5° quinto/a

11 Escucha y coloca estas instrucciones en el orden correcto. / Listen and put these directions in the correct order.

Dobla a la izquierda	____	Sigue todo recto	____
Ve todo recto	1	Coge la primera calle a la derecha	____
Dobla a la derecha	____	Coge la segunda calle a la izquierda	____

ve go **dobla** turn **sigue** continue **coge** take

12

Using the map in Section 1, follow these directions from the railway station (RENFE) and put a cross on the map where you end up.

Desde la estación ve todo recto hasta el cruce.
Dobla a la izquierda y sigue hasta los semáforos.
Dobla a la derecha y coge la primera calle a la derecha.
Ve todo recto y coge la segunda calle a la derecha.
En el cruce dobla a la izquierda.
Sigue todo recto y está al final de la calle.

desde	from
hasta	to
el cruce	the crossroads
los semáforos	the traffic lights

13

Send your partner on a wild goose chase round the town. S/He has to follow your directions.

14 Coge el autobús.

Escucha y escribe el número del autobús y dónde hay que subir y bajar. / Listen and write down the number of the bus and where to get on and off.

	número	sube en ...	baja en ...
a	____	____	la Plaza Nueva
b	____	____	____
c	____	____	____

baja	get off
sube	get on
la parada	the bus stop

15

Practise telling each other which bus to catch and where to get on and off.
For example:
Coge el autobús número 10. Sube en el cine y baja en la calle Calella.

a No 11 – on at supermarket – off at Parque Santa Eulalia

b No 21 – on at Plaza Real – off at football stadium (**el estadio de fútbol**)

c No 42 – on at museum – off at Plaza España

d No 14 – on at Avenida de la Constitución – off at cathedral

gramática

To give directions to friends and young people you can use the imperative (see Grammar Section).

(to one person)	**dobla**	turn	**sigue***	continue
	coge	take	**ve**	go

*Root-changing

16 ¡No hay pérdida! / You can't miss it!

Read this invitation and decide where you think Julio's house is.

Hola, ¿Qué tal?

Voy a dar una fiesta el sábado 24 de junio, para celebrar el fin de curso. ¿Quieres venir?

Te voy a decir cómo llegar a mi casa: Coge el autobús número 19 que sale de la parada que está enfrente de la universidad. Baja en la Plaza Colón y ve todo recto hasta los semáforos. En el cruce dobla a la derecha. Coge la segunda calle a la derecha. Sigue todo recto, y mi casa está a la izquierda. ¡No hay pérdida!

Hasta luego; un abrazo,

Julio

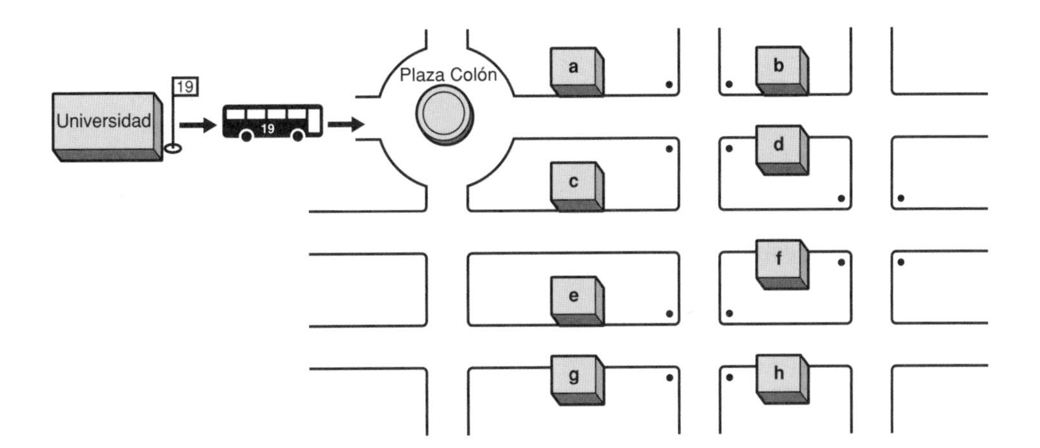

17

Give your partner directions to another house on the map. Did s/he make it to the right one?

18

Tell your partner how to get to your house from where you are now, and how long it takes.

19 Tengo cita. / I have an appointment.

Escucha y contesta a las preguntas.

Carmen has an appointment with the manager of the Excelsor company.

a Where is Reception?

b Where is the lift?

c Where is the secretary's office?

d Where is the manager's office?

en un edificio:	
la recepción	Reception
los servicios	the toilets
el ascensor	the lift
el despacho	the office
el pasillo	the corridor
el piso	the floor

20

Ask for and give locations inside an office building. For example:

A **¿Dónde está el departamento de Marketing?**

B **Está en el segundo piso, al final del pasillo a la izquierda.**

Marketing Department	2nd floor; at the end of the corridor, on the left.
Secretary's office	4th floor, next to the lift, on the right.
Manager's office	5th floor, opposite Reception, on the left.
IT Centre (**Centro de informática**)	2nd floor, between the toilets and the lift.

21 Siéntate. / Sit down.

Escucha y coloca estas instrucciones en el orden correcto.

In her office the secretary tells Carmen what to do.

a Put the instructions into the order in which they are given.

b Match them with their English equivalents.

Escribe tu nombre.	____	Come in.	1
Siéntate aquí.	____	Wait a moment.	____
Espera un momento.	____	Close the door.	____
Pasa.	1	Write your name.	____
Dame tu currículum.	____	Sit down here.	____
Cierra la puerta.	____	Give me your CV.	____
Rellena este formulario.	____	Fill in this form.	____

22

You are the secretary and your partner is the interviewee. S/He has to follow your instructions. For example:

A **Rellena el formulario.** (B fills in a 'form')

A **Abre la puerta.** (B opens the door)

¡Extra!

23 Escucha y contesta a las preguntas en inglés. / Listen and answer the questions in English.

Jorge has left this message on your answerphone.

a What is he inviting you to?

b How does he suggest you get there?

c What directions does he give you?

d How long will it take you?

e When does he say he'll meet you?

24 ¡Hoy es fiesta! / It's party time!

Answer the questions in English.

¡Hola!

Voy a dar una fiesta, ¿quieres venir? Es en mi casa y
empieza a las once. Ven con tus amigos y trae algo
para comer o beber.

Mi dirección es: c/Calella, 3, 2° Dcha. Para ir desde
la universidad coge el metro y baja en la Plaza Colón.
Ve por Los Reyes Católicos hacia el centro.
En el cruce dobla a la izquierda – ésta es la calle
Calella. Mi casa está enfrente del Hostal Bienestar.
Sube hasta la segunda planta y mi piso está a la
derecha.

¡Hasta luego!

Carmen

a When does the party start?

b What and who does she ask you to bring?

c What means of transport does she suggest you use?

d Where in her building is her flat?

traer	to bring
algo	something
por	along

Gramática

- **How to describe where something is:**

a la izquierda/derecha	**al lado del cine**	**al final de la calle**
en la esquina	**enfrente del bar**	**cerca de aquí**
entre el bar y el café		**lejos de la comisaría**

Some prepositions have more than one equivalent in English:

a	'to' or 'at'	**de**	'from' or 'of'
Voy al centro.	I go to the centre.	**Soy de Cádiz.**	I am from Cádiz.
Voy a las tres.	I go at 3 o'clock.	**Un libro de arte.**	'A book of art.' (an art book)

- **Estar** (to be) is the verb used to describe where something or someone is.

estoy	I am	**estamos**	we are
estás	you are	**estáis**	you are
está	he/she/it is; you are	**están**	they/you are

- **How to give instructions and orders:**

In most cases you can use the simple present tense. See page 34.
The imperative (below) is only used when addressing a person or people informally. To give formal instructions the subjunctive is used, which is beyond the scope of this book.

	Talking to one person:		Talking to two or more:
doblar	**dobla**	turn	**doblad**
coger	**coge**	catch/take	**coged**
subir	**sube**	go up	**subid**

With root-changing verbs the vowel only changes when talking to one person.

seguir	**sigue**	continue	**seguid**

Some verbs are irregular in the singular form, i.e. when talking to one person.

salir	**sal**	leave	**salid**
ir	**ve**	go	**id**

With reflexive verbs the reflexive pronoun is attached to the verb and the **d** in the plural forms is omitted.

levantarse	**levántate**	get up	**levantaos**
sentarse	**siéntate**	sit down	**sentaos**

Ejercicios de gramática

1 Write the following in Spanish:
My house is next to the church, opposite the park. On the left there is a small hotel. At the end of the road between the swimming pool and the sports centre there is a large cinema.

2 a Tell your friend how to get to your house by changing the form of the verbs in brackets.
For example:
Coge el autobús número 16.

a (Coger) el autobús número 16.
b (Subir) en el cine.
c (Bajar) en el centro deportivo.
d (Ir) por la calle Mola.
e (Doblar) a la derecha.
f (Seguir) todo recto.

b Give two other friends the same instructions by changing the verbs again.
For example:
Coged el autobús número 16.

3 a You are the secretary in an office. A job applicant has come to see the manager. Tell him what to do by using the imperative form of the appropriate verb.

sentarse	esperar	pasar	escribir	cerrar	rellenar

a Hola, … .
b … la puerta, por favor.
c … un momento.
d … aquí. ¿Quieres café?
e … el formulario.
f … los datos aquí.

b Two applicants have turned up at the same time. Give them the instructions above.

4 How many commands can you make from the verbs on the left of each column combined with the rest of the sentence on the right?

(abrir)	el teléfono.	(leer)	la leche.
(escuchar)	inmediatamente.	(beber)	de la casa.
(levantarse)	la ventana.	(salir)	las verduras.
(coger)	la música.	(comer)	el libro.

Vocabulario

1

banco (m)	bank
estación (f)	station
tren (m)	train
RENFE (f)	train station
catedral (f)	cathedral
supermercado (m)	supermarket
Correos (m)	post office
farmacia (f)	chemist
museo (m)	museum
hospital (m)	hospital
comisaría (f)	police station
perdone	excuse me
coger	to take/catch
al final de	at the end of
todo recto	straight on
a la derecha	on/at the right
a la izquierda	on/at the left
primero	first
segundo	second

3

galería (f)	gallery
telefónica (f)	telephone office
iglesia (f)	church
oficina (f)	office
turismo (m)	tourism
ayuntamiento (m)	town hall

7

al lado de	next to
delante de	in front of
enfrente de	opposite
entre	between
en la esquina	on the corner
cerca (de)	near (to)
lejos (de)	far (from)
parada (f)	stop
mezquita (f)	mosque
escuela (f)	school
esquina (f)	corner
campo (m)	ground
deportivo	sports (adj)
comercial	commercial
a	to, at, ...away
aquí	here
a pie	on foot
andando	walking
en coche	by car
en autobús	by bus

10

piscina (f)	swimming pool
iglesia (f)	church
librería (f)	book shop

16

dar	to give
fiesta (f)	party
celebrar	to celebrate
fin (m)	end
decir	to tell
que	which

24

hoy	today
dirección (f)	address
metro (m)	underground
hacia	towards
planta (f)	floor

Museo von Thyssen, Madrid

Práctica en parejas

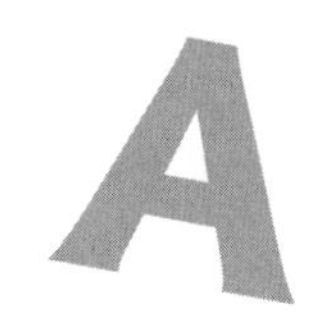

1 **Jugando al escondite.** Playing Hide and Seek.
Imagine you are somewhere on the map in Section 1. Describe your exact location to your partner, and see if s/he can find you. For example:
A **Estoy delante del ayuntamiento.** B **¿Estás en la Plaza Mayor?**
A **Sí.**

Now you try and locate your partner.

2 **a** Your partner will ask how far away these places are. Give the approximate time it would take her/him to get there. For example:
B **¿Está lejos la Plaza Mayor?**
A **No, está muy cerca, a unos 10 minutos andando.**

The police station	5 mins	walking/on foot
The hospital	25 mins	by car

b Now ask how far away the cinema and the cathedral are.

3 Using the map in Section 1, give your partner directions from the train station to these places – without saying where you are directing her/him. Did s/he make it?

the hospital
the bank
the museum

4 **a** You are your partner's own personal fitness trainer. Give him or her instructions to help him or her get into shape. Use some or all of the suggestions below, and if s/he doesn't understand at first, demonstrate what you want your partner to do, without explaining anything in English.
For example: A **Levanta la pierna izquierda tres veces ... toca la pierna derecha con el brazo izquierdo... etc**

(levantar) el brazo cinco veces
(bajar) el brazo
(correr) por la clase dos veces
(tocar) la pierna derecha con el brazo izquierdo

levantarse	to stand up
sentarse	to sit down
levantar	to lift
bajar	to put down
correr	to run
tocar	to touch
el brazo	the arm
la pierna	the leg
cinco veces	five times

b It is now your partner's turn to get her/his revenge. Do as s/he says.

Práctica en parejas

1 **Jugando al escondite.** Playing Hide and Seek.
Your partner is imagining that s/he is somewhere on the map in Section 1. Listen to your partner describing her/his exact location, and see if you can locate her/him. For example:
A **Estoy delante del ayuntamiento.**
B **¿Estás en la Plaza Mayor?**
A **Sí.**

Now your partner will try and locate you on the same map.

2 **a** Ask how far away these places are.
The police station?
The hospital?

b Your partner will now ask about the places below. Give the approximate time it would take her/him to get there. For example:
A **¿Está lejos la Plaza Mayor?**
B **No, está bastante cerca, a unos diez minutos andando.**

The cinema	10 mins	by bus
The cathedral	15 mins	walking/on foot (or 5 mins by car)

3 Using the map in Section 1, give your partner directions from the train station to these places – without saying where you are directing her/him. Did s/he make it?

the bus station
the Post Office
the chemist's

4 **a** Your partner is your own personal fitness trainer. S/He is going to give you some instructions to help you get into shape. Do as s/he says.

b Time for you to get your revenge. Use some or all of the suggestions below, and if s/he doesn't understand at first, demonstrate what you want her/him to do, without explaining anything in English.

(levantar) la mano
(bajar) la mano
(correr) hasta la puerta tres veces
(tocar) el pie derecho
con la mano izquierda

levantarse	to stand up
sentarse	to sit down
levantar	to lift
bajar	to put down
correr	to run
tocar	to touch
la mano	the hand
el pie	the foot
cinco veces	five times

In this unit you will learn how to find your way around by various forms of transport, private and public. You will also learn another way of discussing future plans.

1 ¡Qué será, será! / What will be, will be.

Tick the changes you think will happen to air travel in the future.

En el año 2020 será posible …

- ir a Nueva York por la mañana y volver a Londres para comer.
- ir en un avión comercial, 25 veces más rápido que el sonido.
- ir en un avión sin piloto, dirigido por satélite.
- viajar en un coche volador de alta velocidad.
- viajar en un avión de dos pisos con sala de conferencias y dormitorios.

el sonido	sound	**volador**	flying
alta velocidad	high speed	**dirigido**	guided

2 ¿Cómo viajarás? / How will you travel?

Escucha y rellena los espacios. It's the year 2020. In this survey, students are being asked how they will travel to college tomorrow.

Investigador	¿Cómo irás a la universidad mañana?
Julia	Iré en (a) … de alta velocidad.
Investigador	¿Cómo viajarás a clase mañana?
Tomás	Iré en (b) … dirigida por satélite.
Investigador	¿Cómo llegarás a clase mañana?
Aurora	Viajaré en (c) ….
Investigador	¿Cómo irás a la facultad mañana?
Pedro	Iré (d) … .

tren solar
yate volador
a pie
bicicleta automática
coche ecológico
motocicleta voladora

3

It is still the year 2020. Ask each other how you will get to college tomorrow. Think of as many ways as possible. For example:

A to B: **¿Cómo irás a clase mañana?**
B: **Viajaré en coche solar de alta velocidad.**
B to C: **¿Cómo llegarás a la facultad mañana?**
C: **Iré en bicicleta eléctrica.**

gramática

The future

viajar<u>é</u>	I will travel	**ir<u>é</u>**	I will go
viajar<u>ás</u>	you will travel	**ir<u>ás</u>**	you will go

4 Escucha y contesta a las preguntas en español.

Eduardo is telling Alicia about his trip to Seville tomorrow.

Eduardo	**Alicia**
Mañana iré a Sevilla.	¿Cuándo llegarás?
Llegaré a las seis.	¿Cómo irás desde el aeropuerto al hotel?
Alquilaré un coche.	¿Y cúando volverás?
Volveré el lunes a las dos.	

a ¿Cuándo llegará Eduardo? *Llegará a las ... .*

b ¿Cómo irá al hotel? ________

c ¿Cuándo volverá? ________

gramática

llegará	s/he will arrive
irá	s/he will go
volverá	s/he will return

5

You are going to Madrid tomorrow, arriving at 10.30 and returning on Tuesday at 4.15. You will hire a car and stay in a hotel. Have a conversation similar to the one above, with your partner.

6 En el aeropuerto / At the airport

Escucha y verifica tus respuestas. Listen and check your answers.
Alicia is seeing Eduardo off to Seville at the airport. Fill in the gaps.

Alicia	**Eduardo**
¿A qué hora sale el vuelo?	**a** ________ .
¿Cuánto tiempo dura el viaje?	Dura una hora, aproximadamente.
¿Cuándo llega?	**b** ________ .
¿Cuál es el número del vuelo?	**c** ________ .
¿De qué puerta sale?	**d** ________ .

VUELO	DESTINO	SALIDA	PUERTA	OBSERVACIONES
1B1919	SEVILLA	16.55	2	CONTROL DE PASAPORTES
1B2417	CARACAS	13.45	8	CONTROL DE PASAPORTES
1BI560	ROMA	14.20	6	RETRASO DE 55 MINUTOS

7

Ask and answer similar questions about the other flights. For example:

A **¿A qué hora llega el vuelo de Nueva York?** B **Llega a las ... .**
A **¿A qué hora llega el vuelo de Londres?** B **Llega a las ... .**

LLEGADAS

VUELO	PROCEDENCIA	LLEGADA	OBSERVACIONES
PA9211	NUEVA YORK	10.20	ATERRIZADO
BA347A	LONDRES	11.30	RETRASADO

8 Nos veremos en el bar. / We'll see each other in the bar.

Eduardo sent this e-mail to his colleague Jesús in Seville. Answer the questions in English.

Querido Jesús

Llegaré el miércoles, 10 de octubre a las seis. Alquilaré un coche en el aeropuerto, así que nos veremos en el hotel Sol enfrente del ayuntamiento.

Me quedaré allí la primera noche y te llamaré por teléfono desde el hotel. Si quieres, tomamos una copa en el bar a las ocho o las nueve.

Hasta luego
Eduardo

a Where does he suggest they meet up?

b Where will he stay the first night?

c How will Eduardo contact Jesús?

d What does he suggest they do, and when?

9 Quisiera alquilar un coche. / I'd like to hire a car.

Escucha y escribe las preguntas en español. Eduardo wants to hire a car.

Eduardo	Empleado
Quisiera alquilar un coche pequeño, por favor.	Tenemos un Nissan Micra, un Peugeot o un Ford Fiesta.
Quiero el Peugeot.	¿Para cuántos días?
Para cuatro días.	
a ¿ Cuánto es por día ?	Es €42 por día.
b ¿ ________________ ?	Los seguros son €9.
c ¿ ________________ ?	El depósito es €170.
d ¿ ________________ ?	Sí, está lleno.
e ¿ ________________ ?	Súper sin plomo
¿Acepta usted tarjetas de crédito?	Sí. Su permiso de conducir, por favor. Firme aquí. Aquí están las llaves.

seguros	insurance
lleno	full
permiso	licence
las llaves	the keys

10

Your partner works for a car hire firm in Spain. Arrange to hire a car using the details provided.

Ford Fiesta	
Per day	€40
Insurance	€8
Deposit	€160
Petrol	Super unleaded (full tank)

11 En la RENFE

Escucha y escribe los detalles del viaje. / Listen and write the details of the journey.

¿Adónde va?	Sevilla
¿Sencillo o de ida y vuelta?	______
¿De primera o segunda clase?	______
¿Fumador o no fumador?	______
¿Cuánto es?	______
¿A qué hora sale?	______
¿A qué hora llega?	______
¿Hay que hacer transbordo?	______
¿De qué andén sale?	______

de ida/sencillo	single
de ida y vuelta	return
hay que	you need
hacer transbordo	to change
andén	platform

12 Para ir desde Granada hasta Barcelona

Tren	*Andén*	*Granada*		*Linares-Baeza*			*Barcelona*
		Salida		Llegada	Salida		Llegada
Rápido	10	09.15	____	12.06	12.25	____	22.30
Talgo	12	15.15	____	17.52			
Interurbano	2	18.05	____	21.20	21.58	____	09.00
Expreso	5	23.15	____	02.18			

You are travelling from Granada to Barcelona. Ask your partner for information about the trains above. S/He has to answer your questions by looking at the timetable. For example:

A **¿Hay un tren para Barcelona esta mañana?**
B **Sí, el Rápido.**

A
Ask 'Is there a train for Barcelona this morning?'
Ask 'What time does it leave?'
Ask 'What platform does it leave from?'
Ask 'When does it arrive in Barcelona?'
Ask 'Do I need to change?'

B
Answer.

13 Escucha y contesta a las preguntas en español.

Juana meets her friend Miguel on the station platform.

a ¿Adónde va Juana?
b ¿Adónde va Miguel?
c ¿Cuándo sale el tren?
d ¿De qué andén sale?

14

Juana sent this letter about her trip to Barcelona to Lucía.

> En junio iré a Barcelona. No viajaré en coche – cogeré el tren, porque será más fácil, ¡y más ecológico! Pasaré unos cuatro días allí y me quedaré en un hostal barato. Veré la casa de Gaudí y la Sagrada Familia.

Take the role of another friend and ask your partner questions about Juana's trip. For example:

A **¿Cuándo irá Juana a Barcelona?**
B **Irá en junio.**
¿Cuándo irá …?
¿Cómo viajará?
¿Dónde se quedará?
¿Cuántos días pasará …?
¿Qué verá?

gramática

The future
Add **-é, -ás, -á, -emos, -éis, -án** to the infinitive:

iré	I will go
irás	you will go
irá	s/he will go
iremos	we will go
iréis	you will go
irán	they will go

15 ¿Aceptará su oferta? / Will she accept his offer?

Miguel and Juana are on the train to Barcelona.

Miguel	**Juana**
¿Tienes amigos en Barcelona? ¿Familia?	No.
¿Dónde te quedarás?	Buscaré un hostal.
Llegaremos bastante tarde a Barcelona, ¿sabes? Esta noche podrás quedarte en la casa de mis padres, si quieres. Mañana buscarás un hostal, ¿vale?	Sí.

Underline the phrases in the conversation above that have the same meaning as the ones below. The first has been done for you.

a Where will you stay?

b I shall look for a hostel.

c We shall arrive quite late …

d Tonight you will be able to stay …

e Tomorrow you will look for …

16

Take on the roles of Miguel and Juana and practise the conversation in Section 15. Make up your own ending, with Juana saying 'Sí' or 'No' to Miguel's offer.

17 Juana va en el 'Bus Turistic'.

Escucha y contesta a las preguntas de Juana.

¿Dónde está la parada para el 'Bus Turistic'?	Está en ...
¿Los autobuses son frecuentes?	Vienen cada ... minutos.
¿Para en el Park Güell?	Sí/No ...
¿Cuánto tiempo tarda para ir desde Cataluña hasta la Sagrada Familia?	Tarda ... minutos.

18

Practise asking and answering questions like the ones above, using the bus timetable.

Plaça de Catalunya	09.00	09.20	09.40	etc
Sagrada Familia	09.25			
Park Güell	09.55			
Fútbol Club Barcelona	11.30			

19 Ir en autobús es más barato. / Going by bus is cheaper.

¿Con quién estás de acuerdo? Who do you agree with?

Miguel Quiero alquilar un coche. Ir en coche es más cómodo.
Juana Yo prefiero ir en autobús. Es más barato y contamina menos.
Miguel No es verdad. Ir en autobús contamina más que el coche. Y el coche es más conveniente.
Juana No estoy de acuerdo. Es muy difícil aparcar en Barcelona.

20

Weigh up the relative merits of the forms of transport below. The words in the box might help you. For example:

A **Ir en bici es más ecológico que ir en coche.**
B **Sí, pero ir en coche es más cómodo que ir en bici.**

¿bici o coche? ¿tren o coche? ¿moto o coche? ¿metro o coche?

barato	cómodo	rápido	conveniente	difícil	mejor	saludable
caro	incómodo	lento	inconveniente	fácil	peor	ecológico

gramática

Ir en coche es más caro que ir en autobús. (more than)
Ir en autobús es menos caro que ir en coche. (less than)

21 La contaminación / Pollution

Eduardo is listening to a programme on his car radio.

a What is the programme warning about? Circle the five problems mentioned.

1 la lluvia ácida **2** el calentamiento global **3** la contaminación
4 el tráfico **5** los cambios del clima **6** los incendios en los montes
7 la basura **8** las selvas tropicales **9** las emisiones de CO_2

b Tick the measures which are mentioned by the speaker.
Para solucionar el problema del tráfico:
a Aumentarán los impuestos sobre la gasolina.
b Los empleados que van en el tren recibirán descuentos.
c Se producirán automóviles eléctricos.
d Los conductores pagarán multas por el daño ambiental.
e Conducirán coches con motores ecológicos de bajo consumo.

impuestos	taxes	**descuentos**	discounts
multas	fines	**daño**	harm

22 Por venir

Match the descriptions of the technological inventions to the titles in the box.

1 La compañía petrolera BP instalará células solares en sus gasolineras. De esta forma reducirá en 3.500 toneladas al año las emisiones de CO_2.
2 La 'Rowbike' es una bicicleta sin pedales que se moverá con la fuerza de los brazos. Permitirá ejercitar los brazos.
3 La empresa Car Cosy comercializará una vitrina de microfibra que se abrirá y cerrará electrónicamente y servirá como garaje para cualquier coche.
4 Daimler-Chrysler será la primera compañía en alimentar un vehículo con un combustible diésel sintético que tiene pocas emisiones contaminantes.
5 Las batallas aéreas estarán dominadas por el 'Eurofighter Typhoon'. Alcanzará velocidades supersónicas y dispondrá de sistemas de infrarrojos.

a Un garaje portátil
b Combustible para el coche del futuro
c Gasolineras al sol
d El avión del siglo XXI
e Una bici con remos

Gramática

- **Mode of transport**
  en avión, **en tren**, **en bicicleta**, etc

- **Future: Use**
  There are three ways of expressing the future in Spanish. The second two in particular are often interchangeable.

1 Present tense	for pre-scheduled events:	**El tren sale a las 3.**
2 **Ir a** + infinitive	for intentions and plans:	**Voy a salir esta noche.**
3 Future tense	for predictions:	**En julio iré a África.**

- **Future: Form**
  Add the endings **-é, -ás, -á, -emos, -éis, -án** to the infinitive.

llegaré	I will arrive	**llegaremos**	we will arrive
llegarás	you will arrive	**llegaréis**	you will arrive
llegará	s/he will arrive you will arrive	**llegarán**	they will arrive you will arrive

Irregular verbs have the same endings, but the root of the verb changes:

salir:	**saldré, saldrás**, etc	**tener:**	**tendré, tendrás**, etc
poder:	**podré, podrás**, etc	**venir:**	**vendré, vendrás**, etc
hacer:	**haré, harás**, etc	**decir:**	**diré, dirás**, etc

Reflexive verbs have the pronouns at the beginning:

quedarse:	**me quedaré**	**nos quedaremos**
	te quedarás	**os quedaréis**
	se quedará	**se quedarán**

- **Comparatives**

más que	more than	**El coche es más caro que la bici.** The car is more expensive than the bike.
menos que	less than	**La bici es menos cara que el coche.** The bike is less expensive than the car.

With numbers:
más or **menos** + **de**: **Tiene más de cinco años.**
He is more than five years old.

Ejercicios de gramática

1 Write the questions in Spanish. For example:

¿A qué hora llega el tren? **El tren llega a las seis.**

a ¿ ________________ ? El tren llega a las seis.

b ¿ ________________ ? El autobús sale a las cuatro menos veinte.

c ¿ ________________ ? El viaje dura dos horas.

d ¿ ________________ ? Llega a París a las ocho y diez.

e ¿ ________________ ? El tren sale del andén número cinco.

f ¿ ________________ ? El vuelo sale de la puerta número siete.

2 ¿Cómo vas a viajar?
Write in Spanish:
a I am going to travel by bus.
b They are going to go by bicycle.
c He is going to travel by plane.
d Are you going to arrive by car?

3 These are the things Juana wants to do after her university course.
Change all the verbs to the **yo** form. For example:
Después de la universidad <u>iré</u> de vacaciones ...

Después de la universidad (a) (ir) de vacaciones. (b) (Levantarse) tarde todos los días porque ¡no (c) (tener) que ir a clase! (d) (Salir) todas las noches y (e) (ver) a todos mis amigos. (f) (Hacer) muchas cosas: (g) (escuchar) música y (h) (aprender) a bailar salsa, por ejemplo. Después de uno o dos meses, (i) (buscar) un trabajo ...

4 Itziar and Iñaki want to do exactly the same as Juana. Change the verbs in the above text to the **nosotros** form. For example:
Después de la universidad <u>iremos</u> de vacaciones ...

5 Juana's father is asking her what she thinks she will do after her course. Change the verbs to the **tú** form. For example:
¿Adónde <u>irás</u> después de la universidad?
a ¿Adónde (ir) después de la universidad?
b ¿Cuándo (volver)?
c ¿Qué (hacer) todos los días?
d ¿Cuándo (empezar) a buscar un trabajo?

6 Iñaki's and Itziar's parents ask them the same questions.
Change the verbs to the **vosotros** form. For example:
¿Adónde <u>iréis</u> después de la universidad?

Vocabulario

1

por	by
en	by
que	than
rápido	fast
sala (f)	large room
sin	without

6

destino (m)	destination
durar	to last, take
observación (f)	remark
puerta (f)	gate
retraso (m)	delay
salida (f)	departure
vuelo (m)	flight

7

aterrizado	landed
llegada (f)	arrival
procedencia (f)	from
retrasado	delayed

8

allí	there
así que	so (that)

9

conducir	to drive, driving
firmar	to sign
gasolina (f)	petrol
plomo (m)	lead

14

fácil	easy

17

pararse	to stop
tardar	to take

19

cómodo	comfortable
contaminar	to pollute
difícil	difficult

20

bici(cleta) (f)	bike (bicycle)
incómodo	uncomfortable
lento	slow
mejor	better
metro (m)	underground
moto(cicleta) (f)	(motor)bike
peor	worse
saludable	healthy

21

ácido/a	acid
ambiental	environmental
aumentar	to increase
automóvil (m)	automobile
bajo	low
basura (f)	rubbish
calentamiento (m)	warming
cambio (m)	change
clima (m)	climate
conductor (m)	driver
consumo (m)	consumption
emisión (f)	emission
empleado (m)	employee
incendio (m)	fire
lluvia (f)	rain
monte (m)	mountain
motor (m)	engine
producir	to produce
recibir	to receive
selva (f)	(rain) forest, jungle
solucionar	to solve
tráfico (m)	traffic

22

aéreo/a	air (adj)
alcanzar	to reach
alimentar	to fuel
batalla (f)	battle
célula (f)	cell
combustible (m)	fuel
comercializar	to put on the market
cualquier	any
de esta forma	in this way
disponer	to have
dominado	dominated
ejercitar	to exercise
empresa (f)	firm
fuerza (f)	strength
gasolinera (f)	petrol station
infrarrojo	infra red
moverse	to move
permitir	to allow
poco	few
reducir	to reduce
servir	to be used
siglo (m)	century
tonelada (f)	tonne (metric)
vitrina (f)	glass case

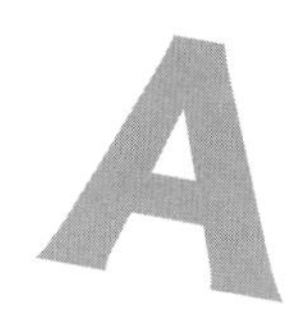

Práctica en parejas

1 **a** You are a fortune teller. Gaze into your crystal ball and answer your partner's questions about the future. Allow your imagination full rein.

b You are now the client. Ask five questions about your future. For example:
¿Ganaré la lotería?
¿Dónde trabajaré después de la universidad?
¿Cuándo conoceré a mi futuro marido/ futura mujer?
¿Aprobaré mis exámenes?
¿Viajaré por el mundo?
¿Cuántos hijos tendré?

2 **a** Answer your partner's questions about what you will do at the end of this course.

b Ask your partner at least four questions about what s/he will do at the end of this course. For example:
¿Qué harás después de la universidad?
¿Viajarás por el mundo?
¿Buscarás un trabajo?
¿Irás de vacaciones?

3 **a** You are going on holiday to Jamaica for two weeks. Answer your partner's questions using the information below.

	FECHA	HORA	LLEGADA
IDA	10/5/03	10.20	21.50
VUELTA	24/5/03	12.10	23.00

b Ask your partner where s/he is going for the holidays, how long s/he is staying, when s/he is leaving and coming back, and how long the journey takes.

4 You want to take the train from Barcelona to Seville. Ask for the departure and arrival times and if you need to change, and the price of a second class return. You are a non-smoker.

Jardín Tropical-Atocha, Madrid

Práctica en parejas

1 **a** Your partner is a fortune teller. Ask five questions about your future. For example:

¿Ganaré la lotería?
¿Dónde trabajaré después de la universidad?
¿Cuándo conoceré a mi futuro marido/ futura mujer?
¿Aprobaré mis exámenes?
¿Viajaré por el mundo?
¿Cuántos hijos tendré?

b Now you are the fortune teller. Gaze into your crystal ball and answer your partner's questions about the future. Allow your imagination full rein.

2 **a** Ask your partner at least four questions about what s/he will do at the end of this course. For example:

¿Qué harás después de la universidad?
¿Viajarás por el mundo?
¿Buscarás un trabajo?
¿Irás de vacaciones?

b Answer your partner's questions about what you will do at the end of this course.

3 **a** Ask your partner where s/he is going for the holidays, how long s/he is staying, when s/he is leaving and coming back, and how long the journey takes.

b You are going on holiday to India for two weeks. Answer your partner's questions using the information below.

	FECHA	HORA	LLEGADA
IDA	21/7/03	12.40	20.55
VUELTA	05/8/03	02.10	10.25

4 Give your partner the information s/he asks for about the train service below.

Barcelona	**Valencia**	**Sevilla**		**Sencillo**	**De ida y vuelta**
0700_______	1100 _______	1940	1ª clase	€100	€150
			2ª clase	€80	€120

Jardín Tropical-Atocha, Madrid

In this unit you will learn how to ring up about jobs advertised, to present yourself at an informal interview and to talk about your experience and what you have done. You will also learn some useful language for working in a Spanish-speaking country.

a

HOSTAL ARIAS
c/ Córdoba, 39, León
Se requiere camarero/a
de buena presencia
para trabajar en el bar.
Diríjanse a Sra Ibáñez
T (987) 42 37 89

b

Se requiere
MOZO/A DE CUADRA
con experiencia.
Diríjanse a CORTIJO
KUPANDA
Cta de Torre
Tel (950) 24 43 34

c

¿Quieres trabajar en una colonia de verano?
Si eres una persona con entusiasmo e iniciativa, y te gustan los niños de 7 – 15 años, llámanos.
T (949) 35 71 20

1 He visto su anuncio. / I have seen your advertisement.

¿Qué experiencia tiene Mike?

Mike wants a holiday job in Spain. Write down details of his work experience.

– Hostal Arias, ¿dígame?
– Hola, buenos días. Quisiera hablar con la señora Ibáñez, por favor.
– Sí, soy yo.
– He visto su anuncio en el periódico, y quisiera solicitar el puesto de camarero.
– ¿Tiene experiencia?
– He trabajado en un bar y un restaurante en Escocia, pero no he trabajado nunca en España.
– ¿Qué hace actualmente?
– Soy estudiante.
– Venga mañana por la mañana a las diez.

2 Underline the phrases in the conversation that have the same meaning as the ones below.

a I have seen your advert in the paper.
b I'd like to apply for the post of …
c I have worked in a bar …
d …but I have never worked in Spain.
e What are you doing at the moment?
f Come tomorrow morning …

3 Ring up about the other jobs, taking turns as the employer and the student. Ask to speak to the owner (**el dueño**) and say 'I have worked in my country but never in Spain'.

4 With a partner, take on the roles of Juana and Mike. Ask and answer questions about his job search.

Juana	**Mike**
¿Has visto el anuncio en el periódico?	Sí, he visto el anuncio.
¿Has decidido solicitar el puesto?	Sí,
¿Has llamado al hostal?	
¿Has hablado con la dueña?	
¿Tienes una entrevista?	
¿Has escrito tu currículum?	

gramática

To say you have done something

		-ar verbs		**-er** and **-ir** verbs	
he		**hablado**	I have spoken	**decidido**	decided
has	+	**trabajado**	you have worked		
ha		**llamado**	s/he has called	**visto** (irreg)	seen
				escrito (irreg)	written

5 Read these references and decide which of the jobs in Section 1 would suit these students. Write down **a**, **b** or **c**.

Juana ha trabajado en una escuela de equitación en Almería. Ha terminado el segundo año de su carrera universitaria y quiere trabajar durante el verano. Le gustan mucho los animales y es una persona trabajadora y responsable. ______

Mike ha trabajado a tiempo parcial en un bar y en un restaurante en Escocia para pagar sus estudios universitarios. Es una persona inteligente con muy buena presencia y buenos modales. ______

Julio es una persona imaginativa e independiente con entusiasmo e iniciativa. Ha completado el primer año de su carrera y ha trabajado como ayudante en un colegio de idiomas. ______

6 Tell your partner about the jobs you have done. For example:

A **¿Qué trabajo has hecho?**

B **He trabajado como dependiente en una tienda de ultramarinos.**

7 Write a reference for your partner and give it to the teacher. Look up any words you need which are not here. When s/he reads out some of the references for the people in the class, guess who they are for.

8 Escucha la entrevista e identifica los errores en el currículum. / Listen to the interview and spot the mistakes in the curriculum vitae.

CURRÍCULUM VITAE

Michael Marshall
20 años

Enseñanza
Primaria
Secundaria
Superior Napier University 1999 – 2003
Carrera Superior de Empresariales

Experiencia Profesional
Marco's Bar 1999 – 2003
Barman (tiempo parcial)
Dispatches Restaurant 1999 – 2000
Camarero (tiempo parcial)
Napier University 2000 – presente
Técnico en informática (tiempo parcial)

9 ¿Por qué no consiguió Dolores el trabajo? Escucha y comenta la entrevista con el resto de la clase / Why didn't Dolores get the job? Listen and discuss her interview with the rest of the class.

10 Tick the best answers to the questions below. Then interview your partner for one of the jobs in Section 1. Would you give her/him the job?

1 ¿Qué estás haciendo actualmente?
- **a** Estoy cursando Ciencias en la universidad de Leeds.
- **b** Nada.

2 ¿Tienes experiencia en este campo?
- **a** No.
- **b** Sí, he trabajado como camarero/a en un restaurante pequeño.
- **c** No, pero estoy dispuesto/a a aprender.

3 ¿Por qué quieres trabajar en esta empresa?
- **a** Porque quiero adquirir experiencia en este sector.
- **b** Porque necesito el dinero.
- **c** Porque la empresa tiene muy buena fama.

4 ¿Sabes trabajar en equipo?
- **a** Prefiero trabajar sólo.
- **b** A mí me gusta trabajar sólo o en equipo.

5 ¿Estás dispuesto/a a hacer horas extras?
- **a** Si es necesario, sí, pero también tengo que estudiar.
- **b** No, de ningún modo.
- **c** Sí, haré todas las horas necesarias.

6 Pagamos €4 por hora. ¿Está bien?
- **a** No. Exijo por lo menos €10 por hora.
- **b** Sí. Necesito este trabajo.
- **c** Lo siento, no. Eso no es suficiente.

11 Los hoteles / Hotels

Dolores did eventually get a placement in a hotel, as a receptionist. Spot the mistakes she made on the hotel register when booking in Señor Serrat.

Estimado señor

Quisiera reservar una habitación doble con baño y balcón, si es posible. Mi mujer y yo llegaremos por la tarde el lunes, 21 de junio y quisiéramos quedarnos cuatro noches hasta el jueves 25. Quisiéramos pensión completa para dos personas.

Le saluda atentamente

Joan M Serrat

NOMBRE	FECHAS	HABITACIÓN DOBLE / INDIVIDUAL	PENSIÓN MEDIA / COMPLETA	BALCÓN	BAÑERA/DUCHA
SERRAT	12-15 junio	individual	media X 2	no	ducha
PONS					

12 Escucha y rellena el registro.

Could you do better? Señora Pons wants to make a reservation.

13

Practise this conversation, then change the items underlined to the ones in brackets.

A **Quisiera una habitación, por favor.**
B **¿Para cuántas noches?**
A **Para <u>dos noches.</u>** (a week)
B **¿Doble o individual?**
A **<u>Individual.</u>** (double)
B **¿Con baño o ducha?**
A **Con <u>ducha</u>.** (bath)
B **¿Media pensión o pensión completa?**
A **<u>Media pensión.</u> ¿Tiene <u>televisión</u>?** (full board; balcony)
B **Todas las habitaciones tienen <u>televisión</u>.** (balcony)
Firme aquí, por favor.

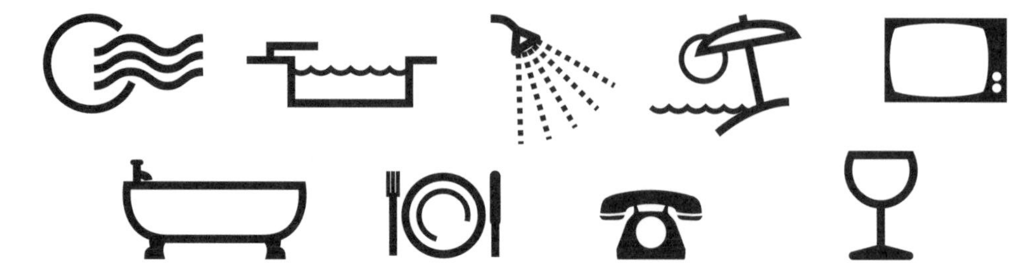

14

Señor Serrat arrives at the hotel on the 21st June. Put the number of each phrase in the box where you think it goes in the dialogue. Then practise the conversation with a partner.

Sr Serrat	Buenas tardes. (a) .1. a nombre de Serrat.
Dueño	¿Para esta noche?
Sr Serrat	Sí. (b) ...
Dueño	Sí, sí, pero (c) ... con la reserva. (d) ... una habitación doble con baño y balcón, y pensión completa, ¿no?
Sr Serrat	Sí. Para cuatro noches.
Dueño	Muy bien; firme aquí.

1 He reservado una habitación
2 Usted ha reservado
3 ¿No ha recibido mi carta?
4 la recepcionista se ha equivocado

15

What can go wrong in a hotel? Join the problems to the solutions.

Huésped

a He dejado mis llaves en la habitación, y la puerta se ha cerrado.

b He perdido mi equipaje. Lo he dejado en el tren.

c He pedido el desayuno en la habitación, pero todavía no ha llegado.

d ¡Me han robado! ¡Mi bolso ha desaparecido!

e Quisiera una habitación para esta noche.

Recepcionista

1 Lo siento, pero el hotel está completo. Aquí hay una lista de hoteles. Puede llamar desde aquí para hacer una reserva, si quiere.

2 Tengo su bolso aquí, señora. Usted lo dejó en el restaurante.

3 Llamaré a la estación, a la oficina de objetos perdidos.

4 Llamaré al portero. Él le abrirá la puerta.

5 La camarera se lo llevará en seguida.

16

With a partner, think of solutions to the problems below. Then take turns to be the receptionist and guest with a problem.

a I have lost my wallet, and can't pay my bill.
b The maid hasn't cleaned my room.

to wash up	**fregar los platos**
to clean	**limpiar**
the police	**la policía**

17 Match the holiday jobs to the duties.

1 Mozo/a de cuadra
2 Animador/a en una colonia de vacaciones
3 Camarero/a
4 Servicio doméstico en la cocina de un restaurante

a Servir a los clientes
b Planear actividades
c Limpiar los compartimientos
d Limpiar las mesas
e Limpiar la cocina
f Dar de comer a los caballos
g Fregar los platos
h Solucionar problemas
i Ser responsable de la seguridad

18 Read Juana's letter and fill in the first part of the table below.

Trabajar en una cuadra es duro, pero a mí, me encanta. Empiezas muy temprano por la mañana - y esto puede ser un problema si las cuadras están muy lejos de la casa. Pero estás fuera todo el día, al aire libre, y puedes montar a caballo.

EMPLEO	VENTAJAS	DESVENTAJAS
Moza de cuadra (Juana)	**Estás fuera todo el día, ... Puedes montar ...**	**Es ... Empiezas ... Las cuadras pueden estar ...**
Camarero (Mike)		
Animador (Julio)		
Servicio doméstico (Dolores)		

19 **Escucha y rellena el cuadro.** / Listen and fill in the table.

Mike, Julio and Dolores are discussing the relative merits of their holiday jobs:

El trabajo es muy duro.
Conoces a mucha gente.
Te dan la comida gratis.
Me gusta el ambiente.
No me gustan mis colegas.
No ganas mucho dinero.
Me llevo muy bien con mis colegas/los dueños/los niños.

20 Tell your partner what it is you like about your work or studies. For example:

A **¿Te gusta tu trabajo?**
B **Sí, porque es muy interesante.**
OR
No, porque es aburrido.

21 ¿Cuánto ganas? / How much do you earn?

Existen nueve comunidades* en las que el salario que se cobra es superior a la media nacional – que es aproximadamente €1.710. No obstante, entre los sueldos de los madrileños – los más elevados – y los de los murcianos – los más bajos – existe una diferencia de €712.

*Spain is divided into 17 **comunidades autónomas.**

a Underline the phrases in the text that mean the same as the ones below.

1. in which the salary earned
2. is above the national average
3. However,
4. the wages of people from Madrid
5. the highest … the lowest
6. those of the people from Murcia

(Adapted from INE, 2° trimestre de 1999; *Quo* Núm 51)

b Escucha y rellena el cuadro.

SALARIO MENSUAL MEDIO POR TRABAJADOR	€ (aprox)
MADRID	
PAÍS VASCO	
CATALUÑA	1.884
CASTILLA Y LEÓN	
BALEARES	1.628
ANDALUCÍA	
GALICIA	1.510
MURCIA	1.378

22 Los seis perfiles más buscados. / The six most sought-after characteristics.

These are the six sorts of worker most sought after by Spanish employers. Match the type of worker to her/his characteristics and to the sort of job which would suit her/him best.

1 INDEPENDIENTE	**a** Paciente, flexible, escucha con interés al cliente.	**i** Labores de electricidad, electrónica, mecánica.
2 ORGANIZADO	**b** Imaginativo, crítico, vanguardista, analítico, observador.	**ii** Enfermería, psicología, ventanillas de reclamaciones, recursos humanos.
3 CON CAPACIDAD DE ESCUCHA	**c** Con gran habilidad manual; le interesan las nuevas tecnologías.	**iii** Marketing, publicidad; las bellas artes y la cultura; el cine.
4 'MANITAS'	**d** Persona ordenada, metódica, con buena memoria.	**iv** Investigación, trabajos científicos, documentación.
5 CREATIVO	**e** Persona extrovertida, sociable y perspicaz.	**v** Trabajos de apoyo, como secretarias.
6 PERSUASIVO	**f** Prefiere trabajar en solitario; analítico y observador con buena memoria, dedicación y constancia.	**vi** Labores comerciales y políticas; expertos en comunicación y turismo; abogados.

Gramática

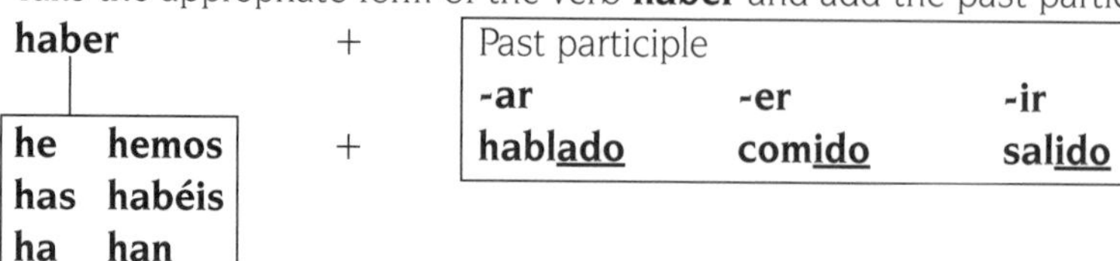

- **The perfect tense**

  This is usually used as it is in English: I *have gone/seen/done, etc.*

  – **Form**

  Take the appropriate form of the verb **haber** and add the past participle:

haber	+	Past participle		
		-ar	**-er**	**-ir**
he **hemos** **has** **habéis** **ha** **han**	+	**habl**<u>**ado**</u>	**com**<u>**ido**</u>	**sal**<u>**ido**</u>

he hablado	I have spoken	**hemos trabajado**	we have worked
has comido	you have eaten	**habéis bebido**	you have drunk
ha salido	s/he/it has left you have left	**han pedido**	they have ordered/asked for you have ordered/asked for

  – **Reflexives**

  The reflexive pronoun always comes first:

  me he levantado I have got up

  – **Direct objects**

  Direct objects come before the verb:

  Lo he visto I have seen it

  – **Irregular**

  There is a small group of frequently used verbs which have irregular past participles:

hacer	to do/make	**hecho**	done/made	**he hecho**	I have done/made
volver	to return	**vuelto**	returned	**has vuelto**	you have returned
escribir	to write	**escrito**	written	**ha escrito**	s/he has written
ver	to see	**visto**	seen	**hemos visto**	we have seen
decir	to say	**dicho**	said	**habéis dicho**	you have said

- **Writing letters and postcards**

  – **Formal**

  Address of recipient Your address
  Date

  Estimado/a señor/a (Name)

  He visto el anuncio y quisiera solicitar el puesto de ...

  Le saluda atentamente

  (your name)

  – **Informal**

  Your address
  Date

  Querido/a (Name)

  ¿Qué tal? Hemos llegado a Puerto Rico y ...

  Un abrazo (muy fuerte) de

  (your name)

Ejercicios de gramática

1 Put the correct form of the verb **haber** into the spaces. For example:
¿Dónde … ido? (tú)? ¿Dónde has ido?

a ¿Dónde …… ido? (tú)
b …… estado en Chile. (yo)
c …… vuelto muy tarde. (vosotros)
d …… terminado. (nosotros)
e ¿…… llegado ya? (ellos)
f El tren …… salido.

2 Change the verb in brackets to the past participle. For example:
He (ser) animador en una colonia. He sido animador en una colonia.

a He (ser) animador en una colonia.
b Hemos (ver) el anuncio.
c Han (decir) que hay televisión.
d ¿No has (escribir) la carta todavía?
e Alfonso ha (hacer) su trabajo.
f ¿Habéis (coger) el tren?

3 Complete this table.

PERFECT	PRESENT	FUTURE
he trabajado	trabajo	trabajaré
____________	____________	llegaré
____________	vuelvo	____________
he salido	____________	____________

4 Change the verbs in brackets. For example:
(Terminar, yo) este ejercicio pero … He terminado este ejercicio pero …
a (Terminar, yo) este ejercicio pero no (empezar, yo) el otro.
b Ana y Bea (llegar) pero Julio no (venir).
c (Ganar, nosotros) la lotería, pero no (comprar, nosotros) una casa.
d ¿(Ver, vosotros) esta película? (Tener, ella) mucho éxito.

5 Translate this e-mail into English.

Querido Jesús

¿Has visto el anuncio para un ayudante en una academia de idiomas? Quiero solicitar el puesto y he llamado a la academia para pedir más detalles. Ya he preparado mi currículum y mi profesor me ha escrito una referencia. ¿Has decidido si quieres trabajar en Francia en julio? Escribe o llámame pronto,

María José

Vocabulario/VOCABULARY

1

¿Dígame?	Hello? (On phone)
actualmente	at the moment
buena presencia (f)	good appearance
colonia (f) de verano	summer camp
diríjanse	apply
mozo/a de cuadra	stable lad/girl
nunca	never
puesto (m)	post
se requiere	required
solicitar	to apply for
venga	come (formal)

5

ayudante (m)	assistant
buenos modales (m pl)	good manners
carrera (f)	course
tiempo parcial	part time
durante	during
equitación (f)	riding
escuela (f)	school
idioma (m)	language
trabajador/a	hard-working

6

tienda (f)	shop
ultramarinos (m pl)	groceries

8

enseñanza (f)	education
informática (f)	Information Technology
técnico/a	technician

10

cursar	to be doing a course
nada	nothing
empresa (f)	firm
adquirir	to acquire
fama (f)	reputation
estar dispuesto/a a	to be willing to
de ningún modo	no way
campo (m)	field
listo/a	keen, clever, ready
equipo (m)	team
solo/a	alone
exigir	to demand
por lo menos	at least
saber	to know (how to)

11

balcón (m)	balcony
doble	double
ducha (f)	shower
Estimado/a	Dear (formal letters)
habitación (f)	room
Le saluda atentamente	Yours faithfully
pensión completa (f)	full board
media pensión (f)	half board

14

equivocarse	to make a mistake
recibir	to receive

15

desaparecido	disappeared
en seguida	right away
equipaje (m)	luggage
huésped (m)	guest
llevar	to bring
objetos perdidos (m pl)	lost property
robar	to rob someone
todavía	still, yet

17

animador/a	activities organiser play leader,
caballo (m)	horse
compartimiento (m)	stalls, stables
mesa (f)	table
planear	to plan
seguridad (f)	security
servir	to serve
solucionar	to solve

18

al aire libre	outdoors
cuadra (f)	stable(s)
duro	hard
esto	this
fuera	outside
montar a caballo	ride

19

aburrido/a	boring
ambiente (m)	atmosphere
colega (m)	colleague
conocer	to (get to) know
ganar	to earn
gratis	free
llevarse bien con	to get on well with
niño/a	child

For more vocabulary turn to the Appendix on p. 181.

Práctica en parejas/PARTNER WORK

1 Ring your partner to tell her/him about a job you have seen advertised. Your partner speaks first.

¿ ______________________________ ?

Say 'Hello, my name is …'.

¿ ______________________________ ?

Reply saying 'I have seen an advertisement in the paper for a job in a bar'.

¿ ______________________________ ?

Say 'I have rung the bar and I have spoken to the boss'.

¿ ______________________________ ?

Say 'I have an interview tomorrow at seven'.

¡ ______________________________ !

2 **a** Your partner is interviewing you for a job as a teaching assistant (**ayudante**) in a school. Either talk about your own work experience, or say you have done the jobs below. Be prepared to answer questions like the ones in Section 10.

Worked as an au pair (**chica/o au pair**) in Spain June, July and August 2000
Worked as a part time lifeguard (**salvavidas**) at a swimming pool 2000 – 2001

b Now you are interviewing your partner for a job as a shop assistant in a clothes shop. Ask her/his age and if s/he has any experience. Then ask two or three questions like the ones in Section 10.

3 **a** You are the receptionist of the Hotel Mayor and your partner is a client who wants to know about the hotel's facilities. Answer her/his questions. For example:
B **¿Hay baño en las habitaciones?** A **Sí, todas las habitaciones tienen baño.**
B **¿Está cerca de la playa el hotel?** A **No, no está cerca de la playa.**

El Hotel Mayor	✓	✓	✓	✓	✓		✓	
El Hotel Colón								

b Your partner is now the receptionist of the Hotel Colón, and you are the client wanting to know about the hotel's facilities.

Práctica en parejas/PARTNER WORK

1 Your partner has rung to tell you about a job s/he has seen advertised. You speak first. Answer the phone (**¿Sí, dígame?**)

____

Ask 'How are you?'

____

Ask 'Have you rung the bar?'

____

Ask 'What did he say?' (i.e. What has he said?)

____

Say 'Good luck!' (**¡Suerte!**).

2 **a** You are interviewing your partner for a job as a teaching assistant (**ayudante**) in a school. Ask her/his age and if s/he has any experience. Then ask two or three questions like the ones in Section 10.

b Your partner is interviewing you for a job as a shop assistant in a clothes shop. Either talk about your own work experience, or say you have done the jobs below. Be prepared to answer questions like the ones in Section 10.

Worked part time in a supermarket 1999 – 2001
Worked part time as an usher/ette (**acomodador/a**) in a cinema 2001 – 2002

3 **a** Your partner is the receptionist of the Hotel Mayor and you are a client who wants to know about the hotel's facilities. Ask questions and complete the table.
For example: **¿Hay baño en las habitaciones?**
¿El hotel está cerca de la playa?

El Hotel Mayor								
El Hotel Colón		✓	✓		✓			✓

b You are now the receptionist of the Hotel Colón, and your partner is the client wanting to know about the hotel's facilities. Answer her/his questions.

In this unit you will learn how to talk about events in your life, what you did yesterday and during visits abroad. You will also develop your understanding of newspaper reports.

1 ¿Dónde estuviste ayer? / Where were you yesterday?

La madre de Miguel quiere saber dónde estuvo ayer. Escucha y completa las respuestas. Miguel's mother wants to know where he was yesterday. Listen and complete the answers.

La madre de Miguel	**Miguel**
Hola, hijo. Te llamé ayer – ¿dónde estuviste?	Por la mañana estuve … .
¿Y por la tarde?	Fui a … .
¿Trabajaste mucho?	Sí, trabajé … .
¿Saliste por la noche?	No, no salí. Pasé toda la noche … .
¿Cuándo te acostaste?	Me acosté a … .
Trabajas demasiado, hijo. Hay que descansar un poquito.	Sí, mamá.

2 ¿Qué hiciste anoche? / What did you do last night?

Bea, la novia de Miguel, también quiere saber qué hizo anoche. Escucha y coloca las preguntas con las respuestas. Listen and match the questions with the answers.

Bea	**Miguel**
a ¿Qué hiciste anoche?	**1** No oí el teléfono.
b ¿Toda la noche?	**2** Nada. Me quedé en casa.
c ¿Adónde fuiste?	**3** Volví a medianoche.
d ¿Cuándo volviste?	**4** Fui al bar con Ricardo.
e Pero te llamé a las doce y media …	**5** Toda la noche no. Salí un rato.

gramática

The preterite tense

Regular:	**-ar**	**llamé**	I phoned	**llamaste**	you phoned
	-er	**volví**	I returned	**volviste**	you returned
	-ir	**salí**	I went out	**saliste**	you went out
Irregular:		**estuve**	I was	**estuviste**	you were
		hice	I did	**hiciste**	you did
		fui	I went	**fuiste**	you went

With reflexive verbs the reflexive pronoun goes first: **me acosté** etc.

3 Practise the two conversations that Miguel has with his mother and his girlfriend.

4 Ask your partner five questions about what s/he did yesterday. For example:

A **¿Qué hiciste ayer por la mañana?**
B **Por la mañana estuve en la biblioteca.**
A **¿Adónde fuiste por la tarde/anoche?**
B **Por la tarde fui a clase. Anoche salí con mis amigos etc**

5 Find out what another partner did last week and write where s/he was each day. For example:

A **¿Qué hiciste el lunes pasado?**
B **El lunes fui al cine.**
(A writes *cine* beside LUNES)

LUNES	
MARTES	
MIÉRCOLES	
JUEVES	
VIERNES	
SÁBADO	
DOMINGO	

the day before yesterday	**anteayer**
last Monday	**el lunes pasado**
last weekend	**el fin de semana pasado**

6 Y Miguel – ¿dónde estuvo anoche? / And Miguel – where was he last night?

Choose what you think is the most likely answer.

Estuvo en casa, estudiando.
Estuvo en el bar con Ricardo.
Estuvo en el bar con una amiga.
Estuvo en un restaurante, trabajando para ganar dinero.
Estuvo en un casino, jugando al black-jack.
Estuvo .... (¿Qué opinas tú?)

7 ¿Dónde estuvo Miguel? / Where was Miguel?

Escucha la conversación entre Miguel y Ricardo para saber la verdad.

8 La historia de la vida de Miguel. / The story of Miguel's life.

Put these events in Miguel's life in the most likely chronological order.

______ Viajó durante un año por América: visitó Chile, Argentina y Paraguay.

__1__ Nació el 10 de octubre de 1979 en Granada.

______ Volvió a España y fue a la Universidad de Granada donde actualmente cursa Cultura Latinoamericana.

______ Aprobó el Bachillerato en junio de 1997.

______ Trabajó en bares y cafés tocando la guitarra.

______ Fue al Colegio de Ave María hasta 1997.

gramática

The preterite tense: 'he', 'she' and 'you' (formal)

Regular			Irregular	
-ar	**trabajó**	s/he/you worked	**estuvo**	s/he was/you were
-er	**nació**	s/he was/you were born	**hizo**	s/he/you did
-ir	**salió**	s/he/you went out	**fue**	s/he/you went

9 Test your partner's memory. Give five facts about Miguel's life, some true and some false in one small detail. Your partner has to say **'Verdad'** or **'Falso'**. For example:

A **Miguel viajó durante dos años por América.**
B **Falso. Viajó durante un año por América.**

10 Write a potted history of your life, including three things you did before going to college or university. For example:

Nací en ... . Aprobé los 'A' Levels en ... . Antes de ir a la universidad fui de vacaciones a Italia, pasé dos meses en Canadá, trabajé como camarero/a en un bar... .

11 In a group of four, put all the life stories on the table, face down. Each person selects one and reads it out. The others have to ask questions to find out whose life it is. For example:

¿Cuándo nació?
¿Qué hizo después de aprobar los 'A' levels?
¿Trabajó/Viajó/Fue de vacaciones antes de ir a la universidad?

12 Lo pasé fenomenal. / I had a great time.

This is part of the presentation Carla gave on her return from an exchange visit. Ask and answer the questions in pairs.

El semestre pasado hice una visita de intercambio a una universidad española. La visita duró tres meses y lo pasé fenomenal.
Cuando llegué a la universidad, fui directo a Relaciones Internacionales, y la secretaria me dio la dirección de una casa. Al día siguiente volví a la universidad y una profesora me ayudó a organizar mi horario. Me sorprendió mucho el número de estudiantes en las clases – unos 70 u 80 –, pero pronto me acostumbré a llegar temprano a clase para poder

a ¿Cuánto tiempo duró la visita?
b ¿Cómo lo pasó?
c ¿Qué le dio la secretaria?
d ¿Quién le ayudó a organizar su horario?

gramática

(me/te/le) dio
s/he gave (me/you/him or her)
(me/te/le) ayudó
s/he helped (me/you/him or her)

¿Cómo lo pasaste/pasó?	How did it go? (for you/her/him)?
¿Cómo lo pasaron?	How did it go (for them)?

13 ¿Cómo lo pasaron? / How did it go?

Estos estudiantes también hicieron un intercambio.

Lo pasó bien ☺		Lo pasó mal ☹
☐	Fernando	☐
☐	Maribel	☐
☐	Itziar	☐
☐	Enrique	☑

14 Escucha otra vez e indica por qué lo pasaron bien o mal.

Match the name to the reason.

Fernando	**a** No le gustó la profesora del intercambio.
Maribel	**b** Tardó seis semanas en encontrar alojamiento.
Itziar	**c** Alquiló un coche y viajó mucho por las afueras de la ciudad.
Enrique	**d** Pronto hizo muchos amigos.

15 Test your memory. Who said the following?

a – Aprendí mucho, sí, pero no en la universidad. No fui muchas veces a clase …
b – Un estudiante argentino me ayudó, y la primera noche me quedé en su casa.
c – Hice muchos amigos, muy pronto …
d – Pero la mañana siguiente traté de buscar una casa – sin éxito.
e – Me quedé en una residencia para estudiantes, que es muy caro.
f – Y cuando traté de verla para pedir más trabajo, no estaba.
g – Después de seis semanas encontré un piso en el centro …, y me trasladé allí …

16 Test your partner. Ask questions about the people above. For example:

A **¿Quién tardó seis semanas en encontrar alojamiento?**
B **Enrique.**
A **¿Dónde se quedó la primera noche?**
B **Se quedó … etc.**

¿Qué le pasó a X?
What happened to X?

17 Fernando had a disastrous evening. Find out what happened by putting the events below in the correct order.

__1__ Cogió la llave de la casa en la agencia inmobiliaria.
_____ Fue al bar de enfrente para esperar a la dueña.
_____ La dueña volvió a la casa a las doce.
_____ Llegó a la casa a las seis.
_____ La dueña no estaba.
_____ Ella abrió la puerta.
_____ En ese momento, Fernando vomitó en la escalera.
_____ Perdió la llave de la casa en el autobús.
_____ Empezó a beber cerveza y tequila, y pronto se puso borracho.

18 Ask questions about what happened to Fernando. Your partner must answer without looking at Section 17. For example:

You	Your partner
¿Dónde perdió la llave?	**Perdió la llave …**

¿A qué hora …?
¿Adónde …?
¿Qué …?
¿Cuándo …?

Palacio Cincuentenario, Barcelona

19 Escucha la entrevista entre el detective y el testigo y rellena los espacios en el artículo.

Listen to the interview between the detective and the witness and fill in the spaces in the article.

Asalto en la calle

Ayer por (a) *la tarde* en la calle Jiménez (b) ...... jóvenes de unos (c) ...... o ...... años amenazaron a una mujer con una navaja y le robaron el bolso. El asalto tuvo lugar a las (d) ...... y duró unos (e) ...... segundos. Los asaltantes se escaparon corriendo por la calle Bogotá.

What happened?
¿Qué pasó?
¿Qué ocurrió?
¿Qué tuvo lugar?

20

With a partner take on the roles of detective and witness to the bank robbery described below. Ask and answer questions about it. For example:

Detective	**Testigo**
¿Cuándo ocurrió el atraco?	Ocurrió ayer por la mañana.
¿A qué hora ...?	__________
¿Qué ...?	__________
¿Cómo ...?	__________

Atraco en el banco

Ayer por la mañana hubo un atraco en el Banco Bilbao Vizcaya en la calle Aragón. Tres jóvenes de unos 18 o 19 años entraron en el banco a las diez, y gritaron «¡Manos arriba!». Amenazaron a los empleados con una pistola y salieron corriendo con €10.000. Se escaparon en un Seat rojo.

gramática

Regular			Irregular	
-ar	**asaltaron**	they attacked	**hicieron**	they did
-er	**volvieron**	they returned		
-ir	**salieron**	they left		

21 Read the first part of an article about a student demonstration.

> **Manifestación en Madrid**
>
> **6.000 estudiantes se manifestaron en Madrid contra la privatización de la Universidad. Colectivos estudiantiles organizaron la protesta, que terminó con una fuerte carga policial.**

22 Escucha las noticias y contesta a las preguntas sobre la manifestación en Madrid.

Listen to the news and answer the questions.

a ¿Cuántos estudiantes vinieron a la manifestación?

b ¿Por qué se manifestaron los estudiantes?

c ¿Quién organizó la protesta?

d ¿Cómo terminó la manifestación?

e ¿Quién resultó herido leve?

f ¿Quién fue detenido?

estudiantil	student (adj)
el enfrentamiento	confrontation
herido (leve)	(slightly) injured
detenido	arrested

23 Replace the misprints in italics in the rest of the article by substituting them with the words given.

> **Colectivos *infantiles* de la *derecha* alternativa convocaron *hoy* en *las afueras* de Madrid a 6.000 *ancianos* para expresar su *aprobación para* la posible *colectivización* de la Universidad. La manifestación *empezó* con enfrentamientos entre un grupo de estudiantes y la policía. Tras la carga, un *policía* resultó herido *grave*. No hubo detenidos.**

ayer — estudiantiles — privatización — leve — protesta — el centro — contra — izquierda — jóvenes — terminó — manifestante

Gramática

- **The preterite tense**
  For expressing something which happened at a particular time or for a defined period of time in the past: It *opened* at 12; They *stayed* for two hours, etc.

Regular

-ar		**-er**		**-ir**	
llamé	I phoned	**volví**	I returned	**salí**	I left
llamaste	you phoned	**volviste**	you returned	**saliste**	you left
llamó	s/he phoned you phoned	**volvió**	s/he returned you returned	**salió**	s/he left you left
llamamos	we phoned	**volvimos**	we returned	**salimos**	we left
llamasteis	you phoned	**volvisteis**	you returned	**salisteis**	you left
llamaron	they phoned you phoned	**volvieron**	they returned you returned	**salieron**	they left you left

Irregular

estar:	to be	**hacer:**	to do	**dar:**	to give
estuve	I was	**hice**	I did	**di**	I gave
estuviste	you were	**hiciste**	you did	**diste**	you gave
estuvo	s/he was you were	**hizo**	s/he did you did	**dio**	s/he gave you gave
estuvimos	we were	**hicimos**	we did	**dimos**	we gave
estuvisteis	you were	**hicisteis**	you did	**disteis**	you gave
estuvieron	they were you were	**hicieron**	they did you did	**dieron**	they gave you gave

- **Ser** and **ir** have the same form in the preterite:

fui	I went	*or*	I was
fuiste	you went		you were
fue	s/he went you went		s/he was you were
fuimos	we went		we were
fuisteis	you went		you were
fueron	they went you went		they were you were

haber: hubo there was

tener: tuve (like **estuve**)

seguir: seguí, seguiste, etc
but **siguió** and **siguieron**

pedir: pedí, pediste, etc
but **pidió** and **pidieron**

Direct object pronouns

- **me ayudó** s/he helped *me*
  te dio s/he gave *you*
  le dijo s/he told *him* or *her*

Reflexive verbs

- **me levanté**
  te levantaste
  se levantó, etc

Ejercicios de gramática

1 Write what you did yesterday. Change the verb forms in brackets.

Ayer por la mañana (a) (ir) *fui* a clase. Por la tarde (b) (trabajar) en la biblioteca y (c) (volver) a casa a las ocho. (d) (Cenar) con mis amigos y después (e) (ver) un poco la tele. (f) (Acostarse) a las once y media.

2 A friend has just come back from an exchange visit in Zaragoza. Fill in the gaps in the questions with the correct forms of the verbs below.

estar	pasar	quedarse	llegar	durar	ir

a ¿Adónde *fuiste*?

b ¿Cuánto tiempo ______ en Zaragoza?

c ¿Cómo lo ______ ?

d ¿Dónde ______ ?

e ¿Cuándo ______ aquí?

f ¿Cuánto tiempo ______ el viaje?

3 Write about the people you met on your exchange visit.
Change the verbs in brackets.

a En Relaciones Internacionales, me (dar) *dieron* la dirección de una casa.

b Me (gustar) todos mis profesores excepto una.

c Unos 70 u 80 estudiantes (asistir) a cada clase.

d Los estudiantes españoles me (ayudar) mucho.

e El primer día dos chicas me (invitar) a cenar.

4 Read the article and write down the questions a detective would ask a witness.
Ask questions beginning with:

a ¿Cuándo (*ocurrió el atraco*?)

b ¿Dónde …?

c ¿Qué …?

d ¿Cuánto tiempo …?

e ¿Adónde …?

f ¿Cómo …?

Ayer a las 11.10 de la mañana hubo un atraco en el supermercado en la calle Orfeo. Tres hombres de edades comprendidas entre los 22 y 30 años entraron gritando en el supermercado por la puerta principal y amenazaron a los empleados y clientes con una pistola. Estuvieron en el supermercado unos cinco minutos exigiendo dinero de las cajas y se escaparon con €2.500 en una furgoneta azul.

Vocabulario

1

saber	to know
ayer	yesterday
pasar	to spend
hay que	it's necessary
descansar	to rest
poquito (m)	a little bit

2

anoche	last night
oír	to hear
nada	nothing
pero	but
rato (m)	while

6

con	with
para	in order to
ganar	to earn
jugar	to play
opinar	to think

8

historia (f)	story
vida (f)	life
nacer	to be born
actualmente	at present
cursar	to take a course
aprobar	to pass
Bachillerato	exam similar in level to A levels
tocar	to play (an instrument)

10

antes de	before

11

después de	after

12

intercambio (m)	exchange
dar	to give
dirección (f)	address
siguiente	following
ayudar	to help
sorprender	to surprise
pronto	soon
acostumbrarse	to get used to
temprano	early
poder	to be able
sentarse	to sit down

14

tardar	to take
encontrar	to find
alojamiento (m)	accommodation
alquilar	to hire
afueras (f pl)	outskirts

15

veces (f pl)	times
tratar de	to try to
buscar	to look for
sin	without
éxito (m)	success
pedir	to ask for
trasladar	to move house

17

coger	to collect
llave (f)	key
agencia (f) inmobiliaria	estate agency
esperar	to wait for
dueño/a	landlord/lady
abrir	to open
vomitar	to be sick
escalera (f)	stairs
perder	to lose
empezar	to start
ponerse	to become
borracho/a	drunk

19

asalto (m)	assault
testigo (m)	witness
artículo (m)	article
jóven (m)	young
amenazar	to threaten
mujer (f)	woman
navaja (f)	knife
robar	to rob
bolso (m)	bag
tener lugar	to take place
asaltante (m)	assailant
escaparse	to escape
correr	to run

20

atraco (m)	robbery
gritar	to shout
¡Manos arriba!	Hands up!
pistola (f)	gun

Práctica en parejas/PARTNER WORK

1 Find out what your partner did yesterday. Ask the questions below. For example:

A **¿Ayer por la mañana estuviste en clase o en la cama?**
B **Estuve en clase.**

¿Ayer por la mañana estuviste en clase/en la cama?
¿Por la tarde fuiste a la biblioteca/a casa de tus amigos?
¿Pasaste la noche estudiando/en el casino con tus amigos?
¿Volviste a casa a medianoche/a las dos de la madrugada?
¿Te acostaste a las doce y media/a las dos y media?

2 Take it in turns with your partner to find out about each other's holidays. Ask about the following:

– Where s/he went
– How long for
– Who s/he went with
– Where s/he stayed
– When s/he came back
– If s/he had a good time

Ask questions beginning with:

¿Adónde ...?
¿Cuánto tiempo ...?
¿Con quién ...?
¿Dónde ...?
¿Cuándo ...?
¿Lo ...?

3 Complete Carla's diary by asking questions about what she did, where there is a blank in the diary. For example:

A **¿Qué hizo Carla el lunes por la mañana?** B **Fue a clase.**
A **¿Salió por la noche?** B **Sí** or **No**, etc

	LUNES	MARTES	MIÉRCOLES
Mañana	________________	Me levanté tarde y me perdí la primera clase.	________________
Tarde	Hablé con Miguel en la librería.	________________	Vi a Miguel en la cantina.
Noche	________________	Esperé toda la noche, pero Miguel no llamó.	________________

Práctica en parejas/PARTNER WORK

1 Find out what your partner did yesterday. Ask the questions below. For example:
A **¿Ayer por la mañana hiciste tu trabajo o hiciste las compras?**
B **Hice las compras.**

¿Ayer por la mañana hiciste	tu trabajo/las compras?
¿Por la tarde jugaste	al fútbol/al tenis?
¿Pasaste la noche	durmiendo/en el bar con tus amigos?
¿Te quedaste en casa	para cenar/para ver la tele?
¿Llamaste por teléfono	a tus padres/a tu amigo?

2 Take it in turns with your partner to find out about each other's holidays. Ask about the following:

– Where s/he went
– How long for
– Who s/he went with
– Where s/he stayed
– When s/he came back
– If s/he had a good time

Ask questions beginning with:

¿Adónde ...?
¿Cuánto tiempo ...?
¿Con quién ...?
¿Dónde ...?
¿Cuándo ...?
¿Lo ...?

3 Complete Carla's diary by asking questions about what she did, where there is a space in the diary. For example:
B **¿Qué hizo Carla el lunes por la tarde?** A **Fue a clase.**
B **¿Fue a clase el martes por la mañana?** A **Sí** or **No**, etc

	LUNES	MARTES	MIÉRCOLES
Mañana	Fui a clase.	______________	Pasé la mañana en la biblioteca.
Tarde	______________	Fui al gimnasio.	______________
Noche	Salí con Miguel. Volví muy tarde a casa.	______________	Invité a Jorge a cenar. Hice una paella. Lo pasamos muy bien – ¡sin Miguel!

In this unit you will consolidate and practise what you have learnt up to now, while also revising your vocabulary in familiar topic areas.

1 Escucha y rellena el formulario. / Listen and fill in the form.

Nombre __________	
Apellidos __________	
Dirección *Calle Colón, núm* __________	
Nacionalidad __________	
Fecha de nacimiento __________	
Lugar de nacimiento __________	
Profesión __________	*Elena Ariza González*

2 Ask your partner questions like the ones on the recording, and take down his or her details.

3 Ask and answer at least five questions each, taking turns to be Elena. Base your answers on the information in the box below. For example:

A **¿Cuántas personas hay en tu familia?** B (Elena) **Somos ...**

> Me llamo Elena. Vivo con mi familia en una casa muy grande en las afueras de Madrid. Somos cinco: mis padres, mi hermana Pino, mi hermano Nacho y yo. Nati, la novia de Nacho, vive bastante cerca con sus padres. Nacho y Nati quieren alquilar un piso en el centro, pero cuesta mucho y en este momento están ahorrando para poder pagar el alquiler.
>
> Voy cada día a la universidad, que está en el centro. Voy en moto, porque es más fácil aparcar. Estoy cursando matemáticas y ciencias. Me gusta bastante pero tengo que trabajar mucho. Salgo los fines de semana con mis amigos y normalmente vamos a algún bar o al cine.

4 Write five sentences about yourself, your family, your house, your job and what you like doing, on a piece of paper. In a group of four, put all the papers on the table, face down. Each person picks one of the papers at random and the others ask questions to find out who wrote it. For example:

¿De dónde es? **¿Cuántos hermanos tiene?** **¿Qué cursa?** etc

5 Discuss your likes and dislikes with your partner and fill in the table.
For example:

A **¿Te gusta hacer el banyi?**
B **Sí, me encanta.** (A writes ✓✓ under B.)

✓✓ me encanta(n)
✓ me gusta(n)
✗ no me gusta(n)
✗✗ no me gusta(n) nada

	A	B
Hacer el banyi		
La música punki		
Las revistas de motos		
Los libros de ciencia ficción		
Las películas románticas		

6 Escucha a Inés, invitando a Juanjo a ir al cine. / Listen to Inés inviting Juanjo to go to the cinema.

Now invite your partner to see the film.

TODO SOBRE MI MADRE
Pedro Almodóvar
Icaria Cineplex
10.00h
Entradas €10

7 Using the menu on page 32, practise ordering a meal in a restaurant. In a group of three, take on the following roles:

A is the waiter/waitress
B is a vegetarian
C doesn't like fish, chicken or olives

To remind you:	
¿Qué quiere tomar?	Quiero/Quisiera
¿Quiere …?	Para mí/ti/él/ella
¿Para beber?	¿Hay …?
No hay …	La cuenta, por favor.

8 Your partner draws a rectangle the same size as the photo to the right. Describe what the people are doing in the photo for your partner to draw them. For example:

A **Un hombre y una mujer sentados en una mesa.**
B draws a man and a woman sitting at a table.

9 **Bea está haciendo las compras. ¿Qué compra? Escucha y rellena el cuadro.** / Listen and fill in the box.

	Prenda	Talla	Color	Problema	Precio
a	una falda	....	....	demasiado pequeña	....
			....	....	–
			....	....	....
			....	–	....
b	unos zapatos	....	....	....	....
			....	–	–

10 Correct the inaccuracies in *italics* in Bea's account of her shopping trip.

He ido a todos los grandes almacenes y ahora estoy en el Corte Inglés. E*l primer vestido* que he probado aquí era demasiado *grande*, y pedí *uno* más *pequeño* a la dependienta. Me ha traído *otro*, pero no me gusta el color. He visto *muchos vestidos* pero por fin me he quedado con *éste*, que me ha costado €25. Pero no he podido encontrar *botas* del mismo color.

11 Jorge is coming to stay with you for a few days. Answer his e-mail.

Hola, ¿qué tal?

La semana que viene, tengo que ir a una conferencia, que es muy cerca de donde tú vives. ¿Puedo quedarme contigo? Voy a llegar el lunes 16, a las 20.10. ¿Vas a venir a la estación parar recogerme? Si no, cogeré un taxi. Al final de la conferencia, voy a tener algunos días libres – ¿qué vamos a hacer? Y tu hermana tan guapa – ¿va a estar en casa? Espero que sí.

Hasta muy pronto,

Un abrazo de

Jorge

12 Jorge is getting ready to leave. Taking on the role of his friend, make sure he hasn't forgotten anything. For example:

A **¿Has cogido tus gafas de sol?** B **Sí, he cogido mis gafas de sol.**
A **¿Has arreglado tu cuarto?** B **No, no he arreglado mi cuarto todavía.**

coger las gafas de sol ✓
arreglar el cuarto
lavar los pantalones ✓
hacer la maleta
planchar la camisa ✓
comprar el billete ✓

13 ¿Dónde tienen lugar estas conversaciones? Escucha y pon el número de la conversacion al lado de la situatión correcta. / Listen and put the number of the conversation next to the correct situation.

a En el aeropuerto
b En la oficina de coches de alquiler
c En la RENFE
d En la estación de autobuses

14 En el aeropuerto / In the airport

Fill in the questions, then practise similar conversations about the other flights.

VUELO	DESTINO	SALIDA	PUERTA	OBSERVACIONES
IB1706	NUEVA YORK	16.25	8	EMBARCACIÓN
IB1918	LISBOA	16.55	2	CONTROL DE PASAPORTE
IB2020	GRECIA	17.05	3	RETRASO DE 1 HORA
IB1519	MEXICO	17.15	4	

<<Señores pasajeros del vuelo Iberia 1706 con destino a Nueva York por favor diríjanse inmediatamente a la puerta 8. >>

¿A qué hora sale el vuelo? — Sale a las cuatro y veinticinco.
¿ ______________________ ? — Iberia 1706.
¿ ______________________ ? — De la puerta número 8.
¿ ______________________ ? — No, no hay ningún retraso.

15

Rearrange Jorge's conversation at the station so that it makes sense, and practise it with a partner.

Jorge
a Quisiera reservar un billete de ida y vuelta a Sevilla.
b ¿Hay uno más temprano?
c ¿Y para volver?
d ¿Hay que hacer transbordo?
e El viernes 28 de marzo.
f ¿A qué hora sale?
g No fumador. ¿Cuánto es?
h El miércoles 2 de abril.

Empleado
1 ¿Cuándo quiere viajar?
2 Sí, el Rápido que sale a las 16.40.
3 A la vuelta sale de Sevilla a las 13.10.
4 No, es directo.
5 ¿Y su fecha de regreso?
6 El Talgo sale a las 20.25 horas.
7 €30
8 ¿Fumador o no fumador?

16 Jorge está hablando con una joven en el tren. Escucha y contesta a las preguntas.

Complete the answers.

a Iré a Estados Unidos.

b Trabajaré en ______________ .

c Viajaré un poco por ______________ .

d Me quedaré en ______________

e y luego iré a ______________ .

f Volveré en ______________ .

17 Ask about your partner's holiday plans.

¿Adónde irás?
¿Cuándo saldrás?
¿Dónde te quedarás?
¿Con quién irás?
¿Qué harás?
¿Cuándo volverás?

18 ¿Quién es el misterioso viajero?

23 de marzo de 1999, 16.45, aeropuerto John Foster Dulles. Los pasajeros del vuelo 3662 de Delta Airlines ocupan sus asientos. La mayoría son hombres de negocios norteamericanos. Todos ignoran al joven alto del traje gris, camisa pálida y corbata verde que ocupa el asiento 1B. Sobre las rodillas tiene un ordenador portátil. ¿Quién es? Parece un ejecutivo, un banquero quizás. No. Es el heredero al trono de un país mediano de la vieja Europa. Se llama Felipe de Borbón.
Tiene 31 años y un día reinará. Ha sido educado desde el día de su nacimiento, y ha crecido con la democracia. Cuando Franco murió tenía siete años. Catorce cuando los socialistas ganaron las elecciones. Sopló las velas de su mayoría de edad jurando la Constitución. Y un día ocupará el trono de España.

Fuente: **El País**

a Describe the appearance of the person in this passage.

b What is his or her job?

c What major events in Spanish history took place when s/he was 7 and 14?

d What did s/he have to swear to uphold on his/her 21st birthday?

19 Imagine your partner is a famous person and you are sitting next to her/him on a plane. Agree who s/he is going to be and ask five questions about his or her life. For example:

A **¿Dónde naciste?** B (As Eva Perón) **Nací en Argentina.**
A **¿Estás casada?** B **Sí, con el presidente de Argentina.**
A **¿Trabajaste antes de casarte?** B **Sí, trabajé en algunos bares ...**
A **¿Siempre has sido rica?** B **No. He sido muy pobre.**
A **¿Te gusta ser famosa?** B **Sí, me encanta.**

20 Have you ever met a famous person? Tick the things your partner has done. For example:

A **¿Has hablado con una persona famosa?**
B **No, no he hablado con una persona famosa.**

¿Has ...

hablado con una persona famosa? ☐
ido a un casino? ☐
viajado en un helicóptero? ☐
robado algo de un supermercado? ☐
besado al novio/a la novia de un/a amigo/a? ☐
comido paella? ☐

nunca or **jamás**
never
No he hablado nunca
I have never spoken

21 **Escucha la vida de Rosario y rellena los espacios.**

Nací en (a) ... en Teruel. Me casé en (b) ... y mis hijos nacieron en (c) ... y (d) ... . Mis padres murieron en (e) ... durante la guerra civil, y el resto de la familia fuimos a América en (f) ... . Volvimos a España en (g) ... .

22 Ask your partner questions about his or her life. For example:
¿Cuándo/Dónde naciste? Nací en ...

¿Cuándo aprobaste el bachillerato/los 'A'Levels?
¿Viajaste/Trabajaste antes de ir a la universidad?
¿Qué cursas actualmente?
¿Trabajas para pagar el curso?
¿Qué harás después de la universidad?

23 Read this Spanish legend and answer the questions.

Los amantes de Teruel

Un joven de 22 años llamado Juan Martínez de Marcilla, se enamoró de Isabel Segura, hija de Pedro Segura, un hombre muy rico. Pidió su mano, pero el padre dijo que no, porque él no era rico. Así que Juan se fue a la guerra, y luchando contra los moros ganó mucho dinero. Después de cinco años volvió, rico, para casarse con Isabel. Pero el día en que Juan llegó a Teruel, Isabel estaba celebrando su boda con otro hombre, y cuando ella se negó a darle un beso (porque estaba casada), él se murió. Un poco más tarde ella murió también, y los dos fueron enterrados juntos en un sepulcro en 1217.

a Why didn't Isabel's father want her to marry Juan?

b What did Juan do when he was away?

c When did he come back?

d What was Isabel doing when he arrived?

e Why wouldn't she kiss him?

f Where were they buried?

24 Study this chronology of Spanish history for a minute. Your partner will then read out each event, changing some details. Say whether it is true or false, without looking at the table. For example:

A **España entró en la Comunidad Europea en 1987.**
B **Falso. España entró en la Comunidad Europea en 1986.**

1588	La Armada Invencible fue vencida por los ingleses.
1826	Las colonias españolas en el Nuevo Mundo ganaron su independencia.
1936	La Guerra Civil española empezó.
1939	La guerra terminó y la dictadura del General Franco empezó.
1975	Franco murió y la democracia fue establecida en España.
1986	España entró en la Comunidad Europea.

25 Test your partner by asking questions.
For example:

A **¿Cuándo empezó la Guerra Civil?**
B **Empezó en …**
A **¿Qué pasó / ocurrió en 1975?**
B …

gramática

In questions with **¿Cuándo …?** the word order is changed.
¿Cuándo murió Franco?

Ejercicios de gramática

1 Complete this conversation by putting the right verbs in the spaces.

Magdalena
Hola. ¿Cómo (a) *te llamas*?
(d) … Magdalena.
No, (f) … en Castellón.
(h) … en un banco.

Martirio
(b) … Martirio. ¿Quién (c) …?
¿(e) … en Alicante?
¿Qué trabajo (g) …?

2 Write what Carlitos does at these times every day.

a (Levantarse, 08.00)
Se levanta a las ocho de la mañana.
b (Salir de casa, 09.00)
c (Llegar a la universidad, 09.15)
d (Comer en la cantina, 13.00)
e (Volver a casa, 18.00)
f (Ir al bar con sus amigos, 22.00)
g (Acostarse, 24.00)

3 Write these numbers in words.

a 41
b 67
c 104
d 552
e 1778
f 9981

4 What are these people doing at the moment?

a (Ana, eating chips)
Ana está comiendo patatas fritas.
b (Gloria, leaving the house)
c (We, working hard)
d (You, arriving at the airport)
e (Vicente and Pepa, buying clothes)
f (I, speaking on the phone)

5 a How would you ask someone if s/he likes the following?
1 Las verduras
¿Te gustan las verduras?
2 Beber cerveza
3 Los animales

5 b How would you express the following?
1 I like the film.
Me gusta la película.
2 I love Cuban music.
3 I don't like football
4 I hate cheese.
5 I like it a lot.
6 I don't like it at all.

Ejercicios de gramática

6 Write what these people are going to do by using the appropriate form of **ir a** before the verb in brackets.

a Manolito (jugar) *va* a jugar al baloncesto.
b Yo (estudiar) esta noche.
c Ellos (ver) al profesor mañana.
d Nosotros (ir) al cine.
e ¿Cuándo (tú, venir) a mi casa?
f (Vosotros, comer) muy pronto.

7 Give directions to these places using the right form of the verbs.

doblar coger seguir ir estar

a from the cinema to the swimming pool
Ve todo recto. La piscina está a la izquierda.
b from the cinema to the hotel
c from the cinema to the bank
d from the cinema to the post office
e from the cinema to the station

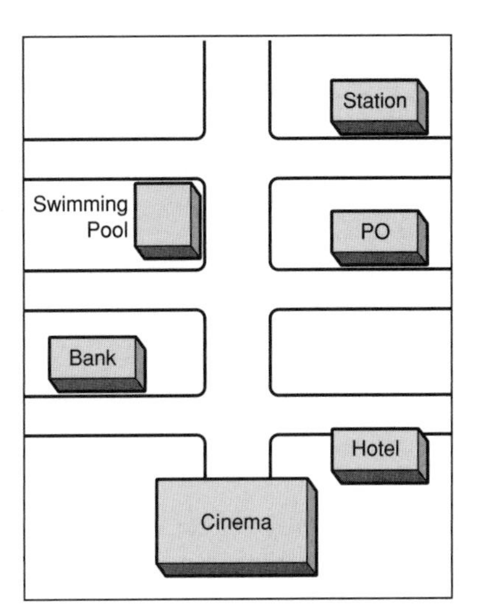

8 Write down these people's future plans.
María irá de vacaciones en junio.

a María	ir de vacaciones en junio.
b Nosotros	volver a América.
c Elías	casarse en junio.
d Yo	poder salir a las seis.
e Tú	acostarse a las doce.
f Ana y Bea	trabajar en Francia en agosto.
g Vosotros	tener que ahorrar dinero.

9 The people in Section 8 have now done what they were planning to do. Change the verbs to the perfect tense.

María ha ido de vacaciones.

10 Change this paragraph so that it describes what the writer did yesterday.

Cada día me levanto a las seis. Preparo el desayuno y salgo a las siete y media. Voy al trabajo en coche y llego a las ocho y cuarto. A mediodía como en un bar enfrente de la oficina. Vuelvo a casa a las ocho y ceno a las nueve y media. Me acuesto a las once o las doce.

Ayer me levanté a las seis. ...

Juegos de palabras/WORD GAMES

1 In the course of this book you have covered the topics listed here. Write down ten words related to each theme. Remember to include the gender of nouns.

La familia La casa La rutina Los estudios La comida El tiempo libre
De compras La ciudad De viajes De vacaciones El trabajo Los intercambios
Las noticias La historia

2 Gender wars

Call out a word with a feminine gender. Your partner must immediately call out a related word of the opposite gender within the same topic area.

For example:	A	**casa** (f)	B	**jardín** (m)
	A	**leche** (f)	B	**azúcar** (m)

3 Put the following words into one of the categories in Section 1 above.

entrevista cita billete entrada dinero sueldo chalet piso

4 Choose three words from one of the topic areas. Your partner has to use them all in one sentence. For example:

A **objetos perdidos** (counts as one word) **andén** **salir** (partner can use any form of the verb)

B **Los objetos perdidos han salido del andén número 10.**

Your partner must now give you four words to combine in a sentence.
Continue, increasing the number of words each time.

5 When you see **-dad** at the end of a Spanish word, it often corresponds to *-ty* in English. For example: **socie<u>dad</u>** means *socie<u>ty</u>*. Can you guess the meanings of the words below? Can you think of any others?

sociedad unidad capacidad prioridad facilidad dificultad normalidad
uniformidad necesidad totalidad

6 All these words have the same five-letter ending. What is it, and what ending does it correspond to in English?

rápida … lenta … general … normal … afortunada … desafortunada …
fácil … difícil …

Práctica en parejas/PARTNER WORK

1 Think of a person in your class. Your partner has to find out who you have in mind by asking no more than five questions like the ones below. You may answer only **Sí** or **No** or **No sé** ('I don't know').

¿Es francés o francesa?
¿Estudia geología?
¿Tiene una casa grande?
¿Es de Amsterdam?
¿Tiene 25 años?
¿Le gustan los animales?

2 Ask questions to fill in the blanks in Elena's timetable below. Then give your partner the information s/he asks for. For example:

A **¿Qué clase tiene Elena el lunes a las 12?**
B **Tiene clase de matemáticas.** (A writes **matemáticas** on the timetable)

	9:00	10:00	11:00	12:00	13:00	17:00	18:00	19:00	20:00
lunes		Inglés							
martes		Ciencias (laboratorio)							
miércoles	Informática					Deportes			
jueves									
viernes			Matemáticas						

3 Ask your partner how far these places are from Tarragona in time and fill in the table. For example:

A **¿A cuántas horas/cuántos minutos está Altafulla de Tarragona?**
B **Está a veinte minutos.**

	hrs		**hrs**
Altafulla	20 mins	Benidorm	
Calella		Sitges	
Reus		La Pineda	

Benidorm	**Reus**	**La Pineda**	**Tarragona**	**Altafulla**	**Sitges**	**Calella**
396km	8km	4km	0	20km	67km	172km

Práctica en parejas/PARTNER WORK

1 Think of a person in your class. Your partner has to find out who you have in mind by asking no more than five questions like the ones below. You may answer only **Sí** or **No** or **No sé** ('I don't know').

¿Es francés o francesa? ¿Es de Amsterdam?
¿Estudia geología? ¿Tiene 25 años?
¿Tiene una casa grande? ¿Le gustan los animales?

2 Ask questions to fill in the blanks in Elena's timetable below. Then give your partner the information s/he asks for. For example:

B **¿Qué clase tiene Elena el lunes a las 10?**
A **Tiene clase de inglés.** (B writes *inglés* on the timetable)

	9:00	10:00	11:00	12:00	13:00	17:00	18:00	19:00	20:00
lunes				*Matemáticas*		*Informática*			
martes									
miércoles			*Ciencias*			*Deportes*			
jueves	*Ciencias (laboratorio)*								
viernes									

3 Ask your partner how far these places are from Tarragona in distance and fill in the table. For example:

B **¿A qué distancia está Altafulla de Tarragona?**
A **Está a 20 kilómetros.**

	km		**km**
Altafulla	20	Benidorm	
Calella		Sitges	
Reus		La Pineda	

Benidorm	**Reus**	**La Pineda**	**Tarragona**	**Altafulla**	**Sitges**	**Calella**
5 hrs	10 mins	5 mins	0	20 mins	50 mins	2 hrs

Más práctica
FURTHER PRACTICE

1 Tú y los demás

1 En la oficina de Incarna / In Incarna's office

Escucha y contesta en inglés. Listen and answer in English.

a What is Jorge's job?
b What is Beatriz's job?
c Where is Jorge from?
d Where does he live?
e Who is Raúl Gomera?

2

Read the conversation and give four details in English about Carla.

– Carla, no eres de aquí, ¿verdad*?
– No. Soy de Puerto Rico, pero vivo aquí en Miami.
– ¿Dónde trabajas?
– Trabajo en la universidad.
– ¿Eres estudiante?
– No. Soy administradora, pero también aprendo italiano.

* Used to confirm something. In the case above it could be translated as '*are you*'?

3 Escucha y habla después de las señales. / Listen and speak after the prompts.

Take part in a similar conversation to the one above.

4

Listen to the numbers and say the next number after the prompt. For example, when you hear **dos** on the recording, say **tres**.

5

What questions would you ask to get the following answers? Write them in Spanish.

a Me llamo Miguel.
b Vivo en Edimburgo.
c No, no soy escocés. Soy inglés.
d Soy estudiante de informática.

6 En una escuela de lenguas en Oviedo / In a language school in Oviedo

Escucha y contesta en español. Listen and answer in Spanish.

Ignacio	**Amanda**
¿De dónde es? Es de ...	¿Es de Bilbao? Sí/No, es de ...
¿Cuántos años tiene?	¿Vive en Santander?
¿Dónde vive?	¿Tiene 24 años?
¿Cuál es su profesión?	¿Es intérprete?

7 You are Laurie Dimock, and you want to enrol on a Spanish course. Complete this letter to a language school with the details given.

Estimado señor/Estimada señora
Quiero matricularme en un curso de español.

Atentamente

Laurie Dimock

Laurie Dimock
22
Welsh, from Bangor
lives in Mexico
hotel receptionist

8 Read the letter from a new friend and write a reply in Spanish.

Querido/a ...

Soy española, de Málaga, pero vivo en Barcelona. Tengo 21 años. Soy estudiante y estudio inglés y alemán. ¡Aprendo mucho aquí! ¿Y tú? ¿De dónde eres? ¿Vives en Barcelona? ¿Cuál es tu profesión? ¿Y cuántos años tienes?
Escríbeme pronto.

Juanita

9 You are working for a Spanish computer dating agency and are responsible for keying in the details of the following people in Spanish. Write a paragraph about each one.

a Kim Lai (female), 25, Chinese, from Hong Kong, lives in Taunton, history teacher.
b Francis Owu (male), 24, from Ghana, lives in Newcastle, researcher.
c Siobhán Harpur (female), 21, Irish, from Dublin, learning French, works in a hotel.

10 Complete the number crossword.

V
E
I
N
T
E

1 Escucha y selecciona. / Listen and choose.

Josefa is telling you about her family. Match the names to the ages of the people she mentions, and their relationship to her.

Nombre	Edad	Relación
Eugenia	46	padre
Paulina	35	madre
Alberto	65	marido
Miguel	28	hermana mayor
Esther	64	hermana menor
Leonardo	40	hermano mayor
José	10	hijo

2 Lee y contesta en español.

Me llamo Charo. Tengo 26 años y soy española, de Valencia. Estoy casada, con dos hijos de seis y cinco años. Trabajo en un banco y mi marido es mecánico. Mis padres están divorciados. Mi madre vive en Valencia y es funcionaria. Mi padre vive en el campo y es agricultor. Tengo una hermana mayor, de 28 años. Se llama Susana. Está separada. Tiene dos hijos pequeños, de dos y cuatro años. Su marido vive en Pamplona. Mi hermano menor, Felipe, es ingeniero. No está casado, pero tiene novia. Su novia trabaja en el aeropuerto.

a ¿Cuántos hijos tienen Charo y su marido?
b ¿Cuál es la profesión del marido de Charo?
c ¿Cuántos hijos tienen los padres de Charo, y cómo se llaman?
d ¿Quién está divorciado, y quién está separado?
e ¿Cómo se llama la hermana mayor de Charo?
f ¿Quién trabaja en el aeropuerto?

3 Escucha y contesta a las preguntas.

Answer Charo's questions about your family. Include as many details as possible about their ages, jobs, marital status, etc.

4

Write a description of a family. It could be your own or a famous one like the British or Spanish royal families.

5 Escucha y completa la tabla. / Listen and fill in the table.

Two people are describing where they live.

	Juan	Ángela
¿Centro o afueras de la ciudad?	afueras	______
¿Casa/piso/chalet/habitación?	casa	______
¿Grande o pequeño/a?	grande	______
¿Número de dormitorios?	______	2
¿Salón o salón-comedor?	______	salón-comedor
¿Cocina grande o pequeña?	______	pequeña
¿Número de cuartos de baño?	______	1
¿Garaje o aparcamiento?	garaje	______
¿Jardín?	2	______
¿Balcón?	______	______

6 You are negotiating a house/flat exchange with a couple from Andalucía. Read the description they have sent you of the accommodation offered and answer the questions.

La casa es muy grande y bastante vieja. Hay dos plantas. Arriba hay cinco dormitorios, tres con cama de matrimonio, y uno con dos camas individuales. El dormitorio pequeño tiene una cama individual y un sofá. Todos tienen balcón. Hay tres cuartos de baño, todos con ducha y lavabo y uno con bañera. Abajo, en la planta baja hay dos salones, uno grande y bastante tradicional y el otro pequeño, con sillones, sofás, alfombras, etc. También hay un comedor, y la cocina es muy moderna con cocina, frigorífico y dos lavadoras automáticas. Hay dos garajes, unos jardines muy bonitos, una piscina y una pista de tenis.

a ¿Cómo es la casa?
b ¿Cuántos dormitorios grandes hay?
c ¿Qué hay en el dormitorio pequeño?
d ¿Dónde están los salones?
e ¿Cómo es la cocina?
f ¿Qué hay en los jardines?

7 You want to rent your own house or flat out for the summer. Write an advertisement describing it, for inclusion in a Spanish newspaper.

1 Escucha y completa la agenda de Isabel. / Listen and fill in Isabel's diary.

Isabel is a busy lawyer and you are her secretary.

	Por la mañana		Por la tarde	
LUNES	10:00	Juicio	______	Cita con Sr. Aznar
MARTES	______	Sra Gómez	______	Restaurante El Juez
MIÉRCOLES	Juicio todo el día		______	______
JUEVES	10:00	______	______	______
VIERNES	______	______	______	______

2

Manuel is Isabel's husband. Reorganize the sentences in this letter describing his day so that it makes sense.

Trabajo hasta las dos. Me levanto a las siete y desayuno a las siete y media. Como en un bar y vuelvo al trabajo a las cinco. Termino a las ocho y ceno con Isabel a las diez. Me acuesto a medianoche. Salgo a las ocho y voy a la oficina.

3

Use the clues to find out what jobs Isabel's five friends have. Fill in the table.

	Andrés	**Bea**	**Carlos**	**Diana**	**Enrique**
Profesión					
Por la mañana	*duerme*				
Por la tarde					*sale*
Por la noche				*trabaja*	

El estudiante y el artista duermen por la mañana.
La recepcionista y la profesora trabajan todo el día.
Andrés y Bea salen por la noche.
Carlos y la profesora trabajan por la noche.
El artista pinta por la noche y sale por la tarde.
El médico visita a los pacientes por la mañana y vuelve a la clínica por la tarde.
Andrés estudia por la tarde.

4 ¿Qué está haciendo Isabel? Escucha y rellena los espacios.

Back in Isabel's office, Señor Aznar is waiting to see her, but she is very busy.

15:55	**Sr Aznar**	Hola, buenas tardes. Tengo cita con Isabel a las cuatro.
	Secretaria	Hola, buenas tardes. Siéntese aquí. Isabel (a) ____________ con un cliente.
16:20	**Sr Aznar**	¿Está libre ahora?
	Secretaria	No. Ahora (b) ____________ por teléfono.
16:40	**Sr Aznar**	¿Qué (c) ____________ Isabel ahora?
	Secretaria	(d) ____________ un informe.
16:50	**Sr Aznar**	¿Sabe que (e) ____________ ?
	Secretaria	Sí, sabe que usted (f) ____________ .
17:10	**Sr Aznar**	¡Isabel (g) ____________ !
	Secretaria	Sí. Tiene otra cita a las cinco. Vuelva usted mañana.

está estoy haciendo esperando hablando saliendo
escribiendo consultando

5 Escucha y habla después de las señales.

Isabel is in the restaurant with her client. Take on the role of the client and speak after the prompts.

4 El tiempo libre

1 What sorts of books and magazines do Eduardo, Carmen and Andrés like? Indicate whether the sentences below are true or false.

	Verdad	Falso
a Carmen dice «A mí no me gusta leer.»	☐	☐
b A Eduardo le encantan las novelas policíacas.	☐	☐
c Andrés dice «No me gustan nada las revistas de motos.»	☐	☐
d Carmen pregunta «¿A ti no te gustan los libros de ciencia ficción?»	☐	☐
e A Eduardo le gustan bastante las revistas de moda.	☐	☐

2 Write the answers to the questions in Spanish.

Querido Ramón

... ¿Lo que me gusta en Barcelona? Pues todo. Hay muchos edificios muy interesantes desde el punto de vista arquitectónico – me gustan la casa de Gaudí y la Sagrada Familia, por ejemplo. También me encantan las calles que se llaman Las Ramblas. Siempre hay teatro en la calle: me gustan los títeres y las estatuas humanas, y hay muchos pintores y artistas de todo tipo ...

Un abrazo a todos

Ángela

a ¿Cómo se llama el arquitecto que le gusta a Ángela?
b ¿Qué le gusta ver en Las Ramblas?

el edificio	building
los títeres	puppeteers
siempre	always
la calle	street

3 ¿Quieres ver una película?

Match the film title to the description given.

a *La vida es bella* (Benigni)	**1** llena de acción y con mucha violencia
b *Titanic* (Cameron)	**2** humor, imaginación, romanticismo y amargura en la Italia fascista
c *Arma Letal* 4 (Donner)	**3** una biografía de Eva Perón, con Madonna
d *Evita* (Parker)	**4** amor y muerte con Leonardo di Caprio

4 No quiero salir contigo. / I don't want to go out with you.

Match the questions with the right answers so that this conversation makes sense.

a Miguel, ¿quieres salir mañana?	Todo el día.
b ¿Por qué?	No, no quiero salir contigo.
c ¿Por la noche?	Mañana no puedo.
d ¿Puedes salir el martes?	Porque prefiero salir con Juana.
e ¿Todo el día?	Por la noche.
f Miguel, ¿no quieres salir conmigo?	Tengo que trabajar.
g ¿Por qué?	No. El martes tengo clase.

conmigo with me **contigo** with you

5 Escucha y habla después de las señales.

A friend has rung to invite you out.

6

Susana is rather distracted and makes several mistakes in her diary. Listen to her three phone calls, and correct her diary entries.

LUNES	MARTES	MIÉRCOLES
De compras con Alicia a las 10.00h Cine con Carlos 10.30h	Gimnasio con Bea a las 4.30h	Exposición de Arte con Alicia. 12.00h en la entrada del museo

5 El dinero

1 Read the TV guide and say what sort of programme **'Ámame o Mátame'** is.

2 In this episode the action revolves round three notes.

a ¿Quién va a viajar a Estambul?
b ¿Quién va a París?
c ¿Quién va a estar en el Bar Jinete a las 10.00?

Ámame o Mátame

¿Qué va a pasar en este último episodio? ¿Margarita se va a dar cuenta de que su novio y su mejor amiga son amantes? ¿Cómo pueden estar juntos para siempre Leonardo y Livia? ¿Y quién es el misterioso Salvador? Esta noche miles de espectadores van a saberlo todo …

Una nota en la puerta del frigorífico. Viernes.

Querida Margarita, Tengo que viajar urgentemente a Estambul. Te voy a llamar desde el aeropuerto. Voy a volver el lunes.
Hasta luego, Leonardo

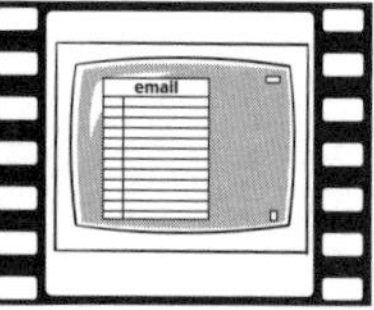

Un email recibido más tarde.

Querida Margarita
No puedo salir contigo esta noche. Este fin de semana voy a París. Voy a comprar mucha ropa (me gusta la moda francesa). Vuelvo el lunes por la tarde.
Un abrazo
Livia

Una nota en el casillero de Margarita.

Querida Margarita
Este fin de semana, tu novio no va a viajar a Estambul, y Livia no va a ir a París. Van a estar juntos en el Bar Jinete esta noche a las 10.
Salvador (camarero en el Bar Jinete)

3 **¿Qué va a suceder?** / What is going to happen?

Guess the rest of the story and write it down. For example:

Margarita va a ir al Bar Jinete. Va a matar a Livia y a Leonardo y después va a comprar un yate y viajar por el mundo.

4 **¿Qué pasa en el bar?** / What happens in the bar?

	Verdadero	Falso
a Margarita llega al bar a las 9.00.	☐	☐
b Pide un coñac.	☐	☐
c Leonardo y Livia no están en el bar.	☐	☐
d Margarita habla con Salvador.	☐	☐
e Margarita no va a salir con Salvador.	☐	☐

5 **¿Qué compran?** / What do they buy?

Margarita and Salvador have gone shopping.

6 **¿Cuánto van a dar a cada persona?**

Leonardo and Livia have won the lottery.

a La madre de Leonardo € ______

b Los padres de Livia € ______

c La hermana de Leonardo € ______

d El hermano de Leonardo € ______

e Los hermanos de Livia € ______

f El padre de Leonardo € ______

7

Livia has changed her plans. Take her part in the conversation at a car showroom. Speak after the prompts.

rápido	fast	**aire acondicionado**	air conditioning
reproductor de CDs	CD player	**cierre centralizado**	central locking
altavoces	loudspeakers		

8

The next day Leonardo receives this letter from Livia. What does it say?

Queridísimo Leo

Mañana voy a ir a Palm Springs con César, el vendedor de coches. Vamos a casarnos en Las Vegas.

Hasta luego; un abrazo

Livia

6 En la ciudad

1 Escucha y coloca los edificios en el plano.

Put the buildings on the map. The first one has been done for you.

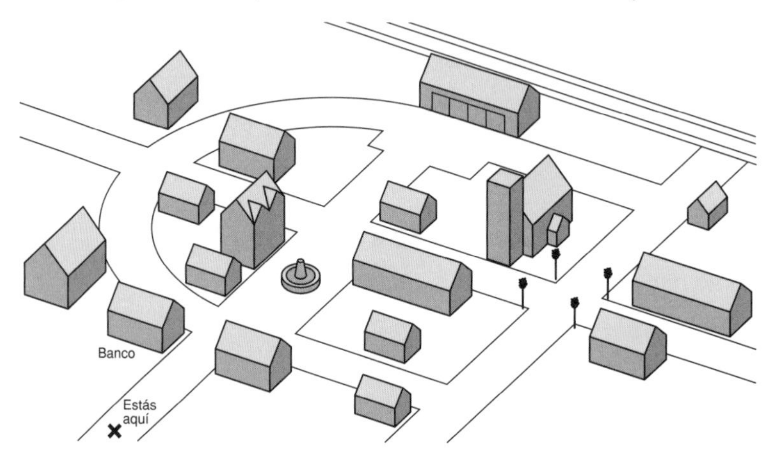

2 Escucha y contesta a las preguntas.

Give the locations of the buildings on the map above, speaking in the pauses. You will hear the correct answer after each pause on the recording.

3 Place the buildings on the plan by putting **A, B, C** etc where you think they go.

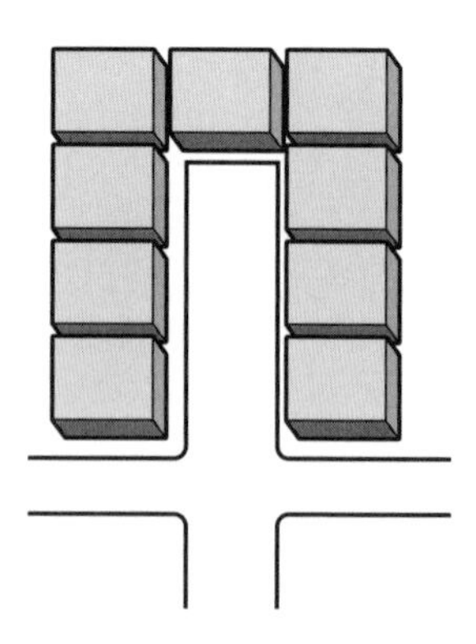

La academia **A** está en la esquina.
El banco **B** está entre la academia y el cine **C**.
El cine está enfrente del centro deportivo **D**.
El centro deportivo está al lado de la estación **E** en la esquina.
La farmacia **F** está entre la estación y la galería **G**.
El hospital **H** está entre el centro deportivo y la iglesia **I**.
La iglesia **I** está a la izquierda.

4 How far away are these places in your own town from each other? Write some sentences. For example:

La comisaría está a 10 minutos andando del parque.

a Police Station/Park
b Hospital/Sports Centre
c Bank/Shopping Centre
d Cinema/University

5 Ve por la calle Ferrán. / Go along Ferrán Street.

Using the map below, give the directions requested, from the Arco Youth Hostel (**albergue**).
Speak after the prompts.

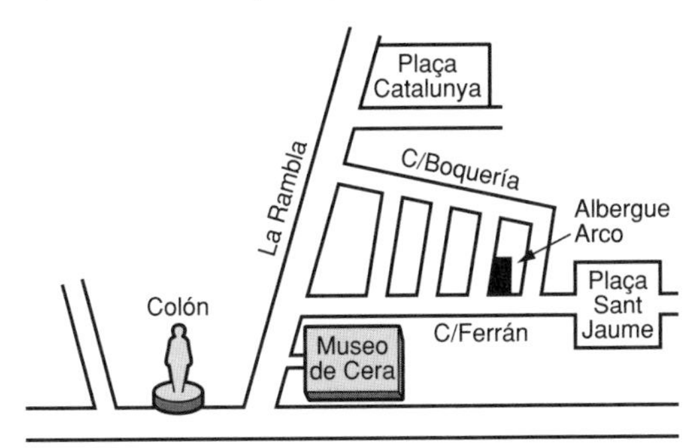

Al salir del edificio
On leaving the building

6 Using the map above write directions to the **Albergue Arco** from the following places:

a The Plaça Sant Jaume.

b The Plaça Catalunya

c The Wax Museum (**el museo de cera**)

7 Match the questions to the answers on this problem page.

Querida Tía María ...

a Todos los días son iguales. Voy a la universidad por la mañana, salgo con mis amigos por la tarde, bebo demasiado y fumo sesenta cigarrillos al día. Me aburro. ¿Qué puedo hacer?

b Mi novia bebe y fuma y no hace ejercicio. Tampoco va a la universidad. Me preocupo por ella. ¿Cómo puedo ayudarla?

c Mi novio nunca quiere pagar la cuenta cuando estamos en un restaurante. ¡Pero yo no soy rica, y no puedo pagarlo todo! ¿Qué puedo hacer?

d Trabajo en un bar para pagar mi curso, pero no me gusta el trabajo, y no tengo tiempo para estudiar. ¿Qué puedo hacer?

Tía María dice ...

1. Busca otro trabajo.
2. Busca otro novio.
3. Habla con ella. Pregúntale por qué bebe y fuma tanto y no quiere estudiar.
4. Es muy fácil. Busca otros amigos, deja de beber y de fumar y practica un deporte como el banyi.

1 Fill in the gaps in these horoscopes.

a Acuario Conocerás a la … de tus sueños.
b Piscis Los … te aportarán buena fortuna.
c Aries Tu … te traicionará.
d Tauro Ganarás mucho … .
e Géminis Viajarás a un país … .
f Cáncer Tendrás un nuevo … .

empleo
amante
dinero
extranjero
números 5 y 10
persona

2 En el año 2020

Write down three of your own predictions for the year 2020.
For example:
Tendré un buen trabajo y ganaré mucho dinero.
Viviré en una granja en el sur de Francia con dos caballos y un perro.
Hablaré cinco idiomas y seré un intérprete importante para la ONU … etc.

3 En el aeropuerto

Señor Alberti wants to change his flight. Write down the details.

	FECHA	VUELO	DESTINO	SALIDA	LLEGADA
Change from:					
Change to:					

4 En la sala de embarque

What does the girl say she will do in the holidays?

	Verdadero	Falso
a «Iré a los Estados Unidos.»	☐	☐
b «Trabajaré en Colombia en el verano.»	☐	☐
c «Después viajaré un poco por América.»	☐	☐
d «Me quedaré en Macedonia.»	☐	☐
e «Luego iré a casarme con un amigo en Miami.»	☐	☐
f «Iré en octubre.»	☐	☐

5 ¡Buen viaje! / Have a good journey!

Write an answer to this e-mail from Claudio. Tell him you can't come with him because you have to work. Tell him about one other thing you expect to do this weekend, and say you will see him next week.

> ¡Hola!
>
> Este fin de semana voy a salir al campo – ¿quieres venir?
>
> Iré con algunos amigos y vamos a acampar, pero la primera noche nos quedaremos en un hostal barato. Iremos en bicicleta, porque es más agradable y menos caro que ir en coche. Es más saludable también. Volveremos el domingo, por la noche.
>
> Espero que puedas venir. De todas formas, te veré la semana que viene. ¡Qué pases un buen fin de semana!
>
> Hasta luego,
>
> Claudio

6

Answer your friend's questions about what you'll do in the holidays.

7

Which of the following points of view best reflects your own views on the traffic problem?

a Hay demasiado tráfico y produce mucha contaminación. Ir en bicicleta o en autobús es mucho más ecológico. Para solucionar el problema de la contaminación, hay que mejorar el transporte público y prohibir los coches en la ciudad.

b No tenemos un problema con la contaminación y el calentamiento global. Cada persona tiene derecho a viajar como quiera. Hay que construir más carreteras y bajar el precio de la gasolina.

8

Vostradamus is the lesser known brother of the famous Nostradamus. He also made predictions about the future, but they were less successful. Rewrite what he got wrong.

> *En el siglo XXI los seres humanos volarán por el aire en barcos, y cruzarán el mar en bicicletas. Viajarán por tierra en submarinos. Cada día irán al trabajo a caballo. Será posible viajar alrededor del mundo en menos de un minuto.*

9

Write down two or three predictions of your own for 22nd century modes of transport.

En el siglo XXII los seres humanos …

1 Escucha y habla después de las señales.

You have seen an advert for an assistant (**un ayudante**) at a language school. Ring the school to ask for an application form (**una solicitud**). Listen and speak after the prompts.

2 ¿Cómo es el trabajador más buscado?

Dinámico, comunicativo, seguro de sí mismo, resolutivo, con conocimientos de informática y dominio de, al menos, un segundo idioma. Así es el trabajador que piden actualmente las empresas. Y es que, hoy en día, la actitud hacia el trabajo es tanto o más importante que la formación.

Fuente: *Quo* Núm 37 (adapted)

a Which of the six most sought after qualities above do you have?
b What is as important as training nowadays?

3

If you were an employer, which of the qualities below would you look for in a prospective employee? Rank them in order of importance.

a Facilidad para trabajar en equipo
b Adaptación a la cultura de la empresa
c Tolerancia al fracaso
d Vida personal equilibrada
e Capacidad de comunicación
f Confianza personal
g Deseo de aprender
h Capacidad de trabajo
i Flexibilidad
j Iniciativa
k Resolución

4 Las cualidades más valoradas / The most highly valued qualities

Listen to the employer talking about some of the above qualities and tick the ones he mentions.

5

Fill in this application form the language school sent you for the assistant's post.

NOMBRE ______________________ APELLIDOS ______________________

DOMICILIO ACTUAL ______________________

EDAD ______________________ ESTADO CIVIL ______________________

ENSEÑANZA (CON FECHAS) ______________________

____

EXPERIENCIA PROFESIONAL (CON FECHAS) ______________________

____

____

6 You are working in a hotel. Who will you call to sort out the guests' problems? Match the problem to the person who can help.

No se preocupe, señor/a. Llamaré …

a El ascensor no funciona.	**1** al fontanero.
b El wáter está bloqueado.	**2** al ingeniero.
c No hay papel higiénico en el baño.	**3** al portero.
d No puedo cerrar la ventana.	**4** a la policía.
e ¡Me han robado!	**5** a la criada.

7 Cómo quejarse en el trabajo / How to complain at work

There are always several ways of voicing a complaint. Choose the better option.

a **1** La fotocopiadora no funciona y no he podido hacer el trabajo. OR
2 Voy a llamar al técnico, a ver si puede reparar la fotocopiadora.

b **1** Antonio y yo tenemos el mismo trabajo, pero él cobra más que yo. OR
2 Yo trabajo mucho más que Javi (que es muy vago) pero él cobra más que yo.

c **1** Esta semana he trabajado 15 horas, pero me has pagado sólo 12. OR
2 ¿Por qué me has pagado sólo 12 horas cuando he trabajado 15?

d **1** No voy a hacer todas estas horas extras. Busca a otra persona. OR
2 No quiero hacer las horas extras, pero las haré. OR
3 No puedo hacer todas las horas extras pero haré dos o tres para ayudarte.

8 Rewrite the letter shown on the right, with everything as a negative experience.

For example:

He empezado el trabajo y <u>no</u> me gusta nada.

Querida Lucía

He empezado el trabajo y me gusta mucho. Empiezo muy temprano por la mañana y termino tarde, pero el trabajo es interesante y variado. Me llevo muy bien con mis colegas y los dueños, y me gusta conocer a los clientes. No pagan muy bien pero ha sido una experiencia importante y he podido practicar el español.

¿Qué tal tu trabajo?

Escríbeme pronto.

Un abrazo de

Juana

9 Describe your holiday job in a letter to a friend. Mention the following:

- the hours you work
- your duties
- the advantages and disadvantages of the job
- whether you like it or not, and why.

aburrido boring
siempre igual always the same

9 ¿Dónde estuviste ayer?

1 ¿Qué tal las vacaciones?

Put the sentences in the right order.

Tomé el sol, me bañé en el mar
Volví a la playa por la tarde,
Pasé toda la mañana en la playa,
y a mediodía fui a comer en un restaurante.
y pasé el resto de la semana en la cama.
Sin embargo, al día siguiente cogí una insolación,
y salí a una discoteca por la noche.
Llegué Mojácar a las siete de la mañana
y fui directo al apartamento.

2 ¡Qué desastre! ¿Qué les pasó a Mariví, Nicolás y Manolo?

Listen and put the name in the space.

Escucha y coloca el nombre en el espacio.

¿Quién –

- **a** olvidó su bolso en el taxi? Mariví
- **b** dejó sus llaves en la habitación? __________
- **c** se puso enfermo después de comer gambas? __________
- **d** perdió el avión y el tren? __________
- **e** llegó tarde al espectáculo? __________
- **f** vomitó en la cama? __________

3 Escucha y contesta a las preguntas sobre unas vacaciones que has pasado recientemente. / Answer the questions about a holiday you have had recently.

4

Write a postcard home from your holiday in Spain. Include the following information:

- **a** Say you arrived yesterday evening at 7.30 and you went straight to your apartment.
- **b** Say you had a meal in a restaurant and spent the rest of the evening in a bar.
- **c** This morning you went to the beach and had lunch in a café.
- **d** You returned to the beach in the afternoon and swam in the sea.
- **e** Now you are in your apartment, about to go out.

4 Quiz

¿Qué sabes de la Unión Europea?

1 ¿En 1946 quién propuso la creación de los Estados Unidos de Europa?
A El norteamericano Woodrow Wilson
B El británico Winston Churchill
C El alemán Karl Marx

2 ¿El tratado de Roma se firmó en qué año?
A 1967
B 1977
C 1957

3 ¿Cuál es el país que tiene menos habitantes en la Unión Europea?
A Finlandia
B España
C Bélgica

4 ¿Quién no volvió a las negociaciones de Luxemburgo en 1966?
A Konrad Adenauer
B Harold Wilson
C Charles de Gaulle

5 ¿Dónde está el Tribunal Europeo de Justicia?
A Maastricht
B Luxemburgo
C La Haya

6 ¿Cuántos miembros hay en el Parlamento Europeo?
A 500
B 626
C 824

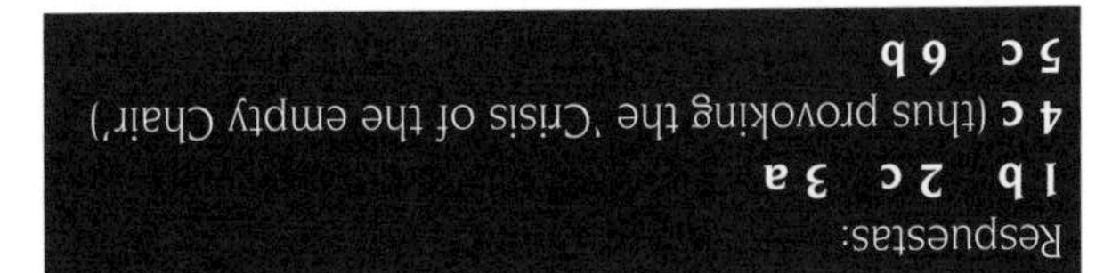

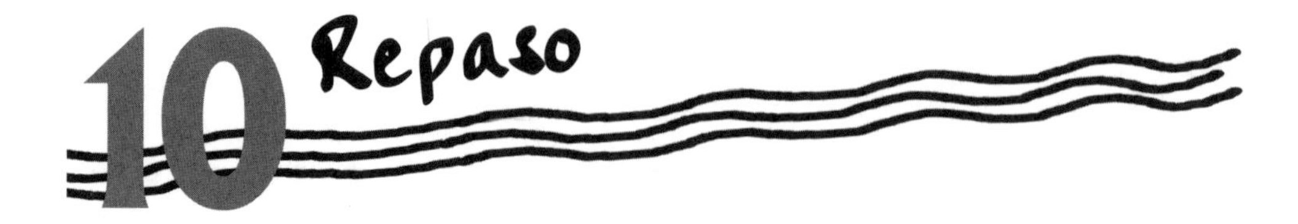

1 Rank the reasons given why young Spanish people prefer to live at home, according to which you think are the most and least common. See if you were right by looking at the Answers and fill in the percentages.

España es uno de los países de la Unión Europea donde mayor porcentaje de jóvenes menores de 24 años vive con sus padres, según la Comisión Europea. ¿Por qué tardan tanto en independizarse?

	%
La vivienda es cara.	____
Prefieren las comodidades sin responsabilidades.	____
Los padres no son muy estrictos.	____
Los jóvenes se casan más tarde.	____
No tienen posibilidades de independizarse antes.	____
Los padres necesitan la ayuda económica de los hijos.	____
Quieren tener una situación estable antes de vivir solos.	____

[Adapted from *Quo* No 47, source: 'Young Europeans', European Commission 1997.]

2 ¿Cuáles son los gastos mensuales de alquilar un piso en España?

Escucha y rellena los espacios. Listen and fill in the spaces.

GASTOS MENSUALES

Alquiler	€______		
Luz	€______	Gas (sin calefacción): natural	€______
Agua	€______	Butano	€______
Teléfono	€______	Calefacción (de gas natural)	€______
Comunidad de vecinos:		sin servicios (ascensor, calefacción)	€______
		con servicios	€______

El alquiler varía desde €______ a €______ . Es más caro en Cataluña, el País Vasco y Madrid y menos caro en Huelva, Cáceres y Huesca. Además, en España cuando alquilas un piso tienes que pagar el primer mes de alquiler y también una fianza de €______ a €______ .

[Adapted from *Quo* No 47, several sources.]

3 Answer the questions about the two historical figures below.

Dolores Ibarruri
Hija y esposa de mineros, la dirigente comunista nació en 1895 en Bilbao. Participó en la lucha obrera desde muy joven, mostrando una gran capacidad oratoria. Salió de España durante la guerra civil y continuó su actividad política en el exilio. Volvió en 1977.

Montezuma
Nació en 1480 y fue gobernante del imperio Azteca en México. Cuando llegó Hernán Cortés en 1519, creyó que era el dios Quetzalcoatl. Cortés lo tomó como rehén. Cuando los aztecas se sublevaron en 1520, Montezuma intentó apaciguarlos, pero murió apedreado.

a Where was the Aztec empire?
b Where was the communist leader born?
c Who was politically active from a young age?
d Who fought on the side of the workers?
e Who was a great speaker?
f Who thought Cortés was a god?
g Who was taken hostage?
h Who was exiled from Spain?
i Who tried to calm the Aztec revolt?
j Who was stoned to death?

4 ¿Qué sabes de la historia española?

1 ¿Cuántos años duró la ocupación romana de España?
A 200 años
B 400 años
C 600 años

2 ¿Cuántos años duró la ocupación árabe de España?
A 400 años
B 600 años
C 800 años

3 ¿Qué pasó en 1492?
A Los moros fueron vencidos en Granada.
B Los judíos fueron expulsados de España.
C Cristóbal Colón viajó a las Américas.

4 ¿Qué pasó en 1808?
A Napoleón invadió España.
B Los británicos tomaron Gibraltar.
C Se abolió la Inquisición

Clave
1 B **3** A, B & C
2 C **4** A

Language learners often feel unsure about grammatical terms. The following list gives some simple definitions. Examples are underlined, terms used which are defined elsewhere in the list are given in bold. Examples are drawn from English: reference is made to Spanish only when something distinctive about that language needs to be noted. This Guide is concerned only with the meanings of grammatical terms: there is a Spanish Grammar Summary beginning on page 146.

Adjective A word used to describe a **noun** ("an interesting woman"; "the curry is hot"). See also **demonstrative adjective**, **possessive adjective**.

Adverb A word which describes the action of a **verb** ("She sings beautifully", "He cooks well") or modifies (= gives further information about) an adjective ("It's a really expensive car") or another adverb ("She sings really well").

Agree In English, **adjectives** don't change their form but in Spanish they have to agree with the noun they are describing in **gender** and **number** : if the noun is feminine, the adjective must be in the feminine form, if the noun is plural, so is the adjective.

Article The (called the definite article), a or an (the indefinite article).

Auxiliary verb A **verb** combining with another verb to form a **compound tense**. ("She has gone" = auxiliary verb "to have" here used to form the Perfect tense by combining with the **past participle** of the verb "to go".)

Comparative Form of an **adjective** ("That room is bigger than this one"; "They've bought a more expensive car") or **adverb** ("She sings more beautifully than I do") expressing a greater degree.

Compound tense A **tense** formed by combining an **auxiliary verb** with another verb. For example the future tense ("He will see you next week" – auxiliary verb "will" combined with the **infinitive** "see"), the perfect tense ("We have already seen him" – auxiliary verb "Have" combined with the **past participle** "seen").

Conjunction A word which joins parts of a sentence ("He was tired and he wanted to go home"; "They arrived early because they wanted a good place").

Demonstrative adjective These "point out" **nouns** (this chair/these chairs; that house/those houses).

Direct object The word which directly undergoes the action of the verb. In the sentence "She sent her mother a present", what she sent was a present, so that is the direct object. She didn't send her mother! See also **indirect object**.

Gender In Spanish, all **nouns** have a grammatical **gender**, masculine or feminine, and **adjectives** have to **agree**.

Imperative Verb form used in giving commands and instructions ("Turn left now!").

Indirect object A secondary **object**. In the sentence "She sent her mother a present", the **direct object**, the thing which is sent, is the present. It was sent to her mother, the indirect object.

Intransitive verb Verb that doesn't take a **direct object**, e.g. "to arrive" ("She arrived at one o'clock").

Infinitive The basic form of a **verb** ("to sing"; "to write").

Irregular verb **Verb** that varies from the standard pattern.

Noun Word denoting a person ("student"), thing ("book") or abstract idea ("happiness").

Number Whether a word is **singular** or **plural**.

Object The **noun** or **pronoun** which undergoes the action of the verb. "We bought a house"; "I saw him."

Object pronoun **Pronoun** used when it's the **object** of the **verb**. Me, you, him, her, it, us, them.

Past participle Part of the **verb** which combines with an **auxiliary verb** to form the Perfect tense ("they have arrived"; "I have seen").

Plural More than one: the plural of "man" is "men".

Possessive adjective e.g. "my house", "your friend", "his car" etc.

Preposition e.g. "on the table"," under the chair", "to the station", "for the teacher" etc.

Pronoun Word taking the place of a **noun**. "Peter saw the waitress" becomes "He saw her."

Reflexive verb In Spanish, a **verb** formed with an extra pronoun (called a reflexive pronoun). E.g. llamarse (to be called, literally "to call oneself"): me llamo Carlos (I'm called/my name is Carlos, literally "I call myself Carlos"); se llama Ana (she's called Ana).

Regular verb **Verb** that follows a standard pattern.

Relative pronoun **Pronoun** used to refer back to a noun earlier in the sentence. e.g. "The man who lives there is very old"; "The book which he chose ..."; "The woman/film that he saw...".

Singular One rather than many: the singular of "bananas" is "banana".

Subject Who or what carries out the action of the **verb**. "A student sent me this email."; "We are travelling next week."; "The letter arrived yesterday".

Subject pronoun **Pronoun** used when it's the **subject** of the **verb**: I, you, he, she, it, we, they.

Transitive verb **Verb** which takes a direct object, unlike an **intransitive verb**, which doesn't e.g. "to catch" ("She caught a train").

Tense Form taken by a **verb** to show when the action takes place. e.g. Present tense: "They live in New York"; Past tense: "They lived in New York"; Future tense: "They will live in New York" etc.

Verb Word indicating an action ("They ate their dinner") or state ("The book lay on the table"). Different **tenses** are used to show when something happened.
See also **auxiliary verb**, **intransitive verb**, **irregular verb**, **reflexive verb**, **regular verb**, **transitive verb**.

The alphabet

There used to be 30 letters in the Spanish alphabet, and in some old dictionaries you will find the four 'extra' ones – **ch**, **ll**, **ñ**, and **rr** – listed in separate sections. Thus **chico** will be found under **ch**, not **c**. However, now the only 'extra' letter is **ñ** – so in new dictionaries **chico** is found under **c** and **llegar** is found under **l**.

There are five **vowels** in Spanish, as in English. They are **a**, **e**, **i**, **o** and **u**, and they only have one sound each. All the other letters are called **consonants**.

El alfabeto									
A	B	C	D	E	F	G	H	I	J
K	L	M	N	Ñ	O	P	Q	R	S
T	U	V	W	X	Y	Z			

Nouns and articles

A noun is the grammatical term for a thing, person, place, animal, event or idea. All nouns have a gender in Spanish. That is, they are either masculine or feminine. Masculine nouns frequently end in **-o** and feminine ones in **-a**:

un piso (masculine)	a flat	**una casa** (feminine)	a house

As in English, they also have a number, singular or plural:

un piso (singular)	a flat	**unos pisos** (plural)	some flats
una casa	a house	**unas casas**	some houses

In Spanish articles have the same number and gender as the noun. Thus **el**, **la**, **los** and **las** all mean 'the'; **un** and **una** both mean 'a'; **unos** and **unas** mean 'some':

Gender	Number			
	singular		plural	
masculine	**el libro**	the book	**los libros**	the books
feminine	**la novela**	the novel	**las novelas**	the novels
masculine	**un colegio**	a college	**unos colegios**	some colleges
feminine	**una escuela**	a school	**unas escuelas**	some schools

Some nouns end in other letters, so the only way you can tell what gender they are is by looking at the article. Thus **la calle** is feminine; **el restaurante** is masculine. Others may end in **-a** and be masculine, or end in **-o** and be feminine: **la mano** is feminine; **el día** is masculine.

Adjectives

Adjectives describe nouns and they have to 'agree' in number and gender with the nouns they are describing. Most adjectives go after the noun in Spanish.
Many Spanish adjectives end in **-o**, like **moderno**:

	masculine	feminine
singular	**un piso moderno** a modern flat	**una casa moderna** a modern house
plural	**unos pisos modernos** some modern flats	**unas casas modernas** some modern houses

Other adjectives end in **-e**, like **grande**. These have only two forms – singular and plural:

	masculine	feminine
singular	**un piso grande** a big flat	**una casa grande** a big house
plural	**unos pisos grandes** some big flats	**unas casas grandes** some big houses

Adjectives like **popular**, which end in a consonant, often have only two forms. To form the plural, **-es** is added:

	masculine	feminine
singular	**un libro popular** a popular book	**una novela popular** a popular novel
plural	**unos libros populares** some popular books	**unas novelas populares** some popular novels

Possessive adjectives

You can use possessive adjectives to indicate who owns the noun. **Mi** (my), **tu** (your) and **su** (his, her, their, your*) have only two forms, singular and plural:

One thing owned		More than one thing owned	
mi coche	my car	**mis coches**	my cars
tu coche	your car	**tus coches**	your cars
su coche	his car, her car, their car, your* car	**sus coches**	his cars, her cars their cars, your* cars

*formal

Nuestro (our) and **vuestro** (your) have four forms:

One thing owned		More than one thing owned	
nuestro libro	our book	**nuestros libros**	our books
nuestra novela	our novel	**nuestras novelas**	our novels

Demonstrative adjectives

These are used to specify a particular object or person, and they have four forms:

	masculine		feminine	
singular	**este libro**	this book	**esta novela**	this novel
plural	**estos libros**	these books	**estas novelas**	these novels

Comparative of adjectives

To compare two things you can use **más ... que** or **menos ... que**:

El coche es más caro que la bici. The car is more expensive than the bike.
La bici es menos cara que el coche. The bike is less expensive than the car.

¿Cuánto?

When **¿Cuánto?** is used as an adjective (when it comes before a noun), it has four forms:

¿Cuánto tiempo tienes? How much time do you have?
¿Cuánta sopa quieres? How much soup do you want?
¿Cuántos hermanos tienes? How many brothers do you have?
¿Cuántas hermanas tienes? How many sisters do you have?

But when you are asking the price of something, **¿Cuánto?** doesn't change:

¿Cuánto es la falda? How much is the skirt?
¿Cuánto son los zapatos? How much are the shoes?

Questions

To ask a question you can use a verb. Note that verbs can be both questions and statements:

Vive en Málaga. He lives in Málaga.
¿Vive en Málaga? Does he live in Málaga?

You can also use question words and verbs:

¿Quién eres? Who are you?
¿Cómo estás? How are you?
¿Dónde vives? Where do you live?
¿Qué haces? What do you do?
¿Adónde vas? Where do you go (to)?
¿Cuál es? Which is it?
¿Cuándo empieza? When does it start?

Pronouns

A pronoun can be used in place of a noun, often to avoid repetition:

John went to the supermarket where John bought some wine.
John went to the supermarket where he bought some wine.

'He' is a pronoun.

Subject pronouns

Singular		**Plural**	
yo	I	**nosotros**	we (all male or male and female)
tú	you	**nosotras**	we (all female)
él/ella	he/she	**vosotros**	you (all male or male and female)
usted*	you	**vosotras**	you (all female)
		ellos/ellas	they (male/female)
		ustedes*	you

*Also written **Vd./Vds.**

You

There are five words for 'you' in Spanish. The one you use depends on whether you are being formal or friendly, how many people you are talking to and what sex they are:

Informal

tú for when you are addressing one person
vosotros* for when you are addressing more than one person, and they are all male, or male and female
vosotras* for when you are addressing more than one person, and they are all female

Formal

usted for when you are addressing one person
ustedes for when you are addressing more than one person

*In Spain only. In Latin America different forms are used.

Tú and **vosotros** are generally used when speaking to people you know by their first names – young people, members of your family, neighbours, teachers. **Usted** and **ustedes** are for people you would normally address by their title, (Mr or Mrs, Dr, Professor), or to whom you wish to show particular respect. If you are a young person you will be addressed as **tú** in almost all situations, including in shops and most interviews. To use **usted**, even to a friend's parents (if they are youngish), can be seen as being standoffish. However, to use **tú** can be seen as being rude, so it is best to start with **usted** when addressing someone you don't know well who is of retirement age or older. They will let you know if they want you to use **tú**.

Subject pronouns are often omitted in Spanish, because in most cases the verb endings make it clear who is performing the action:

Viv<u>o</u> en Ecuador can only mean <u>I</u> live in Ecuador.
Tien<u>es</u> dos hermanas can only mean <u>You</u> have two sisters.

But

Viv<u>e</u> en Ecuador can mean <u>He</u> or <u>She</u> lives in Ecuador.
or <u>You</u> live in Ecuador.

Thus the subject pronoun can be used to avoid misunderstandings, or for emphasis:
Juan y María fueron a la playa. <u>Él</u> se bañó y <u>ella</u> tomó el sol.
Juan and María went to the beach. <u>He</u> bathed in the sea and <u>she</u> sunbathed.

Object pronouns

The object of a verb can be described as the 'recipient' of the action.

She sees the boy.	'The boy' is the object.
She sees him.	'Him' is the object pronoun, often used to avoid repetition.
She gives the book to the boy.	'The book' is the direct object and 'the boy' is the indirect object.
She gives it to him.	'It' is the direct object pronoun and 'him' is the indirect object pronoun in this sentence.

In this course you have seen these object pronouns:

me	**te**	**le, lo**	**la**	**los, las**
(to) me	(to) you	(to) him/it	(to) her/it	(to) them

dime la verdad tell me the truth **lo he visto** I have seen it

Verbs

A verb can indicate the action, mental or physical, in a sentence. Verbs are often used to say someone does (has done, did, will do etc) something. They are also used to express a condition or state: he is, she seems, and so on.

All Spanish verbs belong to one of three groups, depending on whether the infinitives end in **-ar**, **-er** or **-ir**: **estudiar** (to study), **aprender** (to learn), **vivir** (to live). The form of the verb changes according to who or what is the subject (often the person doing the action) and when the action is being performed (in the past, present or future). Most of the verbs within each of the three groups are regular, that is their endings change in the same way, but there are many irregular verbs.

Present tense

Verbs in the present form are often used to express generalities and to describe habitual actions: It *rains* in Spain; He *goes* to work; She *gets* up at seven (every day).

subject pronoun	**estudiar**	to study	**aprender**	to learn	**vivir**	to live
yo	**estudio**	I study	**aprendo**	I learn	**vivo**	I live
tú	**estudias**	you study	**aprendes**	you learn	**vives**	you live
él, ella, *usted*	**estudia**	s/he studies you study	**aprende**	s/he learns you learn	**vive**	s/he lives you live
nosotros/as	**estudiamos**	we study	**aprendemos**	we learn	**vivimos**	we live
vosotros/as	**estudiáis**	you study	**aprendéis**	you learn	**vivís**	you live
ellos, ellas *ustedes*	**estudian**	they study you study	**aprenden**	they learn you learn	**viven**	they live you live

Two irregular verbs in the present

ser	to be			**ir**	to go		
soy	I am	**somos**	we are	**voy**	I go	**vamos**	we go
eres	you are	**sois**	you are	**vas**	you go	**vais**	you go
es	s/he is	**son**	they are	**va**	s/he goes	**van**	they go
	you are		you are		you go		you go

Some verbs are irregular in the **yo** (I) form of the present:

estar (to be) — **estoy** (I am)
hacer (to do) — **hago** (I do)

Verb tables can be found in most dictionaries.

Ser and estar

Ser and **estar** both mean 'to be', but they work in different ways. **Ser** is often used when you want to express something that never changes, while **estar** is for temporary states or conditions. Study their different uses.

Ser is always used in the following situations:

- with an adjective for describing unchanging traits or characteristics:
  Soy alta y morena. — I am (and always will be) tall and dark.
- with a noun for identifying someone or something:
  Es una casa. — It is a house.
- to express nationality and origin:
  Soy de Nigeria; soy nigeriana. — I am from Nigeria; I am Nigerian.
- to show possession:
  Es mi coche. Es el coche de Juan. — It is my car. It's Juan's car.
- for telling the time:
  Es la una; son las dos. — It's one o'clock; it's two o'clock.

Estar is always used in the following situations:

- to express location:
  Está a la izquierda. — It's on the left.
- to discuss health:
  ¿Cómo estás? Estoy bien. — How are you? I am well.
- with an adjective for describing a (usually temporary) state or condition:
  Estoy cansado. — I am tired.

Note that in Spanish other verbs are sometimes used where 'to be' is used in English:

Tener (to have)	**Tengo 20 años.**	I am 20 years old.
Haber (to have)	**Hay un libro en la mesa.**	There is a book on the table.
	Hay dos libros en la mesa.	There are two books on the table.

Reflexive verbs

Reflexive verbs have the normal **-ar**, **-er** or **-ir** endings, but also have a reflexive pronoun to indicate that the person is doing something to, by or for him/herself. These are **me** (myself), **te** (yourself), **se** (himself/herself/yourself), **nos** (ourselves), **os** (yourselves), and **se** (themselves/yourselves):

llamarse to be called (literally to call oneself)

me llamo	I am called (I call myself)	**nos llamamos**	we are called
te llamas	you are called	**os llamáis**	you are called
se llama	s/he is called; you are called	**se llaman**	they/you are called

Root-changing verbs

The root of a verb is the part before the **-ar**, **-er** or **-ir** ending. Root-changing verbs have the normal endings, but a vowel in the root of the verb also changes in most of the verb forms in the present. They do not change in the **nosotros** and **vosotros** forms. These changes are:

- **e** to **ie** (**querer**, **tener**, **venir**, **sentarse**)
- **o** to **ue** (**poder**, **almorzar**, **acostarse**)
- **e** to **i** (**decir**, **pedir**)
- **u** to **ue** (**jugar** – the only verb in this group)

querer	to want	**poder**	to be able to	**pedir**	to ask for
quiero	I want	**puedo**	I can	**pido**	I ask for
quieres	you want	**puedes**	you can	**pides**	you ask for
quiere	s/he wants you want	**puede**	s/he can you can	**pide**	s/he asks for
queremos	we want	**podemos**	we can	**pedimos**	we ask for
queréis	you want	**podéis**	you can	**pedís**	you ask for
quieren	they/you want	**pueden**	they/you can	**piden**	they/you ask for

Tener, **venir** and **decir** are root-changing verbs which are also irregular in the **yo** form: **tengo** (I have); **vengo** (I come); **digo** (I say). Some verbs are reflexive and root-changing: **sentarse** (to sit down): **me siento** etc; **acostarse** (to go to bed): **me acuesto** etc

Present continuous

The present continuous is used to describe an action that is in progress at a particular moment: What are you doing? I am writing a letter. It is formed with part of **estar** and the present participle (saying, doing):

estar + present participle

estoy llegando	I am arriving
estás bebiendo	you are drinking
está saliendo	s/he is leaving you are leaving
estamos hablando	we are speaking
estáis comiendo	you are eating
están escribiendo	they are writing you are writing

present participle

-ar verbs:	
llegar:	**llegando**
-er verbs:	
beber:	**bebiendo**
-ir verbs:	
salir:	**saliendo**

Talking about the future

There are three ways of expressing the future in Spanish. They are often interchangeable.

1 Present tense – for pre-scheduled events:
El tren sale a las 3. The train leaves at 3.

2 'Going to' (**Ir a** + infinitive) – for plans and intentions:
Voy a salir a las 3. I'm going to leave at 3.

3 Future tense – for predictions and intentions:
Saldré a las 3. I'll leave at 3.

Present tense

The present is used as in English for pre-scheduled events: 'The shop opens at 6'; 'The plane arrives at 8', and so on. See above for the verb forms.

Going to ...

Use part of the verb **ir** (*to go*) + **a** + infinitive to say what you are going to do:

voy a ver	I'm going to see	**vamos a llegar**	we're going to arrive
vas a salir	you're going to leave	**vais a viajar**	you're going to travel
va a volver	s/he's going to return	**van a venir**	they're going to come

With a reflexive verb the pronoun often goes on the end:
voy a quedarme I'm going to stay; **vas a levantarte** you're going to get up, etc

Future tense

Add the endings **-é**, **-ás**, **-á**, **-emos**, **-éis**, **-án** to the infinitive:

llegaré	I will arrive	**llegaremos**	we will arrive
llegarás	you will arrive	**llegaréis**	you will arrive
llegará	s/he/you will arrive	**llegarán**	they/you will arrive

Irregular verbs have the same endings, but the root of the verb changes:

salir	to leave:	**saldré**, **saldrás**	I//you you will leave, etc
tener	to have:	**tendré**, **tendrás**	I//you you will leave, etc
poder	to be able to:	**podré**, **podrás**	I/you will be able to, etc
venir	to come:	**vendré**, **vendrás**	I/you will come, etc
hacer	to do:	**haré**, **harás**	I/you will do, etc
decir	to say:	**diré**, **dirás**	I/you will say, etc

Reflexive verbs have the pronouns at the beginning:

quedarse	to stay		
me quedaré	I will stay	**nos quedaremos**	we will stay
te quedarás	you will stay	**os quedaréis**	you will stay
se quedará	s/he/you will stay	**se quedarán**	they/you will stay

Talking about the past

In this book you have looked at two ways of talking about something in the past.

1 The Perfect is usually used as in English: I have gone/seen/done, etc.
2 The Preterite or simple past: I went/I saw/I did, etc.

Perfect tense

To form the perfect you take the appropriate form of the verb **haber** (to have) and add the past participle of the main verb. To form the past participle of **-ar** verbs add **-ado** to the root. For **-er** and **-ir** verbs add **-ido**:

haber		+	past participle		
			-ar	-er	-ir
he	**hemos**	+	**hablado**	**comido**	**salido**
has	**habéis**				
ha	**han**				
-ar	**hablar**		to speak	**he hablado**	I have spoken
-er	**comer**		to eat	**has comido**	you have eaten
-ir	**salir**		to leave	**ha salido**	s/he has left/you have left

Reflexive verbs

The reflexive pronoun always comes first: **me he levantado** I have got up

Direct object pronouns

Direct object pronouns always come before the verb: **lo he visto** I have seen it

Irregular past participles

There is a small group of verbs which have irregular past participles. Here are some of them:

hacer	to do	**hecho**	done	**he hecho**	I have done
volver	to return	**vuelto**	returned	**has vuelto**	you have returned
escribir	to write	**escrito**	written	**ha escrito**	s/he has written
ver	to see	**visto**	seen	**hemos visto**	we have seen
decir	to say	**dicho**	said	**habéis dicho**	you have said

Preterite tense

For expressing something which happened at a particular time or for a defined period of time in the past: 'It opened at 12'; 'They stayed for two hours', etc. Add the endings below to the root.

-ar		**-er**		**-ir**	
llamé	I phoned	**volví**	I returned	**salí**	I left
llamaste	you phoned	**volviste**	you returned	**saliste**	you left
llamó	s/he/you phoned	**volvió**	s/he/you returned	**salió**	s/he left
llamamos	we phoned	**volvimos**	we returned	**salimos**	we left
llamasteis	you phoned	**volvisteis**	you returned	**salisteis**	you left
llamaron	they/you phoned	**volvieron**	they/you returned	**salieron**	they left

Irregular verbs

estar		hacer		dar	
estuve	I was	**hice**	I did	**di**	I gave
estuviste	you were	**hiciste**	you did	**diste**	you gave
estuvo	etc	**hizo**	etc	**dio**	etc
estuvimos		**hicimos**		**dimos**	
estuvisteis		**hicisteis**		**disteis**	
estuvieron		**hicieron**		**dieron**	

Ser and **ir** have the same form in the preterite:

fui	I went	*or*	I was
fuiste	you went		you were
fue	s/he went		s/he was
	you went		you were
fuimos	we went		we were
fuisteis	you went		you were
fueron	they went		they were
	you went		you were

haber:		**hubo** there was
tener:		**tuve** (like **estuve**)
seguir:		**seguí**, **seguiste**, etc
	but	**siguió** and **siguieron**
pedir:		**pedí**, **pediste**, etc
	but	**pidió** and **pidieron**

Direct object pronouns come before the verb

me ayudó	s/he helped me
te dio	s/he gave you
le dijo	s/he told him or her

Reflexive verbs

me levanté,
te levantaste
se levantó, etc

Imperative

The imperative is used to give instructions and orders. In most cases you can also use the simple present tense. See Page 70.

The imperative forms below are only used when addressing a person or people informally. To give formal instructions the subjunctive forms are used. These are not presented in this book.

	Talking to one person		Talking to two or more
doblar	**dobla**	turn	**doblad**
coger	**coge**	catch/take	**coged**
subir	**sube**	go up	**subid**

With root-changing verbs the vowel changes only when talking to one person.

seguir	**sigue**	continue	**seguid**

Some verbs are irregular in the singular form, i.e. when talking to one person.

salir	**sal**	leave	**salid**
ir	**ve**	go	**id**

With reflexive verbs the reflexive pronoun is attached to the verb and the **d** in the plural forms is omitted.

levantarse	**levántate**	get up	**levantáos**
sentarse	**siéntate**	sit down	**sentáos**

Prepositions

Prepositions show the relationships between other words in a sentence, for example 'in', 'on', 'to', 'from', etc. They are often used differently in Spanish, so at first it is best to learn them in context.

Mode of transport

To say 'by' train, car, bike, use **en**: **en tren, coche, bicicleta**, etc
But to say 'by' plane, use **por**: **por avión**

To describe where something is:

a la izquierda/derecha	on the left/right
al lado del cine	next to the cinema
al final de la calle	at the end of the street
en la esquina	on the corner
enfrente del bar	opposite the bar
cerca/lejos de aquí	near to/far from here
entre el bar y el café	between the bar and the cafe

Some prepositions have more than one equivalent in English:

a	can mean 'to' or 'at':	**Voy al centro.**	I go to the centre.
		Voy a las tres.	I go at 3 o'clock.
de	can mean 'from' or 'of':	**Soy de Cádiz.**	I am from Cádiz.
		Un libro de arte.	'A book of art'. (an art book)

The personal 'a'

When the direct object of the verb is human, you must use **a**: **Voy a ver a Juan.**

Gustar

Gustar means 'to please', and it is used to express likes and dislikes.
To say you like one thing:

(a mí*) me gusta	**(a ti*) te gusta**	**(a él/ella/usted*) le gusta**
I like it (it pleases me)	you like it	he/she likes it; you like it

***A mí, ti, él, ella, usted** etc are often used for emphasis, to express a contrast or to eliminate any possible misunderstanding. They mean to me/you/him/her/you, etc.

To say you like more than one thing:

me gustan	**te gustan**	**le gustan**
I like them	you like them	he/she likes them; you like them

To express dislike use **no**:

no me gusta I don't like it **no te gustan** you don't like them

Please note:

1 Several of the words here have different meanings. The ones given here are only the ones needed in this book, and you should take care when using them in other contexts. If you are in doubt, refer to a dictionary.
2 Genders of nouns are given here, but you will need to refer to a dictionary to find out if a particular word is an adjective, preposition, verb, etc.

A

a	away
a menos que	unless
a pie	on foot
abajo	downstairs
abogado/a	lawyer
abrazo (m)	embrace
un abrazo de (in letters)	Love from
abrigo (m)	coat
abril	April
abrir	to open
absolutamente	absolutely
aburrido/a/s	boring/bored
acabar	to finish
acabar de	to have just
academia (f)	academy
acceptar	to accept
aceituna (f)	olive
ácido/a/s	acid
acomodador/a	usher/ette
acompañar	to go with
acostarse	to go to bed
acostumbrarse	to get used to
actividad (f)	activity
actriz/actor	actor
actual	now, present
actualmente	at the moment
acuerdo, de	all right; agreed
adiós	good bye
administrador/a	administrator
¿Adónde?	To where?
adorar	to adore
adquirir	to acquire
adverbio (m)	adverb
aéreo	air (adj)
aerobic (m)	aerobics
aeropuerto (m)	airport
afueras (f pl)	outskirts
agencia (f) inmobiliaria	estate agent's
agosto	August
agua (f)	water
ahorrar	to save
aire (m); al aire libre	air; outdoors
alcanzar	to reach
alcohol (m)	alcohol
alemán/ana	German
Alemania	Germany
alfombra (f)	rug
algo	something
alimentar	to fuel, to feed
allí	there
almacén (m)	department store
almorzar	to have lunch
almuerzo (m)	lunch
alojamiento (m)	housing, lodging
alquilar	to rent, hire
alternativa (f)	alternative
alto	high
ama (f) de casa	housewife
amante (m/f)	lover
amarillo	yellow
ambiental	environmental
ambiente (m)	atmosphere, environment
amenazar	to threaten
amigo (m)	friend
amueblado	furnished
analítico	analytical
anciano (m)	old person
andén (m)	(railway) platform
animador/a	activities organiser, play leader
animal (m)	animal
año (m)	year
anoche	last night
anteayer	the day before yesterday
antes de	before
anuncio (m)	advertisement
apagar	to turn off
aparcamiento (m)	car park
aparcar	to park
apellido (m)	surname
apoyo (m)	support

aprender	to learn
aprobación (f)	approval
aprobar	to pass (an exam)
aproximadamente	approximately
aquí	here
argentino/a/s	Argentinian
Armada (f)	Armada
armario (m)	cupboard, wardrobe
arreglar	to fix
arriba	upstairs
arte (m)	art
artículo (m)	item, article
artista (m)	artist
asado	roast
asaltante (m)	assailant
asaltar	to assault
asalto (m)	assault
ascensor (m)	the lift
así que	so
asiento (m)	seat
asignatura (f)	subject
asistir	to be present
Atenas	Athens
aterrizar	to land
atraco (m)	robbery
atractivo	attractive
auditorio (m)	auditorium
aumentar	to increase
autobús (m)	bus
automático	automatic
automóvil (m)	automobile
avión (m)	aeroplane
ayer	yesterday
ayudante (m)	assistant
ayudar	to help
ayuntamiento (m)	town hall
azúcar (m)	sugar
azul	blue
azulejo (m)	tile

B

Bachillerato (m)	Final High School qualification (like A level or Highers)
bailar	to dance
bajar	to put down, to get off
bajo	down, low, short
balcón (m)	balcony
banco (m)	bank
bañera (f)	bath
baño (m)	bathroom
banquero (m)	banker
banyi (m)	bungee jumping
bar (m)	bar
barato	cheap
barman (m)	barman
bastante	quite, rather
basura (f)	rubbish
batalla (f)	battle
beber	to drink
bebida (f)	drink
bellas artes (f pl)	Fine Arts
benéfico	charitable
besar	to kiss
beso (m)	a kiss
biblioteca (f)	library
bicicleta (f)	bicycle
¡Bienvenido!	Welcome!
billete (m)	ticket
black-jack (m)	blackjack
blanco	white
bocadillo (m)	sandwich
boda (f)	wedding
bolso (m)	handbag
bonito	pretty
borracho	drunk
bota (f)	boot
brazo (m)	arm
buceo (m)	scuba diving
bueno	good
buscar	to look for

C

caballo (m)	horse
cada	each
café (m)	coffee
caja (f)	box, crate
caja (f) de ahorros	savings bank
calamares (m pl)	squid
calentamiento (m)	warming
calle (f)	street
cama (f)	bed
camarero/a	waiter/ress
cambiar	to change
cambio (m)	change
camisa (f)	shirt
campo (m)	ground, the country(side), field
canal (m)	canal, channel
cantina (f)	canteen
capacidad (f)	capacity, ability
carga (f)	charge
carne (f)	meat
caro	expensive
carrera (f)	course, career

carta (f)	letter
cartera (f)	wallet
casa (f)	house
casado/a	married
casino (m)	casino
catedral (f)	cathedral
celebrar	to celebrate
célula (f)	cell
cena (f)	dinner
cenar	to have dinner
centro (m)	centre
centro deportivo	sports centre
cerca (de)	near (to)
cereal (m)	cereal
cerrar	to close
cerveza (f)	beer
chalet (m)	house
champaña (f)	champagne
champiñón (m)	mushroom
chaqueta (f)	jacket
charlar	to chat
cheque (m)	cheque
chico/a au pair	Au pair
chino/a	Chinese man/woman
ciclismo (m)	cycling
ciencia ficción (f)	science fiction
ciencia (f)	science
cigarro (m)	cigar
cine (m)	cinema
círculo (m)	circle
cita (f)	appointment
ciudad (f)	city; town
clase (f)	class, lecture
cliente (m)	customer
clima (m)	climate
club (m)	club
cobrar	to earn
coche (m)	car
cocina (f)	cooker; kitchen
coger	to take, to catch
colectivización (f)	collectivisation
colectivo (m)	collective
colega (m)	colleague
colegio (m)	school, college
colocar	to put
colombiano/a	Colombian
colonia (f)	colony
colonia (f) de verano	summer camp
colonia (f) de vacaciones	holiday camp
color (m)	colour
combustible (m)	fuel
comedia (f)	comedy
comedor (m)	dining room
comer	to eat
comercial	commercial
comercializar	to put on the market
comida (f)	meal; food
comisaría (f)	police station
¿Cómo?	How?
cómodo	comfortable
compañero (m)	classmate; companion; mate
compañía (f)	company
compartimiento (m)	stall, stable
completar	to complete
completo	full; completed
componente (m)	component
compras, de	shopping
comunicación (f)	communication
comunidad (f) autónoma	autonomous community
Comunidad (f) Europea	European Community
con	with
coñac (m)	brandy; coñac
concierto (m)	concert
concluir	to conclude; finish
concurso (m)	competition
conducir	to drive, driving
conductor (m)	driver
conferencia (f)	lecture, conference
conocer	to (get to) know
conseguir	to get (a job)
constancia (f)	perseverance
constitución (f)	constitution
consumismo (m)	consumerism
consumo (m)	consumption
contado, al	in cash
contaminación (f)	pollution
contaminar	to pollute
contemporáneo	contemporary
contestar	to answer
conmigo/tigo	with me/you
contra	against
conveniente	convenient
conversación (f)	conversation
convocar	to call (together)
copa (f)	drink; glass
corbata (f)	tie
correcto	correct
corregir	to mark; correct
Correos (m)	post office
correr	to run
costar	to cost

creativo	creative
crecer	to grow
crédito (m)	credit
creer	to believe
críquet (m)	cricket
crítico	critical
cruce (m)	crossroads
cuadra (f)	stable(s)
cuadro (m)	chart; picture
¿Cuál?	Which?
cualquier	any
¿Cuánto/a/s?	How much; many?
cuarto (m)	room; quarter
cuarto (m) de baño	bathroom
cuarto/a	fourth
cuenta (f)	bill
culebrón (m)	soap opera
cultura (f)	culture
currículum (m)	c.v.
cursar	to be doing a course
curso (m)	course

D

danés/esa	Dane; Danish
daño (m)	harm
dar	to give
dar miedo	to frighten
dar un paseo	to go for a walk
de	of/from
debajo de	beneath; under
decidir	to decide
decir	to say/tell
dedicación (f)	dedication
dejar de	to stop
delante de	in front of
demasiado	too; too much
democracia (f)	democracy
departamento (m)	department
dependiente (m)	shop assistant
deporte (m)	sport
deportivo	sports (adj)
depósito (m)	deposit
derecha (f)	right
desaparecer	to disappear
desayunar	to have breakfast
desayuno (m)	breakfast
descuento (m)	discount
desde	from
despacho (m)	office
después de	after
destino (m)	destination
detective (m)	detective
detener	to arrest
día (m)	day
diciembre	December
dictadura (f)	dictatorship
diesel (m)	diesel
¿Dígame?	Hello? (on the phone)
diferencia (f)	difference
difícil	difficult
dificultad (f)	difficulty
dinero (m)	money
dirección (f)	address
dirigido	guided
dirigirse	to apply to
discoteca (f)	disco
diseñador/a	designer
diseño (m)	design
disponer de	to have available
dispuesto	prepared; willing
divorciado	divorced
doblar	turn
doble	double
documentación (f)	documentation
documental (m)	documentary
doméstico	domestic
domicilio (m)	dwelling; residence
dominar	to dominate
domingo	Sunday
¿Dónde?	Where?
dormir	to sleep
dormitorio (m)	bedroom
drama (m)	drama; play
drama (m) psicológico	psychological play
ducha (f)	shower
dueño/a	owner; landlord/lady
durante	during
durar	to last; take
duro	hard

E

ecológico	ecological
economía (f)	economy; economics
edad (f)	age
edificio (m)	building
Edimburgo	Edinburgh
educar	to educate; bring up
efectivo, en	in cash
efecto, en	in fact
ejecutivo/a	executive
ejercitar	to exercise
él	he; him
el/la/los/las	the
elección (f)	election; choice
electrónico	electronic
elevado	high

ella	she; her
emisión (f)	emission
empezar	to start
empleado (m)	employee
empresa (f)	firm
empresariales (f pl)	business (studies)
en	in, on, by
enamorarse	to fall in love
encantar	to delight
encontrar	to find; meet
enero	January
enfermería (f)	nursing
enfermero/a	nurse
enfermo	ill
enfrentamiento (m)	confrontation
enfrente de	opposite
ensalada (f)	salad
enseñanza (f)	education
enterrado	buried
entrada (f)	entrance; ticket
entrar	to enter
entre	between
entrevista (f)	interview
entusiasmo (m)	enthusiasm
equipaje (m)	luggage
equipo (m)	team
equitación (f)	riding
equivocarse	to make a mistake
error (m)	mistake
escalera (f)	stairs
escaparse	to escape
escocés/escocesa	Scot; Scottish
escondite (m)	hiding place
escribir	to write
escuchar	to listen
escuela (f)	school
escultura (f)	sculpture
espacio (m)	gap; space
español/a	Spaniard; Spanish
espejo (m)	mirror
esperar	to wait
esquina (f)	corner
establecer	to establish
estación (f)	station
estadio (m)	stadium
estantería (f)	shelves
estar	to be
estéreo (m)	stereo
Estimado/a	Dear (formal letters)
esto/a/s	this; these
estrella (f)	star
estrés (m)	stress
estudiante (m)	student
estudiantil	student (adj)
estudiar	to study
estudio (m)	study
euro (m)	euro
evadirse	to escape
evitar	to avoid
exámen (m)	exam
exigir	to demand
existir	to exist
éxito (m)	success
experiencia (f)	experience
exposición (f)	exhibition
exterior, al	outside
extrovertido	extroverted

F

fácil	easy
facilidad (f)	facility; ease
facultad (f)	faculty
falda (f)	skirt
falso	false; untrue
faltar	to lack; be needed
fama (f)	reputation
familia (f)	family
famoso	famous
farmacia (f)	chemist's
febrero	February
fecha (f)	date
fenomenal	great
festival (m)	festival
fiesta (f)	party
fila (f)	row
filosofía (f)	philosophy
fin (m)	end
final (m)	end
firmar	to sign
física (f)	physics
flamenco (m)	flamenco
flan (m)	crème caramel
flexible	flexible
florero (m)	flower vase
footing (m)	jogging
forma (f)	way
formulario (m)	form
fortalecer	to strengthen
francés/francesa	French
Francia	France
frase (f)	sentence
frecuencia (f)	frequency
frecuente	frequent
fregar los platos	to wash up
frigorífico (m)	fridge
fruta (f)	fruit

fuente (f) | fountain
fuera | outside
fuerte | strong
fuerza (f) | strength
fumador | smoking
fumar | to smoke
funcionario/a | civil servant
furgoneta (f) | van
fútbol (m) | football

G

gafas (f pl) de sol | sunglasses
galería (f) | gallery
galés/galesa | Welsh
galleta (f) | biscuit
ganar | to earn
garaje (m) | garage
gasolina (f) | petrol
gasolinera (f) | petrol station
gastar | to spend
gazpacho (m) | cold soup
gente (f) | people
geografía (f) | geography
gimnasio (m) | gymnasium
global | global
grabar | to record
grande | big
gratis | free
gratuita | free
grave | serious
griego/a | Greek
gris | grey
gritar | to shout
grupo (m) | group
guapo/a | handsome; goodlooking; pretty
guerra (f) | war

H

habilidad (f) | skill
habitación (f) | room
hablar | to speak
hacer ejercicio/gimnasia | to work out
hacer transbordo | to change (trains)
hacer | to do
hacia | towards
hasta luego | see you soon
hasta | until
hay que | you have to, it's necessary to
hay | there is/are
heavy (m) | heavy metal music
helado (m) | ice cream
helicóptero (m) | helicopter
heredero (m) | heir
herido | injured
hermano/a | brother/sister
hijo/a | son/daughter
hijos (m pl) | children
hola | hello
hombre (m) | man
hora (f) | hour; time
horario (m) | timetable
hospital (m) | hospital
hotel (m) | hotel
hoy | today
huésped (m) | guest

I

ida, de | single (ticket)
ida y vuelta, de | return (ticket)
idioma (m) | language
iglesia (f) | church
ignorar | to be unaware of; not to know
ilusión (f) | hope
imagen (f) | picture; image
imaginativo | imaginative
impuesto (m) | tax
incendio (m) | fire
incómodo | uncomfortable
inconveniente | inconvenient
independencia (f) | independence
independiente | independent
indicar | to indicate
infantil | childish; for/of children
informática (f) | Information Technology
informe (m) | report
infrarrojo | infra red
ingeniero/a | engineer
Inglaterra | England
inglés/inglesa | English
iniciativa (f) | initiative
inmediatamente | immediately
inmunológico | immunising, immune
instalar | to instal
inteligente | intelligent
intercambio (m) | exchange
interés (m) | interest
interesante | interesting
internacional | international
invencible | invincible
investigación (f) | investigation

investigador/a	researcher
ir de compras	to go shopping
ir de vacaciones	to go on holiday
ir	to go
Irlanda	Ireland
irlandés/irlandesa	Irish
italiano/a	Italian
izquierda (f)	left

J

jamás	never
jamón (m)	ham
japonés/japonesa	Japanese
jardín (m)	garden
jardinero/a	gardener
jazz (m)	jazz
jerez (m)	sherry
joven	young
juego (m)	game
juego de azar	game of chance
jueves	Thursday
jugar	to play
julio	July
junio	June
juntar	to match; join
junto	together
Júpiter	Jupiter
jurar	to swear

K

kárate (m)	karate

L

labor (m)	labour; work
laboratorio (m)	laboratory
lado; al lado de	side; next to
lámpara (f)	lamp
lavabo (m)	basin
lavadora (f)	washing machine
lavar	to wash
lavarse el pelo	to wash one's hair
Le saluda atentamente	Yours faithfully
leche (f)	milk
leer	to read
lejos (de)	far (from)
lengua (f)	language
lenguado (m)	sole
lento	slow
letra (f)	letter (as in A, B, C etc)
levantar	to lift
levantarse	to get up, to stand up
leve	slight
libre	free
librería (f)	book shop
libro (m)	book
limonada (f)	lemonade
limpiar	to clean
lista (f)	list
listo/a	keen, clever, ready
llamarse	to be called
llave (f)	key
llegada (f)	arrival
llegar	to arrive
lleno	full
llevar	to bring
llevarse bien	to get on well
lluvia (f)	rain
lo que	what; that which
Lo siento	I'm sorry
lotería (f)	lottery
luchar	to fight; struggle
luego	then
lugar (m)	place
lujo (m)	luxury
luna (f)	moon
lunes	Monday

M

madre (f)	mother
madrileño/a	person from Madrid
madrugada (f)	early morning; dawn
mal	bad; badly
maleta (f)	suitcase
mañana (f)	morning; tomorrow
manifestación (f)	demonstration
manifestante (m)	demonstrator
manitas (m)	handyman (colloquial)
mano (f)	hand
¡Manos arriba!	Hands up!
mantequilla (f pl)	butter
manual	manual
marido	husband
marketing	marketing
martes	Tuesday
marzo	March
más	more; else
más ... que	more ... than
matemáticas (f pl)	mathematics
materialista	materialistic
matricularse	to enrol
matrimonio (m)	married couple
mayo	May
mayor	older
mayoría (f)	majority

mayoría (f) de edad	age at which one becomes an adult
me	(to) me; myself
mecánico/a	mechanic
media (f)	average
mediano	medium
medianoche	midnight
medias (f pl)	tights
médico (m)	doctor
mediodía (m)	midday
mejor	better
memoria (f)	memory
menor	younger
menos	less, except
mensual	monthly
mermelada (f)	jam
mes (m)	month
mesa (f)	table
mesita (f) de noche	bedside table
metálico, en	in cash
metódico	methodical
metro (m)	underground
mezquita (f)	mosque
mi/s	my
miedo (m)	fear
miércoles	Wednesday
mil (m)	(one) thousand
minuto (m)	minute
mirar	to look; watch
misterioso	mysterious
moda (f), de	fashionable
modales (m pl)	manners
moderno	modern
modo, de ningún modo	way; no way
momento (m)	moment
monedero (m)	purse
monstruo (m)	monster
monte (m)	mountain
montañismo (m)	mountaineering
montar a caballo	ride (horse)
morir	to die
moro (m)	Moor
motocicleta (f)	motorbike
motor (m)	engine
moverse	to move
mozo/a de cuadra	stable lad/girl
mucho/a/s	a lot; many
mueble (m)	(item of) furniture
muebles (m pl)	furniture
mujer (f)	wife; woman
multa (f)	fine
mundo (m)	world
murciano/a	person from Murcia
museo (m)	museum
música (f)	music
músico/a	musician
muy	very

N

nacer	to be born
nacimiento (m)	birth
nacional	national
nacionalidad (f)	nationality
Naciones (f pl) Unidas	United Nations
nada	not at all/nothing
naranja (f)	orange
natación (f)	swimming
navaja (f)	pocket knife
necesidad (f)	necessity
necesitar	to need
negar	to deny
negocio (m)	business
negro	black
niño/a	child
no	not; no
noche (f)	night
nombre (m)	name
normal	normal
normalidad (f)	normality
normalmente	normally
norteamericano/a	American
nosotros	we
noticias (f pl)	news
novela (f)	novel
novelista (m)	novelist
noviembre	November
novio/a	boy/girlfriend
Nueva Zelanda	New Zealand
nuevo	new
número (m)	number
nunca	never

O

o	or
objetos (m pl) perdidos	lost property
obra (f) de arte	work (of art)
observación (f)	remark
observador	observant
obstante, no	however
octubre	October
ocupar	to occupy
ocurrir	to happen
oferta (f)	offer
oficina (f)	office
oliva (f)	olive
ópera (f)	opera

opinar	to think
ordenado	tidy
ordenador (m)	computer
organizado	organized
otro	other; another

P

paciente	patient
padre (m)	father
padres (m pl)	parents
paella (f)	paella
pagar	to pay for
pagos (m pl)	payment
pálido	pale
pan (m)	bread
pan (m) tostado	toast
pantalones (m pl)	trousers
para	(in order) to; for
parada (f)	bus stop
pararse	to stop
parecer	to seem
pared (f)	wall
pareja (f)	couple; partner
parque (m)	park
pasado	last
pasajero (m)	passenger
pasaporte (m)	passport
pasar	to spend (time), to come in
pasillo (m)	corridor
patatas (f pl) fritas	chips or crisps
patinaje (m)	skating
pedal (m)	pedal
pedir	to ask for; order
película (f)	film
pensar	to think
pensión (f) (media/completa)	half/full board
peor	worse
pequeño	small
perder	to lose
perdone	excuse me
perfil (m)	profile; background
periódico (m)	newspaper
periodista (m)	journalist
permiso (m)	licence
permitir	to allow
pero	but
persona (f)	person
perspicaz	perceptive
persuasivo	persuasive
pescado (m)	fish
petrolero	(of) petrol
pie (m)	foot
pierna (f)	leg
piloto (m)	pilot
pintar	to paint
pintor/a	painter
pintura (f)	painting
piscina (f)	swimming pool
piso (m)	flat, floor
pistola (f)	gun
planchar	to iron
planear	to plan
Planetario (m)	Planetarium
plano	flat
planta (f) baja	ground floor
planta (f)	floor; plant
playa (f)	beach
plaza (f)	square
plomo (m)	lead
pobre	poor
poco (m)	(a) little, a bit, few
poder	to be able to
polaco/a	Polish
polar	polar
policía (m)	police officer
policíaco	police, detective
policial	police (adj)
política (f)	politics
pollo (m)	chicken
pollo (m) asado	roast chicken
Polonia	Poland
poner (una película)	to put on a film
ponerse	to become
pop	pop (music)
por	in; during; through; by; along
por favor	please
por fin	finally
por lo menos	at least
porcentaje (m)	percentage
¿Por qué?	Why?
porque	because
portátil	portable
portero/a	porter
posible	possible
postre (m)	dessert
precio (m)	price
preferir	to prefer
pregunta (f)	question
prenda (f)	garment
preparar	to prepare
presencia (f)	appearance
primario	primary
primero	first
prioridad (f)	priority

no hay prisa	there's no hurry
privatización (f)	privatisation
probar	to try; prove
problema (m)	problem
procedencia (f)	from
producir	to produce
profesión (f)	profession; job
profesional	professional
profesor/a	teacher
programa (m)	programme
pronto	soon
protesta (f)	protest
psicología (f)	psychology
psicológico	psychological
publicidad (f)	publicity
público	public
puerta (f)	door, gate
puesto (m)	post
pulsera (f)	bracelet
punki (m)	punk

Q

que	who, which, than
¿Qué?	What?
quedarse	to stay
querer	to want
querido/a	dear
¿Qué tal?	How are you?
¿Quién?	Who?
química (f)	chemistry
quinto	fifth
quisiera	I would like
quizás	perhaps

R

radio (f)	radio
rápido	fast
rato (m)	while
realidad (f)	reality
recepción (f)	reception
recepcionista (m/f)	receptionist
recibir	to receive
recurso (m)	resource
reducir	to reduce
regalo (m)	present
regional	regional
reinar	to reign
relación (f)	relation
relax (m)	relaxation
rellenar	fill in
remo (m)	oar
RENFE (f)	train station; national rail network
repetir	to repeat
requerir; se requiere	to require; required
reserva (f)	reservation
reservar	to book
residencia (f)	residence
responder	reply
responsable	responsible
respuesta (f)	answer
restaurante (m)	restaurant
resultar	to become; get
retrasado	delayed
retraso (m)	delay
reunión (f)	meeting
rico	rich
robar	to rob someone
rock (m) duro	hard rock
rodilla (f)	knee
rojo	red
romántico	romantic
ropa (f)	clothes

S

sábado	Saturday
saber	to know (how to)
sala (f)	large room
salario (m)	salary
salida (f)	departure
salir	to go out
salón (m)	sitting room
salsa (Salsa) (f)	sauce (dance)
saludable	healthy
saludo (m)	greeting
salvavidas (m)	life guard
salvo	except
sano	healthy
satélite (m)	satellite
Saturno	Saturn
se(p)tiembre	September
secretario/a	secretary
sector (m)	sector
secundario	secondary
seguida, en	right away
seguir	to continue
segunda mano (f)	second hand
segundo (m)	second
seguridad (f)	security
seguros (m pl)	insurance
selva (f)	rainforest
semáforos (m pl)	traffic lights
semana (f)	week
semana que viene	next week
semestre (m)	semestre
seminario (m)	seminar

señalar	indicate; tick
sencillo	single (ticket)
senegalés/senegalesa	Senegalese
señor	Mr; Sir
señora	Mrs; Madam
sentarse	to sit down
separado	separated
sepulcro (m)	sepulchre; tomb
ser	to be
serie (f) policíaca	detective series
servicio (m)	service
servicios (m pl)	toilets
servir	to be used, to serve
si	if
sí	yes
siempre	always
siesta (f)	siesta
siglo (m)	century
siguiente	following
silla (f)	chair
sillón (m)	armchair
sin	without
sintético	synthetic
sistema (m)	system
sobre todo	above all
sociable	sociable
socialista (m)	socialist
sociedad (f)	society
sociología (f)	sociology
sofá (m)	settee
solar	solar
soldado (m)	soldier
solicitar	to apply for
solitario	solitary
solo/a	alone
soltero/a/s	single person/people
solucionar	to solve
sonido (m)	sound
sonrisa (f)	smile
sopa (f)	soup
soplar	to blow
sorprender	to surprise
soul (m)	soul (music)
su	his; her; their; your
subir	get on; up; in; to rise
subrayar	underline
sudamericano/a	South American
sueldo (m)	wage
suelo (m)	floor
sueño (m)	dream
¡Suerte!	Good luck!
suficiente	sufficient; enough
súper	super; 4 star petrol
superior	superior; above
supermercado (m)	supermarket
supersónico	supersonic
su/s	his; her; their; your

T

talla (f)	size
también	also
tampoco	neither
tanto	so much
tapa (f)	snack; appetiser
tardar	to take; to last; to be late
tarde (f)	afternoon; evening
tarde	late
tarjeta (f)	card
tarjeta (f) de crédito	credit card
te	(to) you; yourself
teatro (m)	theatre
técnico/a	technician
tecno (m)	tecno
tecnología (f)	technology
tele(visión) (f)	TV
telefónica (f)	telephone office
teléfono (m)	telephone
telescopio (m)	telescope
televisor (m)	TV set
temprano	early
tender	to tend
tener	to have
tener lugar	to take place
tener que	to have to
tenis (m)	tennis
tequila (f)	tequila
tercero	third
terminar	to finish
testigo (m)	witness
tiempo (m)	time
tiempo (m) parcial	part time
tienda (f)	shop
tirar	to throw out
tocador (m)	dressing table
tocar	to play (an instrument), to touch
todavía	still, yet
todo	all; every
todo recto	straight on
tomar	to have/to take
tomar el sol	to sunbathe
tonelada (f)	ton
tónica (f)	tonic
tortilla (f)	omelette
total	total

totalidad (f)	totality
trabajador/a	worker; hard-working
trabajar	to work
trabajo (m)	work
tradicional	traditional
traducción (f)	translation
traer	to bring
tráfico (m)	traffic
traje (m)	suit
transporte (m)	transport
tras	after
trasladarse	to move house
tratar de	to try to
trémulo	tremulous; trembling
tren (m)	train
trono (m)	throne
tropical	tropical
tu	your
tú	you
tú mismo	yourself
turco/a	Turkish
turismo (m)	tourism
U	
ultramarinos (m pl)	groceries
un/a	a
únicamente	only
unidad (f)	unit
uniformidad (f)	uniformity
universidad (f)	university
unos	some
urbanización (f)	housing estate
usted/es	you
utilizar	to use
V	
vacaciones (f)	holiday
vale	OK
valer	to be worth
valor (m)	value
vanguardista (m)	forward looking
vegetariano/a	vegetarian
vehículo (m)	vehicle
vela (f)	candle
velocidad (f)	speed
vencer	to conquer; to beat
venezolano/a	Venezuelan
venir	to come
ventana (f)	window
ventanilla de reclamación	customer services
ver	to see/watch
verano (m)	summer
verdad (f)	truth
verdadero	true
verde	green
verduras (f pl)	greens
verificar	to check
versión (f)	version
vestido (m)	dress
vez/veces (f)	time/times
viajar	to travel
viajero (m)	traveller
vida (f)	life
vídeo (f)	video
viejo/a	old
viernes	Friday
vino (m)	wine
violento/a	violent
violeta	purple
visual	visual
vitrina (f)	glass case
vivir	to live
volador	flying
volver	to return
vomitar	to be sick
vuelo (m)	flight
vuelta (f)	return
W	
wáter (m)	toilet
whisky (m)	whisky
Y	
y	and
yate (m)	yacht
yo	I
Z	
zapato (m)	shoe
zumo (m)	juice

Unit 1

8 **a** ¿Quién eres?/¿Cómo te llamas? **b** ¿Dónde vives? **c** ¿Eres de Algeciras? **d** ¿Eres español? **e** ¿Eres policía? **f** ¿Eres soldado?

16 **a** Federico, 22 años **b** Manuel, 19 años **c** Alberto, 20 años **d** Jacinta 23 años.

¡Extra!

19 Segoshi Tanizaki; *japonés*; *estudiante*; *política*; *Barcelona*; Tokio.
Carla Bertolini; *italiana*; diseñadora; arte y diseño; Llobregat; *Milano*.
Peter; *inglés*; periodista; *español*; *Barcelona*; *Salisbury*.
Xavier Marchand; senegalés; ingeniero; *español*; *Barcelona*; Senegal.

20 **a** He lives in the town centre in a big house with 5 university students. **b** He works in a hotel. **c** She is studying English in Durham. **d** She shares with two people. **e** They are Danish and Chinese. The Danish man studies philosophy and the Chinese woman works in the university office.

Ejercicios de gramática

1 **a** vivo; soy; escribo; trabajo; aprendo **b** trabajas; eres; comes **c** estudia; trabaja; vive; es

2 **a** ¿Cúantos años tienes?; ¿Cuál es tu nacionalidad?; ¿Cuál es tu profesión?; ¿Qué estudias?; ¿Dónde vives? **b** ¿Cuántos años tiene?; ¿Cuál es su nacionalidad?; ¿Cuál es su profesión?; ¿Qué estudia?; ¿Dónde vive?

3 **a** estudiante **b** mexicana **c** profesor **d** francés **e** profesora **f** argentina

Unit 2

3 **a** Mi madre se llama Victoria. **b** Mi padre se llama Vicente. **c** Mis hermanos se llaman Mariví y Enrique. **d** Mi hermana está casada. **e** Mi hermano está soltero. **f** No. Enrique no tiene hijos. **g** Mariví y Alfonso tienen dos hijos.

6 **a** Anita, 33 años **b** Jesús, 45 años **c** Fernando, 27. Hermano José, 31 años. **d** Doña Isabel, 89 años **e** Hermanos: 50, 52, 60. Hermana: 54. María: 49 años.

7

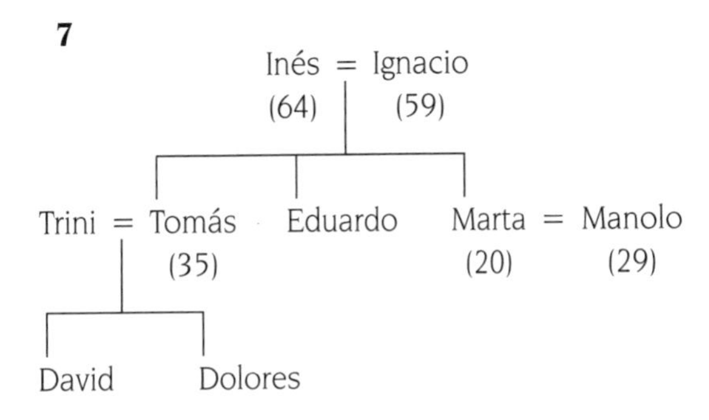

8 **a** Su hermana se llama Marta. **b** Su hijo es David. **c** Su marido tiene 35 años. **d** Sus padres tienen 64 y 59 años.

10 **a 1** **b 3** **c 2** **d 4**

11 **a** grande **b** moderno **c** moderna **d** vieja **e** pequeños

12 All the vocabulary needed is in the vocabulary section on page 22.

13 Conversación 1 No tiene tres dormitorios. Tiene cuatro.
Conversación 2 No es muy vieja. Es bastante moderna. No tiene un dormitorio muy pequeño. Tiene un dormitorio muy grande. No tiene garaje.

14 **a** Elisa is offered a very pretty flat in the centre of town with two bedrooms, a kitchen, a bathroom and a dining/sitting room. **b** It's €4,000 a month.

16 Elisa has all the items except a sofa and stereo.

¡Extra!

18 Grandparents: Isabel (64), Juan (67); daughter: Juana (33), Jorge (45) her husband; sons: Carlos (11), Roberto (8).

19 **a** el salón **b** el dormitorio **c** el cuarto de baño **d** la cocina

20 All the vocabulary needed is in the vocabulary section on page 22.

Ejercicios de gramática

1 **a** No, Andrés es mi marido. **b** No, Lena y Laura son mis hijas. **c** No, Román y Juan son mis hermanos.

2 **a** mis **b** mi **c** mi **d** su **e** sus **f** tus **g** tu **h** tu **i** tus

3 **a** es **b** es **c** está **d** son **e** están **f** está

4 Se llaman Eulalia y Eugenia y son estudiantes. Estudian ciencias y aprenden mucho en la universidad. Están solteras pero tienen muchos amigos.

5 Tengo una casa grande y bonita con tres dormitorios cómodos. En el salón hay tres pequeñas ventanas, un sofá viejo y unos sillones modernos. La cocina también es moderna pero no muy grande.

Unit 3

1 **a** 07:10 **b** 16:15 **c** 23:20 **d** 07:55

2 **b** 12.10 **c** 15.45 **d** 15.05 **e** 00.20 **f** 09.40

3 **b** Desayuno a las ocho menos cuarto. **c** Salgo de casa a las ocho y media. **d** Llego a la universidad a las nueve menos cuarto. **e** Voy a clase a las nueve. **f** Como en la cantina a las dos. **g** Vuelvo a casa a las ocho. **h** Ceno a las diez.

4 **a** Me levanto a las ocho menos cuarto. **b** Desayuno a las ocho. **c** Salgo de casa a las nueve menos veinte. **d** Voy a clase a las nueve. **e** Como a la una y media. **f** Vuelvo a casa a las siete. **g** Ceno a las diez.

6 lunes: 12:00–14:00 ciencias, 17:00–19:00 conference; martes: 17:00–19:00 seminario; miércoles: 11:00–14:00 ciencias; jueves mañana biblioteca; viernes 11:00–14:00 ciencias, 17:00–19:00 seminario.

7 **a** Empiezo a las diez. **b** No. Termino a las siete. **c** Voy a la biblioteca. **d** Voy al centro deportivo. **e** Tengo 16 horas en total.

9 *Ve la televisión* is the only correct answer.

10 **a** Se levanta a las diez. **b** Empieza a trabajar a las cinco. **c** Come en un bar. **d** Termina a las nueve. **e** Va (Vuelve) a casa. **f** Vuelve a casa a las diez.

11 **a** ama de casa **b** portero **c** secretaria **d** médico

13 **a** 4 **b** 3 **c** 1 **d** 2

15 **b** Estoy comiendo. **c** Estoy estudiando. **d** Estoy preparando la cena. **e** Estoy escribiendo un informe. **f** Estoy viendo la tele. **g** Estoy desayunando.

18 Pepe: **b** ✗ **c** ✗ **d** ✗ **e** ✗
Ana: **b** ✓ **c** ✓ **d** ✓ **e** ✗

20 **a** Juana pide un whisky con limonada y una ración de calamares. **b** Lucía pide un coñac y olivas.

21 **a** gazpacho **b** lenguado **c** agua mineral **d** flan **e** helados **f** postre

¡Extra!

23 **a** **puede ser**, can be; **más sano**, more healthy; **relax**, relaxation; **fortalecen**, strengthen; **dormir**, to sleep; **todos los días**, every day; **ayuda**, helps; **el estrés**, stress.
b todos los días 62%; dos o tres veces por semana 13%; una vez por semana 10%; con menos frecuencia 15%.

24 The stress of avoiding work.

Ejercicios de gramática

1 **a** vivo **b** estudio **c** aprendo **d** trabajo **e** como **f** escribo **g** veo **h** salgo

2 **a** ¿…vives? Vivo… **b** ¿…te levantas? Me levanto… **c** ¿…llegas…? Llego… **d** ¿…comes…? Como… **e** ¿…terminas? Termino…

3 **a** ¿A qué hora te levantas? ¿A qué hora se levanta (usted)? **b** ¿Dónde comes? ¿Dónde come (usted)? **c** ¿A qué hora terminas? ¿A qué hora termina (usted)? **d** ¿Sales mucho? ¿Sale (usted) mucho?

4 Examples: Vosotros estáis saliendo de clase. Tú estás escribiendo en el libro. Nosotros estamos hablando con Javier. etc

5 Examples: X está escribiendo. X está hablando con Y. X y Y están trabajando. etc

Unit 4

1 **a:** Me gusta tomar el sol. Me gusta dar un paseo en el campo. **b:** Me gusta ir al cine. Me gusta salir con amigos. **c:** Me gusta ver la tele. Me gusta jugar al fútbol.

2 **a** No, no me gusta. **b** No, no me gusta. **c** Sí, me gusta. **d** Sí, me gusta. **e** Sí, me gusta. **f** Sí, me gusta.

4 **a** 3 **b** 5 **c** 4 **d** 1 **e** 2

5 **a** Sí. Me gusta bastante. **b** No, no me gusta mucho. **c** Sí. Me encanta. **d** No, no me gusta nada. **e** Sí. Me gusta mucho.

7 **a** F **b** F **c** F **d** F **e** F

11 Andrés: le gusta la tele; le gustan las vacaciones; no le gusta el deporte; no le gustan los coches.
Bea: le gusta ir de compras; le gustan los coches; no le gusta el deporte; no le gustan las clases.
Carlos: le gusta ir de compras; le gustan las clases; no le gusta la tele; no le gustan las vacaciones.

12 **a** Bea **b** Bea **c** Bea

16 They don't go to any of the clubs. They decide instead to stay in and watch TV.

17 **a** 4 **b** 1 **c** 3 **d** 2

19 **a** Tengo que trabajar. **b** Tengo que estudiar. **c** Tengo que preparar la cena.

21 **a** ¿Cuándo vais? **b** ¿Qué hay? **c** ¿A qué hora empieza? **d** ¿Cuánto cuestan las entradas?

22 **a** 4 **b** 5 **c** 1 **d** 2 **e** 3

¡Extra!

23 **a** los culebrones, los dramas psicológicos, las series policíacas **b** las comedias, las entrevistas con estrellas y los programas concurso **c** las noticias en la tele, los documentales **d** las películas violentas

24 **a** ✓ **b** ✗ **c** ✓

Ejercicios de gramática

1 **a** me gustan **b** te gustan **c** me gusta **d** te gustan **e** me gustan **f** le gustan **g** le gustan

2 **a** Prefiero ir al teatro. **b** Quiero jugar al tenis. **c** Tengo que estudiar. **d** Prefiero ver las noticias.

3

estamos we are	**estáis** you are
queremos we want	**queréis** you want
preferimos we prefer	**preferéis** you prefer
tenemos we have	**tenéis** you have

4 **a** Quieres Prefiero **b** puede Tiene **c** vais **d** queremos podemos

Unit 5

1 He's going to buy a big house in the country, a plane, a luxury yacht and lots of cars. He's not going to save anything, he's going to spend all his money, starting right now.

4 **a** 101 **b** 250 **c** 545 **d** 1995 **e** 3.886 **f** 7.733.571

6 **a** en agosto **b** en septiembre **c** en octubre **d** en noviembre **e** en diciembre **f** en enero **g** en febrero **h** en marzo

7

NOMBRE	DESTINO	SALIDA	VUELTA
Señor Cid	Marruecos	10 de octubre de 2001	24 octubre 2001
Juana Laloca	Lisboa	5 de abril	1 de marzo
Pepe Botella	París	21 de mayo	nunca/4 de junio

11 Look in the **Vocabulario** Section.

12 **1** una falda; 42 **2** un traje; 44 **3** unos pantalones; 50

13 Look in the **Vocabulario** Section.

14 **1** roja **2** azul,verde **3** amarillos **4** violetas, grises

16 **a** Esta falda es demasiado grande. **b** Estos pantalones son demasiado pequeños. **c** Este abrigo es demasiado caro. **d** Estas botas son demasiado pequeñas.

18 Mariví un florero €50; Luis una cartera €45; Raquel una pulsera €40; Alfonso una pintura €150

19 **a** They are all too expensive. **b** A dress for Carolina.

20 It comes to €2.250, and the problem is he doesn't have enough cash.

¡Extra!

22 **a** **1** €186 **2** €117; **b** Because it's a way of escaping from reality.

23 Yo voy a pagar siempre en efectivo. (Miguel) Antes de ir de compras ... (Miguel) Vamos a comer en casa. (Juana) Tú vas a dejar de fumar, ¿no? (Juana) Tú no vas a salir todas las noches, ¿verdad? (Miguel) ¿Cuándo vamos a empezar? (Miguel)

Ejercicios de gramática

1 **a** vas **b** Voy **c** vas **d** Voy **e** vais **f** Vamos **g** vais **h** va **i** van **j** vais **k** vamos

2 **b** el jueves dieciséis de septiembre de 2001 **c** el viernes veintidós de mayo de 1999 **d** el sábado treinta de marzo de 2020 **e** el domingo primero de enero de 2003

3 554 – quinientos cincuenta y cuatro; 6.689 – seis mil seiscientos ochenta y nueve; 17.777 – diecisiete mil setecientos setenta y siete; 43.167 – cuarenta y tres mil ciento sesenta y siete; 122.943 – ciento veintidós mil novecientos cuarenta y tres

4 **b** Estos ... pequeños. **c** Estas ... grandes. **d** Este ... barato.

Unit 6

3

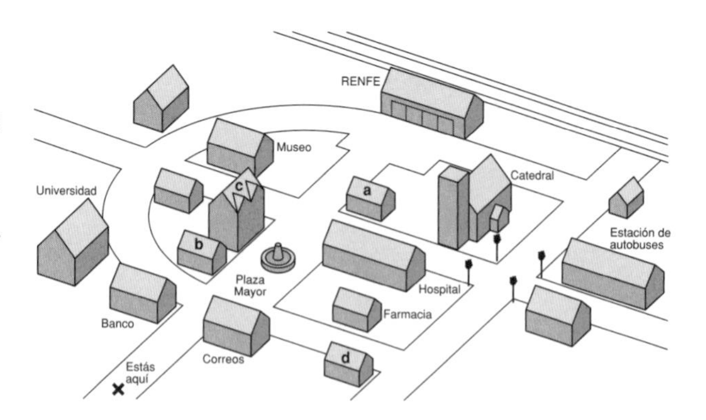

5 **b** lejos; 30 **c** cerca; 10 **d** lejos; 15

7 **b** opposite **c** between **d** on the corner

10 **a** segunda; izquierda; en **b** tercera; derecha; enfrente de **c** al lado de; quinta; izquierda **d** entre; tercera; derecha

11 Dobla a la izquierda 2; Sigue todo recto 4; Ve todo recto 1; Coge la primera calle a la derecha 3; Dobla a la derecha 6; Coge la segunda calle a la izquierda 5

12 You should end up back at the station.

14

	número	sube a	baja a
a	19	centro comercial	Plaza Nueva
b	12	Plaza Nueva	hospital
c	15	Plaza Mayor	biblioteca

16 **g**

19 **a** On the 1st floor on the right. **b** Next to the toilets. **c** On the second floor. Coming out of the lift you turn left and it's the third door on the right at the end of the corridor. **d** Opposite the secretary's office, the third door on the left.

21

Pasa.	1	Come in.
Cierra la puerta.	2	Close the door.
Siéntate aquí.	3	Sit down here.
Rellena este formulario.	4	Fill in this form.
Escribe tu nombre.	5	Write your name.
Espera un momento.	6	Wait a minute.
Dame tu currículum	7	Give me your CV

¡Extra!

23 **a** To the cinema to see **¡Jamón Jamón!** **b** By bus. **c** It's at the Cine Rex, which is in the centre of town. He tells you to get the No 17 bus at the University and get off at the Plaza Mayor. Go straight on to the crossroads and turn left. The cinema is on the right opposite the sports centre. **d** 20 minutes by bus, and 5 minutes on foot. **e** At 9.45, outside the cinema.

24 **a** At 11.00. **b** Bring something to eat or drink and your friends. **c** Underground **d** On the second floor on the right.

Ejercicios de gramática

1 Mi casa está al lado de la iglesia, enfrente del parque. A la izquierda hay un hotel pequeño (*or* un pequeño hotel). Al final de la calle entre la piscina y el centro deportivo hay un cine grande.

2 a **b** sube **c** baja **d** ve **e** dobla **f** sigue

2 b **b** subid **c** bajad **d** id **e** doblad **f** seguid

3 a **a** Pasa **b** Cierra **c** Espera **d** Siéntate **e** Rellena **f** Escribe

3 b **a** Pasad **b** Cerrad **c** Esperad **d** Sentaos **e** Rellenad **f** Escribid

4 The commands you make should be similar to the following:

Abre la ventana. Escucha la música. Levántate inmediatamente. Coge el teléfono. Lee el libro. Bebe la leche. Sal de casa. Come las verduras.

Unit 7

2 **a** motocicleta voladora **b** bicicleta automática **c** tren solar **d** a pie

4 **a** Llegará a las seis. **b** Irá en coche. **c** Volverá el lunes a las dos.

6 **a** Sale a las cinco menos cinco. **b** Llega a las seis. **c** Es Iberia 1919. **d** Sale de la puerta número dos.

8 **a** At the hotel. **b** At the hotel. **c** He will call him from the hotel. **d** He suggests they go for a drink at 8 or 9.00.

9 **a** ¿Cuánto es por día? **b** ¿Cuánto son los seguros? **c** ¿Cuánto es el depósito? **d** ¿Tiene gasolina? **e** ¿Qué tipo de gasolina usa?

11 Sevilla. Ida y vuelta. Segunda clase. No fumador. €13. Sale a las 10.25. Llega a las 12.10. Es directo. Del andén número 15.

13 **a** Juana va a Barcelona. **b** Miguel va a Barcelona también. **c** Sale a las 10.12. **d** Sale del andén número 5.

15 **b** Buscaré un hostal. **c** Llegaremos bastante tarde ... **d** Esta noche podrás quedarte ... **e** Mañana buscarás ...

17 Está en la esquina, enfrente del banco. Vienen cada 20 minutos. Sí, para en el Park Güell. Tarda unos 25 minutos.

¡Extra!

21 a 1, 2, 3, 5, 9

21 b a, b, e

22 1 c **2** e **3** a **4** b **5** d

Ejercicios de gramática

1 a ¿A qué hora llega el tren? **b** ¿A qué hora sale el autobús? **c** ¿Cuánto tiempo dura el viaje? **d** ¿A qué hora llega a París? **e** ¿De qué andén sale el tren? **f** ¿De qué puerta sale el vuelo?

2 a Voy a viajar en autobús. **b** Van a ir en bicicleta. **c** Va a viajar en avión. **d** ¿Vas a llegar en coche?

3 a iré **b** Me levantaré **c** tendré **d** Saldré **e** veré **f** Haré **g** escucharé **h** aprenderé **i** buscaré

4 a iremos **b** Nos levantaremos **c** tendremos **d** Saldremos **e** veremos **f** Haremos **g** escucharemos **h** aprenderemos **i** buscaremos

5 a irás **b** volverás **c** harás **d** empezarás

6 a iréis **b** volveréis **c** haréis **d** empezaréis

Unit 8

1 Mike has worked in a bar and a restaurant in Scotland, but he has never worked in Spain. At the moment he is a student.

2 a He visto su anuncio en el periódico. **b** Quisiera solicitar el puesto de … **c** He trabajado en un bar … **d** … pero no he trabajado nunca en España. **e** ¿Qué hace actualmente? **f** Venga mañana por la mañana …

4 Sí, he decidido … Sí he llamado … Sí he hablado … Sí tengo una entrevista. Sí he escrito …

5 Juana **b** Mike **a** Julio **c**

8 Carrera Superior de Empresariales *e Informática*; Barman 1999–2001; Camarero 2001– ahora; No es técnico

9 Dolores probably didn't get the job because she arrived late for the interview, her attitude was rather off-hand, she didn't bring her CV to the interview, she only wanted the job for the money, and she was negative about her course.

10 1 a **2** b and c **3** a and c **4** b **5** a **6** c

11 & 12

NOMBRE	FECHAS	HABITACIÓN DOBLE / INDIVIDUAL	PENSIÓN MEDIA / COMPLETA	BALCÓN	BAÑERA/ DUCHA
SERRAT	21-25 junio	individual	media X 2	sí	baño
PONS	15-17 mayo	individual	media	sí	ducha

14 b 3 **c** 4 **d** 2

15 a 4 **b** 3 **c** 5 **d** 2 **e** 1

17 1 c, f 2 b, h, i 3 a, d 4 e, g

18 & 19

EMPLEO	VENTAJAS	DESVENTAJAS
Moza de cuadra	Estás fuera todo el día al aire libre; puedes montar a caballo.	Es duro; empiezas muy temprano; las cuadras pueden estar muy lejos de la casa.
Camarero	Conoces a mucha gente; me gusta el ambiente en el restaurante; me llevo bien con todos.	No ganas mucho dinero.
Animador	Me llevo muy bien con los niños; conoces a mucha gente.	No ganas mucho.
Servicio doméstico	Te dan la comida gratis.	El trabajo es muy duro; no me gustan mis colegas; gano casi nada.

¡Extra!

21 a 1 en las que el salario que se cobra **2** es superior a la media nacional **3** No obstante **4** los sueldos de los madrileños **5** los más elevados ... los más bajos **6** los de los murcianos

21 b

SALARIO MENSUAL MEDIO POR TRABAJADOR	€ (aprox)
MADRID	2.090
PAÍS VASCO	2.047
CATALUÑA	1.884
CASTILLA Y LEÓN	1.717
BALEARES	1.628
ANDALUCÍA	1.621
GALICIA	1.510
MURCIA	1.378

22 1 f, iv 2 d, v 3 a, ii 4 c, i 5 e, iii 6 b, vi

Ejercicios de gramática

1 b He **c** Habéis **d** Hemos **e** Han **f** ha

2 b visto **c** dicho **d** escrito **e** hecho **f** cogido

3

he llegado	llego	llegaré
he vuelto	vuelvo	volveré
he salido	salgo	saldré

4 a he empezado **b** han llegado ... ha venido **c** Hemos ganado ... hemos comprado **d** Habéis visto ... Ha tenido

5

Dear Jesús
Have you seen the advertisement for an assistant in a language school? I want to apply for the post and I have rung the college to ask for more details. I have already prepared my CV and my teacher has written me a reference. Have you decided if you would like to work in France in July? Write or ring me soon,
María José

Unit 9

1 Por la mañana estuve en la universidad. Fui a la biblioteca. Sí, trabajé todo el día. Pasé toda la noche estudiando. Me acosté a las once y media.

2 a 2 b 5 c 4 d 3 e 1

7 He was in a bar, playing his guitar with a country and western band.

8 1 Nació el 10 de octubre ... **2** Fue al Colegio de Ave María ... **3** Pasó el bachillerato ... **4** Viajó durante un año ... **5** Trabajó en bares y cafés ... **6** Volvió a España ...

13 Fernando and Itziar had a good time; Maribel and Enrique didn't.

14 Fernando **d** Maribel **a** Itziar **c** Enrique **b**

15 a Itziar **b** Enrique **c** Fernando **d** Enrique **e** Enrique **f** Maribel **g** Enrique

17 1 Cogió la llave ... **2** Perdió la llave de la casa en el autobús. **3** Llegó a la casa a las seis. **4** La dueña no estaba. **5** Fue al bar de enfrente para esperar ... **6** Empezó a beber ... **7** La dueña volvió a la casa a las doce. **8** Ella abrió la puerta. **9** En ese momento Fernando vomitó en la escalera.

19 b dos **c** 17 o 18 **d** tres y media **e** diez

¡Extra!

22 a 6.000 **b** Se manifestaron contra la privatización de la universidad. **c** Colectivos estudiantiles organizaron la protesta. **d** Terminó con una fuerte carga policial. **e** Un manifestante resultó herido leve. **f** No hubo detenidos.

23 Colectivos *estudiantiles* de la *izquierda* alternativa convocaron *ayer* en el *centro* de Madrid a 6.000 *jóvenes* para expresar su *protesta contra* la posible *privatización* de la Universidad. La manifestación *terminó* con enfrentamientos entre un grupo de estudiantes y la policía. Tras la carga, un *manifestante* resultó herido *leve*. No hubo detenidos.

Ejercicios de gramática

1 **b** trabajé **c** volví **d** Cené **e** vi **f** Me acosté

2 There are several possible answers.
b estuviste **c** pasaste **d** te quedaste
e llegaste **f** duró

3 **b** gustaron **c** asistieron **d** ayudaron
e invitaron

4 There are several possible questions.
b ¿Dónde tuvo lugar? **c** ¿Qué pasó?
d ¿Cuánto tiempo duró el atraco?
e ¿Adónde fueron? **f** ¿Cómo se escaparon?

Unit 10

1

Nombre *Elena*

Apellidos *Ariza González*

Dirección *Calle Colón, núm 26, 2°B, 28011 Madrid*

Nacionalidad *Española*

Fecha de nacimiento *28 de agosto de 1982*

Lugar de nacimiento *Madrid*

Profesión *Estudiante*

9

	Prenda	Talla	Color	Problema	Precio
a	una falda	38	roja	demasiado pequeña	€25
			negra/amarilla	no le gustan	-
			azul	demasiado cara	€45
			verde	-	€27
b	unos zapatos	40	todos grises	no los tienen en verde	€36

10 He ido a todos los grandes almacenes y ahora estoy en el Corte Inglés. **La primera falda** que he probado aquí fue demasiado **pequeña**, y pedí **una** más **grande** a la dependienta. Me ha traído **otra**, pero no me gusta el color. He visto **muchas faldas** pero por fin me he quedado con **ésta**, que me ha costado **€27**. Pero no he podido encontrar **zapatos** del mismo color.

11 Your answer should be something like this:

```
Querido Jorge
Sí, puedes quedarte conmigo, y
vendré a la estación para
recogerte. Al final de la
conferencia saldremos al campo
en el coche. Si quieres,
acamparemos. Y mi hermana, lo
siento pero no va a estar en
casa. Está viajando por Francia.
Hasta lunes
Un abrazo
```

13 **a** 2 **b** 4 **c** 1 **d** 3

14 ¿Cuál es el número del vuelo?
¿De qué puerta sale?
¿Hay un retraso?

15 There are a few different possibilities.
a 1 **e** 5 **h** 8 **g** 7 **f** 6 **b** 2 **c** 3 **d** 4

16 **b** Trabajaré en una colonia de verano. **c** Viajaré un poco por América. **d** Me quedaré en la colonia … **e** …y luego iré a casa de mis amigos en Miami. **f** Volveré en octubre.

18 **a** He is tall, wearing a grey suit, a pale shirt and a green tie. He looks like an executive, maybe a banker. **b** He is the heir to the throne of Spain. **c** When he was 7, Franco died. When he was 14, the Socialists won the elections. **d** The Constitution.

21 **a** 1906 **b** 1927 **c** 1928 **d** 1931 **e** 1937 **f** 1938 **g** 1975

23 **a** He wasn't rich. **b** He fought the Moors and earned a lot of money. **c** After five years. **d** Getting married. **e** Because she was married. **f** Together in a tomb.

Ejercicios de gramática

1 **b** Me llamo **c** eres **d** Soy (or Me llamo) **e** Vives **f** vivo **g** haces **h** Trabajo

2 **b** Sale de casa a las nueve de la mañana.
c Llega a la universidad a las nueve y

cuarto de la mañana. **d** Come en la cantina a la una de la tarde. **e** Vuelve a casa a las seis de la tarde. **f** Va al bar con sus amigos a las diez de la noche. **g** Se acuesta a las doce (*or* a medianoche).

3 **a** cuarenta y uno **b** sesenta y siete **c** ciento cuatro **d** quinientos cincuenta y dos **e** mil setecientos setenta y ocho **f** nueve mil novecientos ochenta y uno

4 **b** Gloria está saliendo de casa.
c (Nosotros) estamos trabajando mucho.
d (Tú) estás llegando al aeropuerto.
e Vicente y Pepa están comprando ropa.
f (Yo) estoy hablando por teléfono.

5 **a** **2** ¿Te gusta beber cerveza? **3** ¿Te gustan los animales?

5 **b** **2** Me encanta la música cubana. **3** No me gusta el fútbol. **4** Odio/Aborrezco el queso. **5** Me gusta mucho. **6** No me gusta nada.

6 **b** voy a estudiar **c** van a ver **d** vamos a ir **e** vas a venir **f** vais a comer

7 There are other possible answers.
b Dobla a la derecha. El hotel está a la derecha. **c** Dobla a la izquierda. El banco está a la derecha. **d** Coge la segunda calle a la derecha. Correos está a la izquierda. **e** Ve todo recto y coge la tercera calle a la derecha. La estación está a la izquierda.

8 Your sentences should be similar to these ones. **b** Nosotros volveremos a América. **c** Eliás se casará en junio. **d** Yo podré salir a las seis. **e** Tú te acostarás a las doce. **f** Ana y Bea trabajarán en Francia en agosto. **g** Vosotros tendréis que ahorrar el dinero.

9 Your sentences should be similar to these ones. **b** Nosotros hemos vuelto de América. **c** Eliás se ha casado. **d** Yo he podido salir. **e** Tú te has acostado. **f** Ana y Bea han trabajado en Francia. **g** Vosotros habéis tenido que ahorrar el dinero.

10 Ayer me levanté a las seis. Preparé el desayuno y salí a las siete y media. Fui al trabajo en coche y llegué a las ocho y cuarto. A mediodía comí en un bar enfrente de la oficina. Volví a casa a las ocho y cené a las nueve y media. Me acosté a las once o las doce.

Juegos de palabras

5 Other words which end in **-ad**, and which you have seen in this book are: **nacionalidad**, **universidad**, **ciudad**, **facultad**.

6 **-mente**. It corresponds to *-ly* in English and is an adverb. Thus **rápidamente** means *quickly*, etc.

Más práctica 1

1 **a** lawyer **b** secretary **c** Argentina **d** Madrid **e** company director

2 She is not from here; she is from Puerto Rico; she lives in Miami; she works in the university; she is not a student; she is an administrator; she is also learning Italian.

5 **a** ¿Cómo te llamas?/¿Quién eres? **b** ¿Dónde vives? **c** ¿Eres escocés? **d** ¿Cuál es tu profesión?

6 Ignacio: Es de Perú. Tiene 21 años. Vive en Oviedo. Es estudiante de medicina.
Amanda: Sí. Es de Bilbao. No. Vive en Oviedo. No. Tiene 25 años. Es secretaria.

7 Estimado señor/Estimado señora
Quiero matricularme en un curso de español. Me llamo Laurie Dimock y tengo 22 años. Soy galés/galesa, de Bangor, pero vivo en México. Soy recepcionista en un hotel.
Atentamente Laurie Dimock

8 Example reply:
Querida Juanita
Soy de (where you are from) y vivo en (where you live). Soy (your job) y tengo

(your age) años. Soy (your nationality). Estudio (what you study). Un abrazo de (your name)

9 **a** Kim Lai tiene 25 años. Es china, de Hong Kong, pero vive en Taunton. Es profesora de historia. **b** Francis Owu, tiene 24 años. Es de Ghana, y vive en Newcastle. Es investigador. **c** Siobhán Harpur tiene 21 años. Es irlandesa, de Dublín. Aprende francés y trabaja en un hotel.

10

						S	E	I	S		C
				V		I					A
T	R	E	C	E		E					T
				I		T		O	C	H	O
	Q	U	I	N	C	E					R
				T							C
		D	I	E	C	I	N	U	E	V	E

Más práctica 2

1 Paulina, 28, hermana menor; Alberto, 46, marido; Miguel, 40, hermano mayor; Esther, 64, madre; Leonardo, 65, padre; José, 10, hijo.

2 **a** Tienen dos hijos. **b** Su marido es mecánico. **c** Tienen tres hijos. Se llaman Susana, Charo y Felipe. **d** Los padres de Charo están divorciados y su hermana, Susana, está separada. **e** Se llama Susana. **f** La novia de Felipe trabaja en el aeropuerto.

5 Juan: 5, salón, grande, 3, garaje, 2, no. Ángela: piso, centro, pequeño, aparcamiento, no, 3.

6 **a** Es muy grande y bastante vieja. **b** Hay 4 dormitorios grandes. **c** Hay una cama individual y un sofá. **d** Están en la planta baja. **e** Es muy moderna. **f** Hay una piscina y una pista de tenis.

Más práctica 3

1 lunes: 5:00 – cita con Sr Aznar; martes: 10:00 – a la oficina Sra Gómez, 3:00 – restaurante El Juez; miércoles: juicio todo el día; jueves: 10:00 – juicio, 4:00 – casa de Sr Aznar; viernes: Trabaja en casa todo el día.

2 Me levanto a las siete y desayuno a las siete y media. Salgo a las ocho y voy a la oficina. Trabajo hasta las dos. Como en un bar y vuelvo al trabajo a las cinco. Termino a las ocho y ceno con Isabel a las diez. Me acuesto a medianoche.

3 Andrés: duerme, estudia, sale – estudiante; Bea: trabaja, trabaja, sale – recepcionista; Carlos: visita a los pacientes, vuelve a la clínica, trabaja – médico; Diana: trabaja, trabaja, trabaja – profesora; Enrique: duerme, sale, pinta – artista

4 **a** está consultando **b** está hablando **c** está haciendo **d** está escribiendo **e** estoy esperando **f** está esperando **g** está saliendo

Más práctica 4

1 **a** F **b** F **c** F **d** F **e** V

2 **a** Se llama Gaudí. **b** Le gusta ver los títeres y las estatuas humanas, los pintores y los artistas de todo tipo.

3 **a** 2 **b** 4 **c** 1 **d** 3

4 **a** Mañana no puedo. **b** Tengo que trabajar. **c** Por la noche. **d** No. El martes tengo clase. **e** Todo el día. **f** No, no quiero salir contigo. **g** Porque prefiero salir con Juana.

6

1 lunes	2 martes	3 miércoles
De compras con Alicia a las 12.00h →	~~Gimnasio con Bea a las 4.30h~~ Cine con Carlos 10.30h	Exposición de Arte con Alicia. 12.00h en la entrada del museo

Más práctica 5

1 It's a soap opera.

2 **a** Leonardo va a viajar a Estambul. **b** Livia va a París. **c** Leonardo y Livia van a estar en el Bar Jinete a las 10.

4 **a** V; **b** F (Pide un whisky); **c** V; **d** V; **e** F (Margarita va a salir con Salvador)

5 Compran un traje nuevo para Salvador.

6 **a** €1500; **b** €1200; **c** €2000; **d** €1000; **e** €1400; **f** €1500

8 It says that tomorrow she is going to Palm Springs with César the car salesman, and that they are going to get married in Las Vegas.

Más práctica 6

1

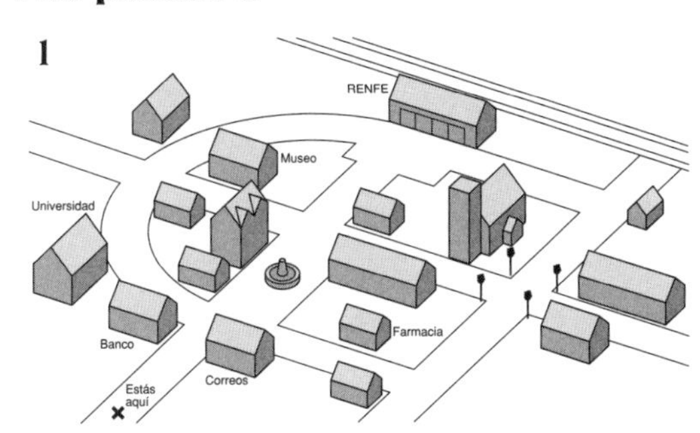

3

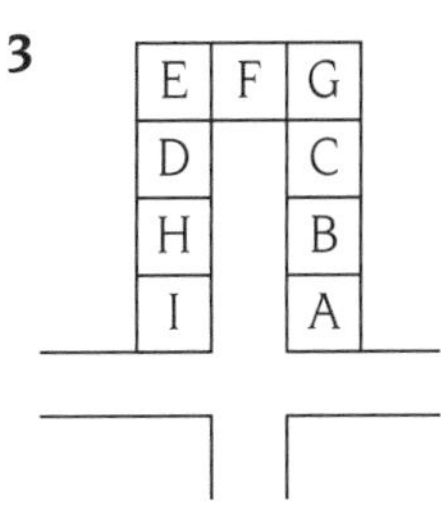

6 Your directions should be similar to the ones below.
a Desde la Plaça Sant Jaume ve por la calle Ferrán. Coge la segunda calle a la derecha y el albergue está a la derecha.
b Desde la Plaça Catalunya ve por la Rambla. Coge la segunda calle a la izquierda. Es la calle Boquería. Coge la tercera calle a la derecha y el albergue está a la izquierda.
c Desde el Museo de Cera dobla a la derecha. Coge la primera calle a la derecha. Es la calle Ferrán. Coge la tercera calle a izquierda y el albergue está a la derecha.

7 **a** 4 **b** 3 **c** 2 **d** 1

Más práctica 7

1 **a** persona **b** números 5 y 10 **c** amante **d** dinero **e** extranjero **f** empleo

3

	FECHA	VUELO	DESTINO	SALIDA	LLEGADA
Change from	24 enero	Iberia 1607	Tenerife	15.40	–
Change to	21 enero	Iberia 1801	Tenerife	17.50	20.30

4 **a** V **b** F **c** V **d** F **e** F **f** F

5 Your answer could be something like this:

Querido Claudio

Lo siento, pero no puedo ir contigo al campo, porque tengo que trabajar. Este fin de semana trabajaré el sábado todo el día, y el domingo voy a ver a mis padres. Te veré la semana que viene.

Un abrazo,

Your name

8 There are a few possible variations to the changes made below:

En el siglo XXI los seres humanos volarán por el aire en aviones, y cruzarán el mar en barcos. Viajarán por tierra en coches. Cada día irán al trabajo en coche. Será posible viajar alrededor del mundo en una semana.

Más práctica 8

2 **b** Your attitude towards the job.

4 He mentions the following: **h**, **g**, **a**, **i**, **d**, **c**

6 **a** 2 **b** 1 **c** 5 **d** 3 **e** 4

7 **a** 2 **b** 1 **c** 1 **d** 3

8

Querida Lucía

He empezado el trabajo y no me gusta nada. Empiezo muy temprano y termino tarde, y el trabajo es aburrido y siempre igual. No me llevo muy bien con mis colegas y los dueños y no me gusta conocer a los clientes. No pagan muy bien, no ha sido una experiencia importante y no he podido practicar el español.

Un abrazo,

Juana

9 Your letter might be something like this:

Querido Jaime

He empezado un trabajo de verano. Trabajo desde las ocho de la mañana hasta las dos y desde las cinco hasta las ocho de la tarde. Tengo que fregar los platos y limpiar la cocina. Me gusta porque me llevo muy bien con mis colegas y he podido practicar el español, pero no se paga muy bien.

Un abrazo de

Your name

Más práctica 9

1 **1** Llegué a Mojácar … **2** Pasé toda la mañana en la playa. **3** Tomé el sol, me bañé en el mar **4** y a mediodía fui a comer en un restaurante. **5** Volví a la playa por la tarde **6** y salí a una discoteca por la noche. **7** Sin embargo, al día siguiente cogí una insolación **8** y pasé el resto de la semana en la cama.

2 **b** Nicolás **c** Manolo **d** Mariví **e** Nicolás **f** Manolo

4 Your postcard should be similar to the following:

Querida María

Llegué ayer por la tarde a las siete y media y fui directo al apartamento. Comí en un restaurante y pasé el resto de la noche en un bar. Esta mañana fui a la playa y comí en un café. Volví a la playa por la tarde y me bañé en el mar. Ahora estoy en el apartamento y voy a salir.

Un abrazo

Your name

Más práctica 10

1

	%
La vivienda es cara	28
Prefieren las comodidades sin responsabilidades	6
Los padres no son muy estrictos	30
Los jóvenes se casan más tarde	32
No tienen posibilidades de independizarse antes	80
Los padres necesitan la ayuda económica de los hijos	15
Quieren tener una situación estable antes de vivir sólos	34

2

GASTOS MENSUALES	
Alquiler	€500–€620
Luz	€30
Agua	€8 o €9
Teléfono	€40 o €45
Gas (sin calefacción):	
natural	€8
Butano	€8
Calefacción (de gas natural)	€50
Comunidad de vecinos:	
sin servicios (ascensor, calefacción)	€50
con servicios	€115

El alquiler varía desde €580 a €300. Es más caro en Cataluña, el País Vasco y Madrid y menos caro en Huelva, Cáceres y Huesca. Además, en España cuando alquilas un piso tienes que pagar el primer mes de alquiler y también una fianza de €500 a €620.

3 **a** In Mexico **b** In Bilbao **c** Dolores Ibarruri **d** Dolores Ibarruri **e** Dolores Ibarruri **f** Montezuma **g** Montezuma **h** Dolores Ibarruri **i** Montezuma **j** Montezuma

Additional vocabulary

Unit 1: Tú y los demás

Other useful words	
su	his/her
tu	your
también	also
un/a	a
y	and

Unit 3: La rutina

Las bebidas (f pl)	Drinks
zumo (m)	juice
agua (f)	water
leche (f)	milk
jerez (m)	sherry

Unit 8: Trabajo de verano

21

bajo/a	low
cobrar	to earn
comunidad (f) **autónoma**	autonomous community
elevado/a	high
madrileño/a	person from Madrid
media (f)	average
mensual	monthly
murciano/a	person from Murcia
No obstante	However
sueldo (m)	wage

22

perfil (m)	profile, characteristic, background
vanguardista (m)	forward looking
enfermería (f)	nursing
ventanilla (f) **de reclamación**	customer services
recurso (m)	resource
habilidad (f)	skill
perspicaz	perceptive
manitas (m)	handyman (colloquial)

Unit 1 **Tú y los demás**	Greetings and saying goodbye Personal information: origin, nationality, job, subjects studied, age	Present tense – first, second and third persons singular Questions and answers Negatives Personal pronouns **yo**, **tú**, **él**, **ella** Numbers up to 25 **tener** for age (first 3 persons singular) **ser** (first 3 persons singular) Nouns and articles
Unit 2 **La familia en casa**	Family Describing your house or flat; renting accommodation	Possessive adjectives **mi/s**, **tu/s**, **su/s** Numbers 26–100 Adjectives **ser** and **estar** (to express permanent and temporary states) Present tense: 3rd person plural
Unit 3 **La rutina**	Telling the time Describing daily routines. Describing current and on-going activities Food and meals	Present continuous Formal form of second person [**usted**] Regular and reflexive verbs in the present Subject pronouns **ser** **ir**
Unit 4 **El tiempo libre**	Evening and weekend activities Making, accepting and rejecting invitations Buying tickets for shows Saying you like something Expressing obligation, desire and ability	**gustar** **tener que** **querer** **poder** Plural forms of verbs Root-changing verbs
Unit 5 **El dinero**	Talking about holidays Saying what you are going to do Describing people and things	**ir** + **a** + infinitive Demonstrative adjectives **este/a/os/as** The personal **a** Adjectives, number and gender **¿Cuánto/a/s?**
Unit 6 **En la ciudad**	Describing where something is Giving directions and instructions Finding your way round a town and within office buildings	Prepositions **estar** Imperative

Unit 7 **Medios de transporte**	Using transport, private and public Discussing future plans	Future tense Comparatives
Unit 8 **Trabajo de verano**	Ringing up about jobs advertised Presenting yourself at an informal interview Talking about your experience and what you have done Working in a Spanish-speaking country Writing letters and postcards	Perfect tense
Unit 9 **¿Dónde estuviste ayes?**	Talking about past events and exchange visits abroad Understanding newspaper reports	Preterite tense
Unit 10 **Repaso**	Consolidation and practice Revison of vocabulary in familiar topic areas	

INDEX

From the publishers of *Breakthrough*

Foundations Languages

Meeting the language teaching needs of today

- Classroom courses
- Specifically designed for IWLPs and similar provision
- Tailored to the needs of a 20-24 week teaching year
- Focused on the needs of HE non-specialist language students including the growing number of international students
- A core classroom section is supported by ample self-study supplements to cater for all student abilities and timetabling provision

The price of cassettes includes a free site licence. Full set of tapescripts available on request, or downloadable from our website.

Series Editor TOM CARTY
Formerly IWLP Programme Leader at Staffordshire University and the University of Wolverhampton

All course books are available on inspection to teaching staff where an adoption would result in the sale of at least 12 copies. Please email lecturerservices@palgrave.com

Contact:
Lecturer Services
Palgrave Macmillan, Houndmills, Basingstoke,
Hampshire RG21 6XS

tel : +44 (0) 1256 302866
fax : + 44 (0) 1256 330688
lecturerservices@palgrave.com

German 1
Tom Carty
Formerly Staffordshire University

Ilse Wührer
Keele University

French 1
Dounia Bissar
Cécile Tschirhart
London Metropolitan University

Helen Phillips
Bristol University

French 2
Kate Beeching
University of the West of England

Italian 1
Mara Benetti
Imperial College and Goldsmiths College, London

Carmela Murtas
Project Coordinator:
Robert di Napoli
University of Westminster

Caterina Varchetta
London Metropolitan University

Spanish 1
Cathy Holden
Edinburgh University